THE
PLANT-FORWARD
SOLUTION

REBOOT YOUR DIET, LOSE WEIGHT & BUILD LIFELONG
HEALTH BY **EATING MORE PLANTS** & LESS MEAT

CHARLOTTE MARTIN, MS, RDN, CSOWM

VICTORY BELT PUBLISHING
Las Vegas

First published in 2021 by Victory Belt Publishing Inc.

ISBN-13: 978-1-628604-34-4

The information included in this book is for educational purposes only. It is not intended or implied to be a substitute for professional medical advice. The reader should always consult their healthcare provider to determine the appropriateness of the information for their own situation or if they have any questions regarding a medical condition or treatment plan. Reading the information in this book does not constitute a physician-patient relationship. The statements in this book have not been evaluated by the Food and Drug Administration. The products or supplements in this book are not intended to diagnose, treat, cure, or prevent any disease. The authors and publisher expressly disclaim responsibility for any adverse effects that may result from the use or application of the information contained in this book.

Cover and author photos by Maddie Kaye Photography

Cover design by Kat Lannom

Interior design by Kat Lannom and Justin-Aaron Velasco

Printed in Canada
TC 0121

For my parents, Lisa and Jean-Paul, who encouraged me to appreciate nutritious foods from a very young age (even when I resisted), and for my mémé Paulette, who inspired me in the kitchen.

And for the reader who considers beans to be nothing more than a "*musical* fruit," may this book persuade you to see them as *magical.*

CONTENTS

INTRODUCTION

Currently, I'm a practicing dietitian, but before that I was a Paleo dieter turned carbophobe turned vegetarian and everything in between, so I've both seen and lived it all. (Well, I haven't tried the keto diet, but trust me, there is no FOMO happening here.) You can call me a glutton for punishment, I suppose. I lived in the extremes, constantly chasing after the solution to some iteration of the question *what should I eat?!*

"What should I eat for optimal health—to feel my best and live a long and vibrant life?"

At first I was wondering what I should eat to continue to fit into my (low-rise, acid wash) jeans from high school. But, over time, my question (thankfully) matured into *what should I eat for optimal health—to feel my best and live a long and vibrant life?* It then evolved into a question of *what should WE eat* as I started working with clients who were desperately asking me that same question. It took me many years to find a sound answer. As a fresh-out-of-school (and very naive) dietitian, I continued to be easily influenced by the people who were shilling the latest and greatest nutrition nonsense, much to my regret now. It wasn't until I furthered my education and learned from and interacted with seasoned experts in my field who lived by a motto of "fact over fad" that I was able to silence the noise and champion fact over fad myself.

We have decades of nutrition research at our disposal, and although nutrition research is not perfect, it's certainly not insignificant. You see, there is a basic and uncomplicated answer to that question (read: what the heck should I/you/we eat?) that a wealth of evidence supports and that most experts and leading authorities in the controversial and increasingly confusing world of nutrition and health now agree on. (When I say "experts," I'm not referring to the self-proclaimed ones on your social media feed.) And while there is no—as the cliché goes—one-size-fits-all approach to eating when you get down to the nitty-gritty details, one general solution can and should be applied by most people. It isn't one of the extreme eating practices that have become so commonplace that they might as well be embedded into our DNA. It's not eliminating grains, it's not eating very low-carb, it's not eating super high fat, it's not eating all meat, and it's not eating no meat at all. The answer doesn't require you to eliminate anything really, nor does it require supplements or tonics.

The answer? Just *eat more plants*. Not necessarily plants *only*—just a lot more of them. If you are here to lose weight, improve overall health, or both, plants are the answer. And not because one dietitian (me) said so or because your neighbor's cousin said she's thriving on a plant-based diet but for the numerous evidence-based reasons discussed in this book. The science you're about to dive headfirst into behind the power of plants is equally as convincing as it is fascinating and exciting.

Now, let me be clear—rebooting your diet in any capacity is no walk in the park. If it were, I'd be out of a job, and this book wouldn't exist. But seeing as how helping you do so is my job, I've put my all into ensuring your transition to a plant-forward lifestyle is as seamless and enjoyable as possible. I left no stone unturned and no questions unanswered when it came to writing this book. Seriously—I even included a myth-busting section that addresses common myths and misconceptions surrounding certain plant foods and plant-centric eating so that you can start your plant-forward journey with a clear conscience and open mind. I wholeheartedly believe in this approach, and I'm confident that if you read through all of the easy-to-digest science in Part 1 and give at least some of the 28-day reset and (delicious) recipes in this book a try, you will, too. So, without further ado, let's start with the basics!

PART 1:

WHY TO GO PLANT-FORWARD

CHAPTER 1:
THE BASICS

———

Diets rich in plants have long been touted for their health benefits. In fact, eating more nutrient-dense plant foods seems to be one of the only things most experts and leading authorities in the controversial and increasingly confusing world of nutrition and health can agree on. If you've picked up this book because you want to lose weight or improve gut, heart, and/or overall health, plants are your silver bullet.

Gone are the days when a plant-rich diet meant endless servings of steamed broccoli; we are now transforming walnuts and lentils into taco meat, cashews into queso, bananas into ice cream, chickpeas into cookie dough, and more. It is easier and, dare I say, more exciting than ever to get more healthful plant foods on your plate. So, why aren't we all doing it? Well, it's one thing to know that eating more plants is great for you and another thing entirely to commit to it.

Unfortunately, pesky media headlines and nutrition misinformation at our fingertips have led us to believe that the dietary approach we choose to follow must lie on one end of the spectrum or the other. And, so, the mere notion of eating more plants can leave some people feeling like they've been forced to choose between "all plants" or "no plants." For many, the perceived barriers to adopting a plant-based diet—the enjoyment of eating meat and the difficulty in abandoning it, nutrient deficiencies (especially protein), convenience, time, taste, dining out, and constraints in social situations, to name a few—greatly outweigh the perceived benefits, making that decision an easy, don't-have-to-think-twice one.

Here comes the good news. Committing to healthy, plant-centered eating does not have to be an all-or-nothing proposition. There lies a solution in the middle ground between the extremes—the plant-*forward* solution.

What Is Plant-Forward Eating, Exactly?

Let's start with what it isn't—it's not yet another diet. I must admit, I'm guilty of a little knee-jerk eye roll whenever I hear someone say, "This isn't a diet; it's a lifestyle!" about the "not-a-diet" diet they're trying to sell you on. Sure, Jim, you keep telling yourself that as you salivate over my slice of pizza. If you can't do it for life, then it's not a lifestyle.

A plant-forward diet *is not* a diet by the modern definition of the word. It's not a temporary means to an end; something you start only to stop soon after. Rather, it's a plant-centric, health-focused, and flexible approach to eating that is meant to be sustained for the long term (for *life*).

At its core, the plant-forward approach focuses primarily on nutrient-dense plant-based foods but is not limited to them. This way of eating allows for you to consume meat, poultry, and seafood (without the sides of guilt and shame), but these foods are no longer *consistently* the main feature of your meals or your diet overall. It is a role reversal of sorts—plant-based foods take center stage (the Beyoncé of the diet, if you will), and animal foods are the backup singers.

Some might call this approach "lazy vegetarian" or "vegetarian with benefits." Some might go so far as to call it a cop-out. As a dietitian, I could not disagree more. I'm disheartened when I hear clients, friends, and family members say they don't eat many plant-based foods because they could "never be vegetarian." The two are not mutually exclusive, my friend. You do not have to commit to a 24/7 vegetarian or vegan lifestyle to enjoy and reap the benefits of a plant-rich diet. I see plant-forward eating as a win-win—a sustainable compromise that celebrates the consumption of a wide variety of plant-based foods without deprivation. And deprivation, after all, is a main reason why most diets fail. There are no hard-and-fast rules here; no eliminating foods or entire food groups, no eat-this-not-that, no calorie- or macro-counting, and no missing out on your brother-in-law's famous burger at the annual family barbecue.

Meat Less Instead of Meatless

Unless you skipped over the book description (which hey, I do that, too), the fact that you're reading this book means that there is at least one burger or burger equivalent in your life you're not looking to give up completely. And why should you have to? I've read a lot of nutrition and diet books, and I mean *a lot*. And every time I read a plant-based one that unjustly demonizes animal foods, all I can think about is how badly I want a juicy fillet with a side of cheese. So, throughout this book, you'll notice that I make it a point *not* to do that. Call it reverse psychology, if you will; the fact is—strictly speaking from a nutritional standpoint here—there is no quality evidence to support the need to *completely* remove animal proteins from your diet for optimal health. As long as you put plants forward, of course (*wink wink*).

The Plant-Forward Pyramid

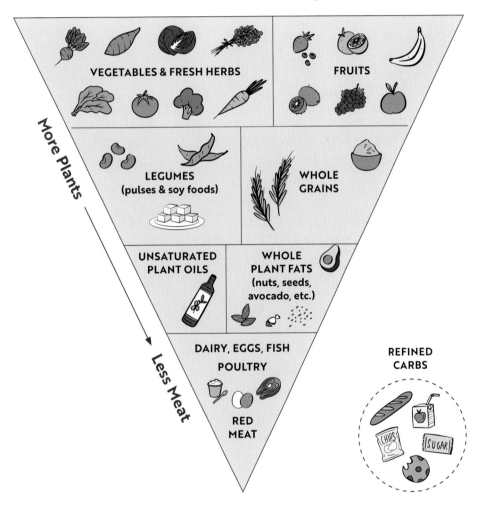

As illustrated in the plant-forward pyramid, produce is a *top* priority here (pun intended). Animal proteins can still be a part of your weekly rotation, but they've fallen to the bottom to make room for more plant-based proteins (like legumes, soy proteins, nuts, and seeds). The pyramid represents the bulk of your food intake. As such, the foods in it are the less-processed and no-added-sugar versions of foods—

think whole grains instead of white grains, roasted potatoes instead of fast-food French fries, ground turkey instead of turkey bacon, and plain yogurt instead of sweetened yogurt. Off to the side, you'll find the other versions of these foods (like refined carbohydrates), which offer little from a nutritional standpoint, but I'd argue they have a lot to offer from a good-for-your-soul standpoint. (I don't know about you, but I've never met a cookie I didn't like, and a life without my local pizza is not a life I want to live.) You can breathe a deep sigh of relief because I've now given you visual confirmation that nothing is off-limits here. We are simply reconfiguring proportions of plant and animal foods in the typical diet with the overall goal of eating more plants and less meat.

Your Plant-Based Glossary

Vegan, vegetarian, flexitarian, plant-based, plant-forward, plant-backward—keeping up with the latest plant-based terminology can be more challenging than keeping up with America's favorite reality TV family. Adding to the confusion is how these terms are often thrown around interchangeably. But there are some key differences among them that I think you should be aware of, so let me clear things up:

- A **vegan** diet excludes *all* animal products from the diet, including the animals themselves and any products that come from them (e.g., eggs, cheese, and milk).

- A **vegetarian** diet excludes the animals themselves but often includes eggs and/or dairy products.

- A **plant-based diet** originally described a diet focused primarily on plant-based foods without completely excluding foods from animals (hmm, sound familiar?). It has since evolved to be almost synonymous with vegan in that it now excludes all animal products from the diet. The difference between plant-based and vegan is that the former emphasizes consumption of whole and minimally processed plant-based foods.

- **Flexitarian** is a combination of the words *flexible* and *vegetarian* used to describe a mostly or semi-vegetarian diet centered on plant-based foods with the occasional inclusion of animal ones. Again, sound familiar?

Flexitarian, semi-vegetarian, and *plant-forward* are essentially different terms that describe the same primarily, but not entirely, plant-based way of eating. They are nearly identical, with the exception that the plant-forward approach puts greater emphasis on *celebrating* the evidence-based benefits of putting plants forward (from both a health and environmental perspective) and on consuming a wide *variety* of plant-based foods (and you'll soon find out why).

Notice how the word exclude *is mentioned for all of the eating approaches except for plant-forward and flexitarian. That is because this approach is not defined by what you* exclude *from the diet but rather what you* include.

At this point, you might be thinking, "Just eat more plants and less meat—sounds a bit ambiguous." And well, that is sort of the point. I want you (and everyone else reading this book) to put plants forward for life, which means this approach must put flexibility at the forefront. That said, if there is one thing I have learned as a dietitian, it is that absolute flexibility sounds great in theory, but what people really need (and want) is *structured* flexibility. That is why Chapter 5 is dedicated to a comprehensive 28-day plant-forward reset plan with easy-to-digest guidelines (and some wiggle room, of course).

"This approach is not defined by what you exclude from the diet but rather what you include."

And fair warning, I use the word *plant* about a million times in this book. Don't let it overwhelm you; the word represents more than just fruits and veggies. It refers to all the nutritious came-from-a-plant foods, like whole grains, legumes, nuts, and seeds, too.

CHAPTER 2:
THE POWER OF PLANTS

You're ready to regain your health, but ultimately, why should you go plant-forward to do so? Making any dietary change is not easy, but understanding the "why" behind the recommendation to make a change can empower you to sustain it for the long term. I want to make sure that my clients (and now you, the reader) understand *exactly* why I recommend what I recommend: because of the incredible life-altering (and perhaps even life-extending) changes that will occur inside you once you put plants forward.

Understanding the "why" behind going plant-forward can help you overcome the days when you are just not feeling the plants. Because let's be honest, if all plant foods (veggies, I'm talking to you) tickled your taste buds like chocolate or a sizzling fillet do, I wouldn't be writing this book.

Let me be *totally* honest here: The temptation to cut back on nutrient-dense plant-based foods in favor of the highly palatable animal products and/or ultra-processed foods that are so readily available to us will inevitably occur at some point during your plant-forward journey—especially when you no longer notice significant changes in your health day to day. Diet-induced changes in certain health and well-being measures, like weight and energy levels, are obvious and become noticeable soon after a person makes the dietary switch. But other equally important changes that stay below the surface, like shifts in your gut microbiome and cholesterol levels, may not be as obvious until they are, which is usually a sign that something isn't quite right. So, keep this section in your metaphorical back pocket to serve as motivation to keep putting plants forward when temptation strikes.

The Power of Plants for Gut Health

Any conversation about the gut involves my second-favorite f-word—*fiber*—which is arguably the most important tool in your health arsenal. When you think of fiber, you probably picture a sad bowl of bran flakes or your grandma's Metamucil. *Hard pass, thanks!* Fiber's reputation is anything but sexy, but get enough of it in its whole food form, and you are sure to feel sexier... eventually.

Fiber is a type of carbohydrate found in plant-based foods like fruits, veggies, legumes, and whole grains. In fact, plant-based foods are the only foods that naturally contain fiber. So if only 5 percent of Americans meet their daily fiber requirements, that means the other 95 percent are not eating enough plants. (Well, unrefined plant foods. We certainly get enough of the refined, fiberless ones.) Yikes!

Unlike with protein, fat, and the other carbohydrate types (sugars and starches), your body can't break down fiber and (directly) uses it for energy because you don't have the digestive enzymes needed to do so. Instead, fiber works its magic by sliding through your gut relatively intact but not unnoticed. It's thought that a lack of dietary fiber is a primary feature of the typical Western diet that has led to a rise in chronic disease. But exactly how does a nutrient that you can't even digest play such a big role in your health? Well, because...

You Are Not Alone in Your Body

Sounds like the title of a low-budget horror film, but it's the reality. There are trillions of microorganisms—bacteria, fungi, and viruses—that call the human body home. In fact, it could be said that half of you isn't human. That is, about half of the cells that make up "you" are bacteria, the majority of which are hitching a ride in your gut. This gut ecosystem—technically referred to as the gut *microbiota* but more often referred to as the gut *microbiome*—has attracted a lot of attention from the scientific community in recent years as research has uncovered the fundamental and, until now, underestimated role the bacteria in it play in many aspects of human health and disease.

Your gut is host to hundreds of different bacterial species, both beneficial and potentially pathogenic. A balanced ecosystem where the species live together in mutual harmony and the "good" greatly outnumber the potentially "bad" is critical because, unlike Vegas, what happens in the gut does not stay in the gut. You have a symbiotic relationship with your gut bugs; you provide them with room and board. In turn, they influence countless processes throughout your body related to digestion, weight management, cardiovascular health, immunity, and much, much more. They can even synthesize vitamins for you—notably vitamin K and most of the B complex vitamins.

"Unlike Vegas,
what happens in the gut
does not stay in the gut."

These guys have been linked to the health of just about every organ in the body; when they're happy, you're happy, both figuratively and literally speaking. (Seriously, the gut is often referred to as the "second brain" because it is in constant bidirectional communication with the brain in your skull, thus influencing mood, behavior, and more.) And like you, your gut friends must eat to survive. Their favorite food? You guessed it—fiber, the hallmark of the plant-forward solution. You see, we humans may not possess the enzymes needed to break down fiber, but our bacterial tenants have an arsenal of enzymes at their disposal, and they are armed and ready to use them.

You Are What Your Gut Bacteria Eat

Digestion 101: Most of the food we eat is digested and absorbed in the upper part of the digestive tract to nourish our bodies. The remainder—the parts of the food that are indigestible to humans (hello, fiber) and small amounts of other food molecules that escape digestion—makes its merry way down to the colon, where the vast majority of gut bacteria reside. Cue the bacterial feast!

As the gut bacteria ferment (their way of "eating") our scraps for their own energy, they gift us with their waste products or "metabolites"—a more polite way of saying bacteria poo, basically. Stay with me here because things are about to come full circle. This "waste" does not actually go to waste. Quite the opposite, actually. Our gut bacteria influence our health largely due to the production of these metabolites, which are either health-promoting or health-impeding. Feed your friendly gut bacteria lots of the fermentable fibers they thrive on—referred to as *prebiotics*— and they will churn out health-promoting metabolites—sometimes referred to as *postbiotics.*

Although we are just scratching the surface of what we know about all the different health-promoting metabolites the bacteria can produce, we do know that an important group of them called short-chain fatty acids (SCFAs) boasts quite a resume. They act as signaling molecules by binding to and activating cell receptors throughout the body that increase fat oxidation; reduce fat storage; trigger the release of appetite-suppressing hormones (leptin, PYY, and GLP-1); regulate blood pressure; and influence the activity of key enzymes involved in blood sugar control, insulin secretion and signaling, and cholesterol production. Translation: SCFAs help you burn body fat, hack your hunger hormones, prevent weight gain, reduce the risk of heart disease, and combat insulin resistance. *Where do I sign?*

It gets better. They even benefit the very bacteria they come from by regulating the gut's pH, enabling these beneficial SCFA-producing bacteria to survive, thrive, and inhibit pathogens' growth. The SCFA butyrate is of particular interest because it suppresses intestinal inflammation and is the main energy source for the cells lining your colon (colonocytes), enabling them to carry out their important functions like preserving the integrity of your gut lining. And since about 70 percent of the immune system resides in the lining of your gut, it's essential that your diet encourages the growth and activity of these butyrate-producing and other beneficial bacteria to support a strong immune system that protects against disease.

"SCFAs help you burn body fat, hack your hunger hormones, prevent weight gain, reduce the risk of heart disease, and combat insulin resistance."

Immune Health

In 2020, the COVID-19 pandemic turned the world upside down, which led to a renewed interest in how to support immunity. Many turned to social media and Google in search of the latest and greatest supplements and superfoods—and understandably so. But has the answer to how to support a healthy immune system been inside us all along? Literally speaking here, the bacteria living inside your gut are separated from the majority of your immune cells by just a single layer of cells, and, so, your immune system and gut microbiome are in constant communication with each other and support one another. After all, they've been across-the-fence neighbors since you came out of the womb. The vitality of your immune system and your body's immune response largely depend on the composition and state of your gut microbiome. It makes sense then that nurturing it could be one of the best ways to help keep your immune system in top shape to fight infectious adversaries not only during a pandemic but for years to come.

So, if these powerhouse SCFAs are the end products of microbial fermentation of (i.e., chowing down on) prebiotic fibers, well, you are in luck. The plant-forward journey you are about to embark on is chock-full of prebiotic grub for your good gut guys, both supporting their growth and survival and enabling them to crank out SCFAs left and right. *Winner winner chickpea dinner!*

Remember, plant foods are your only natural source of fiber. It's no wonder plant-based diets are associated with higher levels of SCFAs and SCFA-producing bacteria in the gut (like *Bifidobacteria* and *Roseburia* species, *Faecalibacterium prausnitzii*, and *Eubacterium rectale*). It also comes as no surprise that the standard American diet (which has an appropriate acronym of SAD and is low in fiber, high in animal fat and protein, and high in sugar) is associated with the opposite. Deprive your beneficial fiber-loving gut bacteria of their cuisine of choice, and they are left to ferment whatever else comes their way to survive or are starved out of commission, which allows the microbial villains to set up camp and throw the balance of your gut ecosystem out of whack (often termed "dysbiosis"). This can lead to a decrease in the production of anti-inflammatory metabolites (like SCFAs) and an increase in the production of pro-inflammatory ones from the fermentation of dietary fats and proteins. (For example, a high-fat diet can increase the production of pro-inflammatory metabolites implicated in colon cancer called secondary bile acids.)

And it doesn't end there—as if it were straight from that hypothetical horror film I mentioned earlier, this fiber-starved gut microbiota may start to munch on the protective mucus layer of your gut, damaging the integrity of your gut lining. Yeah—that same gut lining that houses the majority of your immune system cells. But again, this isn't a movie. This unfavorable and complex sequence of events is thought to play a role in the chronic low-grade inflammation that is associated with numerous conditions, including obesity, type 2 diabetes, cardiovascular disease (CVD) and its risk factors (atherosclerosis and hypertension), inflammatory bowel disease (IBD), Irritable Bowel Syndrome (IBS), and certain cancers.

Go Plant-Forward for Your Gut Microbiome

The good news is, you can tweak the makeup and activity of your gut microbiome to favor health, and quite rapidly, too. I'm talking within twenty-four hours. And how might you do that? Say it with me: Eat. More. Plants. There is mounting evidence that upping your intake of less-processed plant foods and swapping more animal proteins for plant ones has the potential to prevent those *scary* intestinal inflammatory processes via the gut microbiome. But not just *more* plants—you've got to get in a *variety* of them, too! The American Gut Project—one of the largest studies on the human microbiome—found that those with the most diverse gut microbiomes (meaning a greater number of bacterial species in the gut) were consuming upwards of thirty *different* plant foods per week. (Sounds daunting, but I promise you it's not.) A diverse gut microbiome is thought to be more resilient to pathogens and better able to produce higher levels of SCFAs, and it's considered a generally good indicator of a "healthy" gut.

Does this mean you have to go completely plant-based? Nope! Remember, we're Team Pro-Plants, not Team Anti-Meat. Research suggests that dietary efforts for supporting a health-promoting gut microbiome should focus on a greater, but not necessarily exclusive, intake of plant-based foods because it's unlikely that including small amounts of animal foods in the diet, should you choose to, will sabotage these efforts. But a diet rich in animal foods leaves less room for and therefore lacks the foods we know, without a doubt, support a flourishing, harmonious gut microbiome. What are these foods? One more time for the people in the back: PLANTS!

The Power of Plants for Weight Loss and Blood Sugar Control

We now know that a plant-forward approach can positively influence your gut microbiome's composition and activity, which in turn influences satiety, blood sugar control, insulin sensitivity, and inflammation for the better. And all those things play a role in weight management. Beyond its powerful effects on the gut microbiota, how else might going plant-forward help you lose (or maintain) weight? Good ol' carbohydrates—or "carbs" for short. If that word sends shivers down your spine, you are not alone. The decades-long low-carb fad diet craze has made carbohydrate-rich foods public enemy number one, and the more recent popularity of a very low-carb, very high-fat diet (rhymes with *veto diet*) has only furthered the carb controversy, turning one poor soul after the other into a *carbophobe*. (Confession, I was once a carbophobe, too.) Put yourself on a low-carb, high-fat diet, and all of your ailments will be solved! Easy as pie (but no, you can't actually have any pie). Ironically, we've been scared into eating a lot more fat out of fear of getting fat. And since many plant-based foods are carbohydrate-rich, this fear could make you skeptical to start this plant-forward journey. Let's turn that carb confusion into carb confidence.

"Let's turn that carb confusion into carb confidence."

To understand how carbs are more of a hero than a villain in this story, it's important that I briefly mention how they got such a bad rap in the first place. It ties back to their effect on the hormone insulin (*gasp*)—carbs' co-conspirator and public enemy number two. A quick primer: during digestion, digestible carbohydrates (i.e., sugars and starches, not fiber) are broken down by the body into the simple sugar glucose (the body's primary energy source), which then enters the bloodstream for distribution. The rise in blood sugar levels signals the release of insulin to clear the glucose out of the bloodstream and into neighboring cells, where it can be used directly as fuel or converted to fat for long-term storage *if in excess* (emphasis by carb antagonists on the "converted to fat" part). At the same time, the release of insulin tells the body to stop burning stored fat for fuel in favor of using the energy coming in. Put (very) simply, the theory championed by low-carb advocates suggests that carbohydrates are uniquely fattening because they are the primary driver of insulin, which promotes fat gain and—the theory goes—makes you hungrier, too.

I suppose it makes intuitive sense that the proposed solution to our weight struggles as of late has been to ditch carbs to keep secretion of the widely misunderstood hormone that is insulin to a minimum. But if carbs are inherently fattening and drive appetite, wouldn't we expect to see significantly greater fat loss from low-carb diets? Ah yes, but alas, we do not. Tightly controlled studies in which calories and protein were held constant have upheld that low-carb diets offer no fat loss advantage over higher-carb ones. As for the appetite part, in a 2021 metabolic ward study published in *Nature Medicine* in which ad libitum (i.e., eat as much as you want) keto and low-fat, plant-based diets were pitted against each other, those randomly assigned to the plant-based group took in significantly fewer calories over the study period. Yet, despite this—and the fact that this higher-carb diet led to greater secretion of insulin after meals—there was no difference in their hunger or fullness levels when compared to those in the keto diet group. (How is this possible you might ask? Stay tuned.)

And interestingly, putting people on very low-carb diets has been shown to drastically reduce concentrations of SCFAs (you know—the bacterial metabolites that can beneficially affect the control of body weight, among other things) and the bacterial species that produce them. Not exactly surprising, considering that fiber is a type of carbohydrate, and when you cut out carbs, the logic holds you'll cut out fiber, too.

Wouldn't we also expect to see higher obesity rates among vegans and vegetarians, who typically consume a larger percentage of their calories from carbohydrates? Yup. But again, we do not. Both intervention trials and large population studies that analyze various dietary patterns paint a consistent picture that vegans and vegetarians tend to consume fewer calories, have lower body mass index (BMI), lower rates of overweight and obesity and type 2 diabetes, and gain less weight over time than their nonvegetarian peers. (Make no mistake: I'm not saying that these diets make you immune to weight gain and that you can't be an overweight plant-eater—you certainly can be.) Population-based cohort studies enrolling a large percentage of vegetarians (with varying degrees of vegetarianism) provide considerable insight into the relationship between plant-rich diets, weight, and overall health. The two largest studies—the European Prospective Investigation into Cancer and Nutrition–Oxford (EPIC-Oxford) and the Adventist Health Study–2 (AHS-2)—have studied thousands of individuals over decades. And while observational research such as this can only tell us correlation and not causation, the "weight" of the evidence thus far points to a positive effect of these carbohydrate-cherishing dietary patterns on weight.

And I can't skip mentioning the longest living populations in the world—referred to as the "Blue Zones"—have survived and thrived on carb-centric diets for centuries. Sure, these populations also tend to be more active (I'm talking walking five miles a day in comparison to our thirty-minute elliptical sessions) and engage in a variety of other healthy behaviors—but still, if carbohydrate intake were as problematic as mainstream media has made it out to be, we wouldn't expect these populations to be so lean and healthy.

Legumes, whole grains, and fruit have each been independently linked to reduced body weight. Yet, in the carbophobic mind, these extremely nutritious, carbohydrate-rich foods are often lumped together with white bread and bonbons and vilified just the same. (This reminds me of the time I overheard someone ask for no beans on their salad because they were "too high in carbs." I can't help but chuckle at the thought of beans somehow being implicated as a culprit in America's obesity epidemic. They may make you fart, but they won't make you fat. Quite the opposite, in fact. According to data from the National Health and Nutrition Examination Survey 1999–2002, consumers of this "magical fruit" tend to have *lower* body weight and *smaller* waistlines. Pass the beans, please!)

What gives? Why do I lose weight like a fat-burning machine every time I cut carbs? (Emphasis on the "every time," seeing as how most people go low-carb but then don't stay low-carb.) I believe you! But it's not a matter of carbohydrate (or insulin) per se—it ultimately boils down to the fundamental principle of weight manipulation: calorie control. (Although there is more to the simple equation of "calories in versus calories out," I won't belabor that here.) I hate to burst the low-carb bubble, but these weight-loss results are less "magic" and more "thermodynamics" mixed in with some water-weight loss. If cutting carbs forces you to reduce your overall caloric intake over time, you will lose weight. The issue is not that carbohydrates are inherently fattening; it's that many of the carbohydrate-rich foods that are so easily accessible to us are extremely palatable, come at a high-calorie price tag, and do a poor job of filling you up because of how quickly they are processed by the body. You know, the kinds of foods that immediately pop into your head when you hear the word *carbs,* like pizza, bagels, pizza bagels (yes, a real thing), and the endless bowls of pasta and breadsticks at Olive Garden. As you can imagine, it's pretty easy to lose weight (and quite rapidly, too) by going into a caloric deficit when you have to eliminate these foods to stay below some arbitrary carbohydrate number. And thus, all carbohydrate-rich foods (even the nutrient-dense ones like legumes, whole grains, and poor, poor fruit) and *only* carbohydrate-rich foods take the blame for your pre-diet weight woes. (But we forget that many of the calorically dense, carb-rich foods are "guilty by association" and tend to be high in fat, too.)

The real question is, were you able to sustain that low-carb lifestyle for the long term? I'm thinking there's a high probability that you're shaking your head *no* right now, seeing as how you're reading this book. I could be wrong; I recognize that there is no universal approach to eating, and a low-carb lifestyle can work for *some* people and may be particularly useful for some who are managing diabetes (at least, in the short term). However, having started my career as a low-carb dietitian, I've witnessed firsthand that it simply doesn't work out for a vast majority of people (myself—a recovering carbophobe—included). And trust me when I say that I was really rooting for low-carb diets to come out on top—they produce results rapidly (although not often permanently), they're not hard to explain or sell, and they can make the person selling them a lot of dough (i.e., money, not actual dough, which you unfortunately can't enjoy when cutting carbs).

> ## "I think many of us could have saved ourselves a lot of time, stress, money, and missed happy hours had we simply figured out how to incorporate carbohydrate-rich foods into our lives in a way that favors health in the first place."

Even if there were a slight metabolic advantage to living a low-carb life (which, hey, I'm not ruling out entirely), the fact of the matter is, the desire for carbohydrate-rich foods eventually wins out for most. You end up right back where you started—in a love-hate relationship with all carbohydrate-rich foods that leads to you gaining and losing the same 10, 15, 20 pounds over and over again. I think many of us could have saved ourselves a lot of time, stress, money, and missed happy hours had we simply figured out how to incorporate carbohydrate-rich foods into our lives in a way that favors health in the first place.

Hormone Hack

Carbophobia may be affecting your stress levels and sleep, too. Your body treats low blood sugar as a stressor, causing levels of cortisol—your main stress hormone—to rise. Adequate carb intake can help lower cortisol levels and keep them in check, and consequently, not eating enough carbs can increase levels. Plus, carbs help clear the way for the amino acid tryptophan to enter the brain, which ultimately helps us produce melatonin—the hormone you might recognize from your sleeping pill that promotes good sleep. So, by depriving yourself of carbs, you could be hurting your sleep, too. And it doesn't end there. The body perceives lack of sleep as a stressor, too, which puts you right back on the cortisol train. That's a train we'd like to stay off of, thank you very much.

Be Carb-Conscious

I want to make one thing very clear—I am by no means suggesting you drop this book right here and now, go wild on all the carbohydrate-rich foods you want and let your blood sugar levels (and insulin levels) spike without regard. (I'm also not suggesting you go low-fat, either, seeing as how many fat-rich plant foods are extremely nutritious.) Although all carbohydrate-rich foods can have a place in your plant-forward diet, they are not all created equal and should be treated as such. Beans, quinoa, and fruit are on a different tier than refined pasta, white bread, and donuts—and there's overwhelming evidence to support that *overconsumption* of the latter (and thus displacement of the former) has contributed to the problems of obesity, heart disease, insulin resistance, and type 2 diabetes that's plaguing developed nations.

But I want you to rest assured that carbohydrate-rich foods can be your ally when it comes to weight and blood sugar management, and they are your ally when going plant-forward. In the context of this approach, they will neither "make you fat," nor will they prevent you from losing fat should you want to. When you shift your focus from carb *quantity* to carb *quality*, you're able to control satiety, hunger, and overall calorie intake, and therefore your weight, as a by-product—no carb- or calorie-counting necessary. And how do you focus on carb quality? It's simple, really. You look for our five-letter, nondigestible friend. Remember—my second-favorite f-word.

————————————

"When you shift your focus from carb quantity to carb quality, you're able to control satiety, hunger, and overall calorie intake, and therefore your weight, as a by-product—no carb- or calorie-counting necessary."

————————————

Fiber! It Fills You Up Without Filling You Out

I'm guilty of using this line way too often. Even though I cringe a little every time I say it, it gets the point across quite nicely. Fiber—the nondigestible carbohydrate type—is your secret weapon for weight management. Well, more like your not-so-secret weapon because you are now well aware of the gut microbiome–mediated effects it has on satiety. But before fiber even has the chance to be gobbled up by your good gut guys in the large intestine, it provides several metabolic benefits—benefits you're likely missing every time you go low-carb.

It starts in the mouth. Fiber-rich foods generally require more chewing than low-fiber foods, decreasing the rate of ingestion and forcing the body to produce more saliva and gastric juices, which expands the stomach and increases satiety. It doesn't stop there. Once in the stomach, fiber is not broken down and absorbed like the other carbohydrate types (remember, we do not have the necessary enzymes). Instead, a certain fiber type (soluble fiber) absorbs water to form a gel that slows stomach emptying and digestion, which keeps you fuller for longer. In the small intestine, this gel entraps sugars, cholesterol, and fats, slowing their absorption into the bloodstream (even preventing some from being absorbed altogether) and resulting in a lower postprandial blood sugar level and a more steady, sustained release of energy. It's thought that this prolonged presence of nutrients in the gut means that the time over which these nutrients can interact with satiety receptors in the gut is longer, which stimulates a greater release of hormones involved in appetite regulation.

For the grand finale, once in the colon, your gut bacteria break down and ferment the prebiotic fibers, and well, you know what happens next (*cough* SCFAs *cough*). For these reasons, a key component of the plant-forward approach is getting most (but not necessarily all) of your carbohydrate intake from fiber-rich, slow-release sources—which I call "slow carbs."

———— PLANT-POWERED FACT ————

Fiber intake recommendations from the Institute of Medicine for women and men are 25 and 38 grams per day, respectively. (These numbers fall to 21 and 30 grams per day for those over the age of fifty.) The average intake in the United States is somewhere in the neighborhood of 15 grams per day—meaning, most people need to *double* their daily fiber intake. And research suggests that going beyond 30 grams per day can be beneficial, especially for reducing risk of colorectal cancer. Could you get enough fiber on a low-carb diet? Sure—with some planning and eating a boatload of avocado, raspberries, and seeds on the daily, it is possible (although it becomes increasingly difficult the lower carb you go). But to meet or, better yet, exceed the recommended daily fiber intake with *ease* (and without a supplement), your best bet is to recover from carbophobia and embrace the higher-carb, fiber-rich foods, like whole grains, legumes, and fruit, in addition to these lower-carb ones just mentioned.

Fiber Content of Various High-Fiber Foods

ALMONDS	1 ounce	3.5 grams
APPLE	1 medium	4.5 grams
ARTICHOKE	1 medium	7 grams
AVOCADO	1 medium	10 grams
BARLEY, COOKED	1 cup	6 grams
BLACK BEANS, COOKED	½ cup	7.5 grams
BREAD, SPROUTED/EZEKIEL	1 slice	3 grams
BREAD, WHOLE WHEAT	1 slice	2 grams
BROCCOLI	1 cup	5 grams
CHIA SEEDS	2 tablespoons	10 grams
CHICKPEA OR LENTIL SPAGHETTI	1 cup	6 grams
EDAMAME	1 cup	8 grams
GREEN PEAS	1 cup	9 grams
KIWI	2 medium	4 grams
LENTILS, COOKED	½ cup	8 grams
NAVY BEANS, COOKED	½ cup	9.5 grams
OATS, COOKED	1 cup	4 grams
PASTA, CHICKPEA OR LENTIL, COOKED	1 cup	6 grams
PASTA, EDAMAME, COOKED	1 cup	13 grams
PASTA, WHOLE WHEAT, COOKED	1 cup (cooked)	6 grams
PEAR	1 medium	5.5 grams
POPCORN, AIR-POPPED	3 cups	3.5 grams
QUINOA, COOKED	1 cup	5 grams
RASPBERRIES	1 cup	8 grams
SWEET POTATO, WITH SKIN	1 medium	4 grams

The Second-Meal Effect

Okay, so we know that fiber is great for blood sugar control right after a meal we just ate. But guess what? It can also influence how your *next* meal is digested and the blood sugar response it elicits, too. How? SCFAs for the win, *again!* Let me explain.

You eat a bean burrito bowl for dinner; soon after, you get the fiber benefits described previously. When you're chowing down on breakfast the next morning, your gut bacteria in the large intestine are going to town on the prebiotic fibers from the beans in your dinner, producing SCFAs in the process. These SCFAs can affect how your current meal (aka your breakfast) is digested and may lessen the blood sugar response to sugars and starches you consume in this meal. Not only that, but they can influence your appetite at this subsequent meal, too. Researchers fed a group of healthy young adults beans or white bread for dinner, and the next morning, the bean eaters had higher levels of satiety hormones and lower levels of hunger hormones. Pretty neat, right?! This phenomenon was initially referred to as the "lentil effect" because it was first discovered using lentils. Beans, chickpeas, and certain whole grains were also found to have the same effect, and so it has since been dubbed the "second-meal effect." You'll be taking full advantage of this effect going forward—plant forward, that is.

Nutrient-Dense, Calorie-Poor

So, fiber fills you up both directly and indirectly, all while contributing little to no calories—hence the "without filling you out" part of my cringe-worthy line. It's a big part of the reason you can end up eating more going plant-forward and still lose weight (or maintain your current weight).

Sounds gimmicky, I know, but it's true. The scientific principle behind this "magic" is called energy density. Energy or calorie density is the number of calories (amount of energy) in a specific weight of food. Foods with lower energy density provide fewer calories per gram than foods with higher energy density. Why do we care? Well, research shows that, to a certain degree, we tend to consume the same amount (weight) of food each day regardless of calorie content. Let's say that you eat about 4 pounds of food every day (which is pretty spot-on with the average)—it's possible to feel as full from 4 pounds of food totaling 1,700 calories as you would from 4 pounds of food totaling 2,000 calories. And since we know calorie control is important when it comes to weight manipulation, we can use this principle of energy density to our advantage and essentially feel full on fewer calories. The main factors that determine the energy density of food are water, fiber, and fat content. Lower energy density foods tend to have a higher fiber and/or water content; higher energy density foods tend to be higher in fat (no surprise here, since fat is the most calorically dense macronutrient).

> "Generally speaking, whole and less-processed plant-based foods provide bulk, weight, and/or volume in fewer calories, giving you more belly-filling bang for your buck."

Any guesses on which kinds of foods fall on the lower end of the energy density spectrum? Generally speaking, whole and less-processed plant-based foods provide bulk, weight, and/or volume in fewer calories, giving you more belly-filling bang for your buck. Think fruits, vegetables, legumes, and cooked whole grains, which are high in fiber and/or water and low in fat. That keto versus plant-based study I mentioned earlier makes a lot more sense now, doesn't it? No wonder those in the plant-based group were able to feel as full despite consuming significantly fewer calories—the energy density of their diet was much lower than that of the high-fat keto diet.

Now, there is one important thing to be mindful of: Ultra-processed plant-based foods often have a higher energy density because processing tends to remove fiber and water and add fat and/or sugar. Take, for example, the humble potato. Process it into potato chips, and you've now increased the energy density to seven times that of a baked potato (sans the butter and sour cream, of course).

Go Plant-Forward for Weight Loss and Blood Sugar Control

So, given everything you've read thus far, it should come as no surprise that studies have shown that fiber intake is inversely associated with body weight, waist circumference, and risk of developing type 2 diabetes. Because the only way to increase dietary fiber intake is to eat more plant-based foods (and therefore embrace the dreaded c-word, carbs!), well, eating more plants seems like a no-brainer. Luckily, you don't need to limit your diet to *only* plant-based foods to reap these benefits—even semi-vegetarian (i.e., plant-forward) diets have been associated with substantially lower risk of type 2 diabetes and lower BMI compared to nonvegetarian ones. And weight loss as low as 5 percent of total body weight has been shown to trigger a cascade of health benefits, including improvements in blood pressure, cholesterol levels, blood sugar levels, and inflammation.

But losing weight is only half the battle. For many people, the greater challenge is keeping the weight off over the long term. This is where the plant-forward approach is especially advantageous, seeing as how you do not have to cut ties with any of your favorites (whether they come from plants or animals).

The Power of Plants for Heart Health

Cardiovascular disease (CVD) is the leading cause of death in the United States (and globally), claiming a life approximately every thirty-six seconds. Scaring you with health stats was not on my agenda for this book, but I felt it necessary to mention this impactful one. There are many risk factors for heart disease and stroke, some of which are out of your control (e.g., family history, ethnicity, and age), but many of which are in your control. In fact, it's estimated that 80 percent of premature heart disease and stroke can be prevented through healthy behaviors. Could one of those healthy behaviors that improves heart health be eating more plant-based foods? A resounding YES.

When you put together what I've discussed so far, it's easy to see how harnessing the preventative power of plants can lead to a healthier heart. I hate to sound like a broken record, but many of the cardiovascular benefits of the plant-forward

approach tie back to boring but miraculous ol' fiber. I briefly mentioned that a specific gel-like fiber type (soluble fiber) can entrap cholesterol and bile acids (made from cholesterol) in the small intestine, encouraging them to exit the body instead of being absorbed. Soluble fiber essentially helps your body flush out excess cholesterol and forces your liver to pull cholesterol from the blood to make more bile acids, thus decreasing the amount of "gunk" that can build up in your arteries and lead to atherosclerosis (plaque build-up and hardening of the arteries).

Hormone Hack

Speaking of "flushing" things out, fiber can also bind to the cholesterol-based sex hormone *estrogen* in the gut, helping to "flush" excess amounts from the body, decrease reabsorption, and reduce circulating levels in the blood. And no surprise here, a flourishing, fiber-fueled gut microbiome helps to limit estrogen reabsorption, too. Dealing with high estrogen levels (relative to other hormone levels, often referred to as "estrogen dominance") is a challenge some individuals face that can present with symptoms that cause major disruptions in well-being and may increase risk for more serious health concerns.

You also know that a higher intake of fiber is associated with lower body weight, reduced risk of type 2 diabetes, and improved blood sugar control in those with diabetes. What you may not know yet is that a diet rich in fiber can help reduce and prevent high blood pressure (hypertension), too. Hyperlipidemia (high cholesterol, triglycerides, or both), obesity, type 2 diabetes, and hypertension—these just so happen to be the major diet-related and *controllable* risk factors for CVD.

The plant-forward diet includes lots of fiber-rich foods low in energy density that can help you take control of all the above. But fiber doesn't deserve all the credit—after all, every superhero has a team of sidekicks fighting alongside it. Where there is fiber, you will also find a variety of vitamins, minerals, antioxidants, and other plant nutrients (aka phytonutrients) with antioxidant and anti-inflammatory effects tagging along. Many health benefits associated with fiber may partially be mediated by these sidekicks. For example, vitamin C, potassium, magnesium, and polyphenols are found abundantly in fiber-rich plant foods and have all been linked to supporting a healthier heart.

Plant sterols, or phytosterols, are phytonutrients found in plant cell walls that are structurally similar to the body's cholesterol (and the cholesterol in animal foods). They can help lower total and low-density-lipoprotein (LDL) cholesterol (aka the "bad" cholesterol) levels by competing against cholesterol and blocking its absorption in the gut. Phytosterols are found in all plant foods, but the highest concentrations are in unrefined plant oils, including vegetable, nut, and olive oils, whole grains, nuts, seeds, and legumes (especially soy-based ones).

The cardioprotective power of going plant-forward is clearly largely due to what the approach *includes*, but how about what the approach *limits*? Time to address the elephant in the room: saturated fat—the fat type found in large quantities primarily in animal foods (but also in tropical plant oils like coconut oil) that has been the center of a big FAT (pun intended) heart-health controversy for decades now. Long implicated as a leading cause of CVD, it has recently been absolved of any wrongdoing by many in the low-carb, high-fat diet community who go so far as to say it's A-OK in large quantities. Which begs the question...

Is Butter Really Back?

Spoiler alert: If butter really were back, I'd be giving you a reason to return this book right here and now; so, no, you will not be hopping on the butter-in-your-coffee train anytime soon. But the whole story here is *saturated* with complexity. Although it is known that increased intake of saturated fats can increase well-known heart disease risk factors—notably, LDL cholesterol levels—strong evidence of a direct link between saturated fat intake and heart disease itself is lacking.

What gives? For one, the health effects of saturated fat are likely food-specific and depend on the "food matrix"—the various nutritional components of a specific food and how they are arranged in that food. Take, for example, dairy fat, which has a high saturated fat content. Different dairy products have different food matrices—butter lacks the protein, probiotics, and certain vitamins and minerals that cheese and yogurt contain—and this helps to explain why cheese and yogurt have been associated with neutral and even positive effects on measures of cardiovascular health compared to the less-than-stellar effects of butter. (Don't worry, you can still enjoy some butter on the plant-forward approach if you want to.) Now, I'm not giving you the green light to douse your plant-forward meals in cheese (although I do love a good fondue). Saturated fat is simply one piece of a complicated puzzle, further complicated by that fact that its health effects likely depend on what it is replacing—or being replaced by—in your diet.

A large prospective cohort study found that replacing 5 percent of energy intake from saturated fats with equivalent energy intake from unsaturated fats or *unrefined* carbohydrates (from whole grains) was associated with a significant reduction in heart disease risk. But when that same amount of saturated fats was replaced with carbohydrates from *refined* sources, risk remained similar. Basically, swap your bulletproof coffee (aka the coffee with butter I mentioned earlier) for white toast at breakfast, and you probably won't be doing yourself any favors in the heart department.

Saturated fat may not be as inherently villainous as we once thought, but, despite the headlines, it's no celebrity comeback story, either. We know that—on a population level—dietary patterns consistently associated with lower rates of heart disease tend to be lower in saturated fat. We also know that decades of research have indicated that unsaturated fats (polyunsaturated and monounsaturated fats) are preferable to saturated fats when it comes to cardiometabolic health, and replacing the latter with the former may reduce your risk of heart disease. These heart-healthy unsaturated fats just so happen to be predominantly found in plant-based foods and plant-derived oils (with the exception of omega-3-rich fatty fish)—think nuts, seeds, olives, olive oil, and the almighty avocado. You'll notice they aren't as headline-worthy these days because a wealth of research has solidified their role in heart and overall health. They're just *that good*, and you'll be hard-pressed to find evidence to the contrary. The good news is, by putting plants forward, you'll limit saturated fat sources in favor of unsaturated fat sources naturally (as long as you're not slathering all of your meals in coconut oil).

"Decades of research have indicated that unsaturated fats (polyunsaturated and monounsaturated fats) are preferable to saturated fats when it comes to cardiometabolic health, and replacing the latter with the former may reduce your risk of heart disease."

Coconut Oil Conundrum: Should You Eat It or Moisturize with It?

Speaking of coconut oil, this plant-based fat is made up almost entirely of saturated fats (about 90 percent compared to butter's 60 percent). Yet, despite its high saturated fat content, proponents recommend regular consumption of it for the exact reason many health experts caution against high saturated fat intake: heart health (weight loss and cognitive performance are among the host of health claims, too). The rationale? The saturated fatty acids in coconut oil are predominantly *medium-chain* fatty acids, which are metabolized by the body differently than the more commonly found *long-chain* ones and are therefore thought to have positive effects on your health. However, the evidence thus far paints coconut oil as neither a health villain nor a health hero. In fact, a 2020 meta-analysis from the American Heart Association found that coconut oil raises cholesterol levels—both the good and the bad kinds—more than other plant-based oils. Bottom line: Like most foods, there's no need to remove it from the diet entirely—but there's also no need to use it in excess for health reasons. Stick with the fats that have been supported by a large body of evidence for the most part (hello, unsaturated fats), and if you enjoy coconut oil, do so in moderation (and perhaps more so as a moisturizing hair mask).

Fats at a Glance

Saturated fats	Unsaturated fats*			
Raise total and LDL cholesterol	Monounsaturated	Polyunsaturated		
	Lower LDL cholesterol, may raise HDL cholesterol	Omega-3s *Lower triglycerides and blood pressure*		Omega-6s *Lower total and LDL cholesterol*
• Animal fats (meat, butter, and full-fat dairy products) • Tropical oils (coconut, palm oil)	• Avocados • Nuts • Oils (avocado, olive, and nut oils) • Olives	EPA/DHA	ALA	• Nuts • Seeds • Vegetable oils (best sources are corn, safflower, soybean, sunflower)
		• Fatty fish (best sources are mackerel, salmon, sardines, tuna) • Microalgae • Omega-3-enriched eggs	• Chia seeds • Flax seed • Flax seed oil • Hemp hearts • Soy foods • Walnuts	

Unsaturated fats are most beneficial when they replace saturated fats in the diet.

What's the Beef with Red Meat?

Where does red meat—often brought up in the saturated fat versus heart health debate—stand? Experts used to think that red meat wasn't great for your heart simply because of its saturated fat content. That was, until our microbial passengers stepped into the limelight not too long ago. Remember, what you eat shapes your gut's bacterial composition and thus the "metabolites" the bacteria produce. We have discussed the health-promoting metabolites at length—but as a quick refresher, these SCFAs positively influence weight, inflammation, blood sugar control, cholesterol production, and blood pressure through a variety of mechanisms that collectively support cardiovascular health. Now, just as they are produced by friendly bacteria in your gut when you eat fiber, the metabolite *trimethylamine N-oxide* (or TMAO for short—not to be confused with the internet slang LMAO) is produced when meat-loving bacteria in your gut get ahold of carnitine and choline—amino acid–like compounds found abundantly in red meat (and eggs). Within the past decade, high blood levels of TMAO have been linked to increased risk of cardiovascular events in several studies. And, like clockwork, TMAO was quickly crowned the new culprit in the link between red meat and heart disease. But (there's always a but, isn't there?) it turns out TMAO is more likely a *marker* of disease—and possibly of disease mediated by a dysbiotic microbiome rich in the specific bacterial species that produce it—rather than a *cause*. Remember, the more Westernized the diet—red meat and all—the more Westernized the microbiome (and thus the higher risk of disease, including CVD).

Like most complicated relationships, the relationship status between red meat and the heart can (and most likely will) change again in the future. But as it stands currently, it can be summed up quite nicely in five simple words: the dose makes the poison. A growing body of evidence suggests that *high* consumption of red meat increases your risk of heart disease and stroke, as well as CVD mortality and other adverse health outcomes (including diabetes and certain cancers). This is likely due to a combination of factors, including its saturated fat and heme iron (more on this later) content, how you cook it, and more importantly—the bigger picture here—*what it displaces in your diet.*

Consuming red meat (and other foods rich in saturated fat) frequently and in large quantities leaves less space for the protective foods we *know* are jam-packed with fuel for our loyal SCFA-producing bacteria and other good-for-your-heart stuff (unsaturated fats, antioxidants, phytosterols and other phytonutrients, etc.). Yeah, yeah—you know what these foods are (give me a P, give me an L, give me an A...). That doesn't mean that red meat is completely off the table because there is no convincing evidence to support that you can't enjoy modest amounts within the context of a plant-rich diet from a heart and overall health standpoint should you choose to, especially since it can serve as a source of high-quality protein and vitamin B12. But going plant-forward and *limiting* intake in favor of more plant-based proteins, like beans, soy foods, nuts, and protein-rich whole grains—even just swapping one serving a day—is backed by science to support a healthier heart.

Go Plant-Forward for Heart Health

The potentially protective role of plant-based dietary patterns in cardiovascular health has been increasingly recognized, with accumulating evidence linking them to healthier body weights, lower risk of type 2 diabetes, favorable blood pressure levels and blood lipid profiles (i.e., cholesterol, triglyceride, and apolipoprotein B levels), greater presence of specific beneficial gut bacteria, and higher counts of health-promoting metabolites—all of which translate to less CVD risk. Generally, the higher the proportion of nutrient-dense plant-based foods in the diet, the lower the risk and the greater the reward—but a completely plant-based diet is not necessary for cardiovascular health. Plant-forward-style, semi-vegetarian diets consisting of predominantly plant-based foods that contain smaller amounts of animal foods have been associated with favorable blood lipid profiles and blood pressure levels and lower risk of CVD and cardiovascular-related death. In fact, a plant-forward diet falls in line with the most recent American College of Cardiology/American Heart Association diet recommendations for the prevention of CVD, which suggest emphasizing intake of fruits, vegetables, legumes, nuts, whole grains, and fish and prioritizing unsaturated fats over saturated ones to reduce risk. Essentially, putting plants forward in any capacity is good for your heart.

Well, *almost* any. I have to mention this one caveat: Just because something is "plant-based" doesn't make it healthy by default. The infamous Oreo, for example, could be considered a plant-based food because its ingredients—white flour and sugar being the main ones—do indeed come from plants. And while enjoying an occasional cookie (or a few), a bowl of white spaghetti, or some baguette at your favorite Italian restaurant isn't anything to stress about, a diet full of refined, fiberless, and/or added sugar–rich plant-based foods pretty much negates the what-could-have-been benefits of a plant-centric diet.

Unsurprisingly, when researchers analyzed the diets of more than 200,000 participants from three large prospective cohort studies based on the healthfulness of the plant-based foods included, a diet rich in healthful ones (fruits, vegetables, nuts, legumes, plant oils, tea, and coffee) was associated with significantly lower risk of heart disease, whereas a diet that emphasized less-healthy ones (juices, sweetened beverages, refined grains, potatoes, fries, and sweets) was associated with increased risk. This plant-based version of the Standard American Diet is still, for lack of a better word, SAD, and one cannot assume that simply eating more plant-based foods irrespective of the source will produce positive health outcomes. (When you assume things, you make an—well, you know how the saying goes.) That said, a diet rich in healthful plant-based foods like fruits, vegetables, legumes, nuts, and seeds certainly will. And it turns out, it's not only good for *your* health but also for the health of the planet.

Go Plant-Forward for the Planet

The global food system is a major driver of climate change and depletion of resources. It's been estimated that as a result of population growth and the continued consumption of Western diets high in red meats and processed foods, the environmental pressures of our food system could increase 50 to 90 percent by the year 2050 without concerted action.

Put simply, animal-based foods tend to be more resource-intensive than plant-based ones (there are exceptions, of course)—with beef and dairy being the heavy hitters here. Cattle release methane—a potent greenhouse gas (GHG)—through belching as well as in manure. The World Resources Institute has estimated that per gram of protein, beef can require twenty times the land and emit twenty times the GHG emissions compared to common plant proteins, like beans. (Although with advanced technology and innovative farming techniques to improve farm management and feed quality, farmers can significantly reduce their emissions and environmental impact.)

> "Although your main driver for going plant-forward is likely your health, it's nice to know that this dietary shift could help the planet, too."

There is a growing consensus within the scientific community that reducing meat consumption could help mitigate the global climate and water crises as diets higher in plant-based foods than animal ones have been shown to carry a lower environmental footprint in terms of GHG emissions and land, energy, and water use. But just like eating for your health doesn't have to be an all-or-nothing proposition, the same applies to eating for the health of the planet. Leading experts and environmental research groups point out that we *do not* have to abandon meat altogether, as studies suggest that large reductions in GHG emissions are possible without complete exclusion of animal products. In fact, a plant-forward diet is likely a more feasible solution to our planetary health problems than a plant-exclusive one because it's better able to fulfill the nutritional needs of many and would require less change of social and cultural food traditions, and therefore, more people (globally) may be prepared to adopt it. Although your main driver for going plant-forward is likely your health, it's nice to know that this dietary shift could help the planet, too.

Live Long and Prosper with Plants

When I say, "go plant-forward for life," I'm speaking figuratively and *literally*. This approach is not only sustainable for life, but it can also support a healthier and longer life. If we put together everything we have discussed up to this point, it seems pretty obvious that this would be the case. Putting plants forward can help you reduce your risk of heart disease—the number one cause of death in the United States. How about the second leading cause of death—cancer? Well, there is strong evidence that high fiber intake, especially from whole grains, has a protective effect against colorectal cancer (a 10 percent risk reduction was shown for every 10 grams of fiber eaten per day), and that the opposite holds true with high saturated fat and red meat intake, especially processed red meat. And although no diet can guarantee you

won't develop cancer, the leading authorities on cancer research agree on one dietary pattern in particular that can help lower your risk: one that consists predominantly of nutrient-dense foods from a variety of plant sources. Sound familiar?

Exactly how and why plant-rich diets can be protective against certain cancers is being actively researched, but the evidence thus far points to multiple potential mechanisms. For instance, they can protect against inflammation, insulin resistance, and obesity—all of which can increase your risk of certain cancers. Plant foods are rich in antioxidant vitamins and other phytochemicals—like polyphenols, vitamins C and E, and carotenoids—which act as free radical fighters that protect healthy cells from the oxidative damage thought to play a role in cancer development. And our beloved SCFAs produced in abundance by a fiber-fueled gut microbiome may have anti-cancer properties, too. Butyrate, for example, may slow growth of and promote apoptosis (i.e., cell death) in colorectal cancer cells. (And recall that I briefly mentioned secondary bile acids—pro-inflammatory metabolites implicated in colon cancer—are produced by a fiber-famished, fat-fueled microbiome.)

Go Plant-Forward for Life

Many trendy diets promise optimal health and longevity, but the only dietary patterns that decades of research suggest actually deliver on these promises are those rich in healthful plant-based foods. In fact, a review that looked at different dietary patterns associated with longer and healthier lives concluded that the ones that are associated with lower risk of death from CVD, cancer, or any cause are all "built on a common core of a diet rich in plant foods," specifically, "whole grains, a variety of fruit and vegetables, nuts, and legumes." The Mediterranean diet, for example, is characterized by a high intake of vegetables, fruits, nuts, whole grains, and olive oil and is well-established as one of the healthiest eating patterns in the world. Interestingly enough, when data from the landmark Spanish PREDIMED trial was reanalyzed based on how "pro-vegetarian" the participants' Mediterranean-style diets were, those with higher pro-vegetarian scores had a significantly lower risk (41 percent) of premature death compared to those with lower scores—and they were still consuming small amounts of animal proteins regularly. (Think of it as a plant-forward diet with a Mediterranean flair.)

"Many trendy diets promise optimal health and longevity, but the only dietary patterns that decades of research suggest actually deliver on these promises are those rich in healthful plant-based foods."

These findings are consistent with a large body of evidence that suggests plant-rich diets provide exceptional health benefits, including increased longevity. But are we overestimating the power of plants? Let's consider the fact that those who eat more plant-based foods tend to be more likely to exhibit other healthy behaviors—like being more active, less likely to smoke and drink alcohol, etc.—that could contribute to these benefits. It's difficult (pretty much impossible, even) to disentangle a single health behavior—in this case, diet—from the multitude of other lifestyle and dietary factors that influence health, even when researchers attempt to adjust for these confounding factors. But the evidence thus far appears convincing enough for leading national and global health authorities, including the World Health Organization (WHO) and previously mentioned organizations, to agree that for the health of people and the planet, a predominantly, but not entirely, plant-based (better known to you and me as plant-forward) diet is the way to go.

Humans are complex, nutrition is complex, and therefore studying nutrition at the population level and attempting to make general, one-size-fits-all recommendations based on these findings is complex. You can think of it as a multiple-choice test where the answer to most questions is rarely A, B, C, or D, but rather some or all of the above. But if, hypothetically speaking here, you ever find yourself faced with a question on the best dietary approach for *most* people to reduce risk of chronic disease and promote optimal health and longevity and can only choose *one* answer— I'd go for the one that puts plants forward.

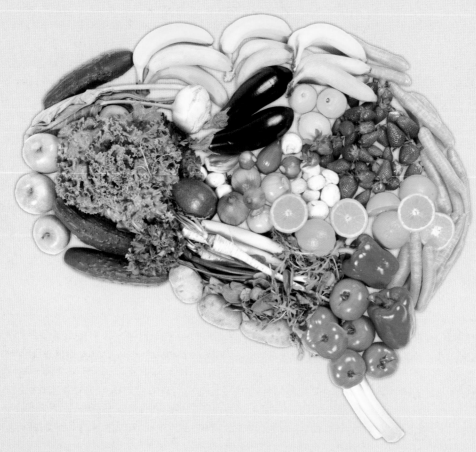

Nourish Your Noggin

It turns out that eating more plants may not only translate to a longer life span but also a longer "brain span"—aka the number of years you have a healthy and highly functioning brain. There is evidence that dietary patterns heavy on fiber- and phytonutrient-rich plant-based foods—like the Mediterranean-DASH Intervention for Neurodegenerative Delay or "MIND" diet—may preserve cognitive function, slow cognitive decline, and reduce the risk of developing Alzheimer's disease and other forms of dementia later in life.

And how might fiber bolster brain health? Well, SCFAs are thought to influence gut-brain crosstalk and brain function through various mechanisms, including their ability to cross the blood-brain barrier where they may exert neuroprotective and anti-inflammatory effects. As for phytonutrients, particularly polyphenols, their antioxidant abilities can protect neurons (brain cells) from oxidative damage and the buildup of beta-amyloid proteins, which can form hardened plaques between them. (Like plaque between your teeth, but in your brain, where a toothbrush and some floss unfortunately cannot help you.)

Although brain health and cognition are an area of health often left to be tackled in old age, taking proactive measures to support them should be a priority no matter your age. Following a plant-forward lifestyle is one such measure—and it's not a bad idea to make extra room in your plant-forward diet for the following plants, which research suggests may be particularly powerful in supporting brain health:

- **BERRIES:** Berries, especially blueberries, are packed with anthocyanins—the polyphenols responsible for their blue, purple, and red hues and that have been associated with enhanced neural activation in areas of the brain involved in memory. Studies have shown that blueberry supplementation is associated with improvements in memory and cognitive performance in both older adults and children. Small but mighty wild blueberries are particularly anthocyanin-rich thanks to their higher skin-to-pulp ratio, offering 33 percent more anthocyanins than their cultivated counterparts.

- **CRUCIFEROUS VEGGIES:** Broccoli (especially broccoli sprouts), cauliflower, bok choy, and cabbage are rich sources of sulforaphane, which has been shown to increase levels of glutathione—a potent endogenous antioxidant and the brain's major free radical scavenger—in certain areas of the brain.

- **LEAFY GREENS:** A prospective study of older Americans found that those who consumed an average of 1 to 2 servings per day of leafy greens, like spinach, kale, and collard greens, over five years were eleven years younger cognitively than those who consumed little to no leafy greens. The lutein, folate, vitamin K, and beta-carotene in leafy greens are thought to account for much of their protective role in age-related cognitive decline. Not a fan of salads? Try the spinach-containing smoothies (page 170) or the nourish bowls (page 248) for salad-free ways to get in more leafy greens.

- **NUTS AND SEEDS:** Nuts and seeds, especially walnuts and flax, chia, and hemp seeds, are among the most concentrated plant sources of omega-3 fatty acids—building blocks for brain cell membranes that are therefore critical for maintaining optimal brain structure, function, and health throughout life (see page 63 for more on omega-3s). Walnuts are exceptionally high in antioxidant nutrients that offer neuroprotection, like polyphenols and vitamin E.

CHAPTER 3:
MYTH BUSTING

If you follow me over on the 'gram, then you may have noticed I enjoy debunking common food- and nutrition-related myths (almost as much as I enjoy staying in on a Friday night with takeout in one hand and a glass of rosé in the other—*almost*). With all the information available at our fingertips, you'd think it would be easy to separate fact from fiction. Yeah, not so much. Nutrition misinformation and food fearmongering are more pervasive than ever, thanks in large part to social media. And as plant-based foods have become more mainstream, so too have the misconceptions that surround them. I don't want these myths and misconceptions to prevent you from reaping the benefits of a plant-forward diet, so let's play a little game of myth or fact to set the record straight once and for all.

You Should Avoid Fruit If You Want to Lose Weight

 MYTH: I give you permission to ignore whoever told you to avoid fruit because it's "too high in sugar." Yes, fruits are naturally rich in sugar (some more so than others), but there is no need to sound the alarm. Fruit antagonists will try to scare you by saying, "a banana is basically a candy bar." When I referred to nutrition nonsense that is being spewed all over social media, this is the type of thing I was talking about. Fruit may be nature's candy, but it's *not* Halloween candy. And if I were a betting woman, I'd bet that the reason you aren't meeting your health and wellness goals isn't that you're eating too much fruit. In fact, research has consistently shown that fruit intake has an *anti-obesity* effect.

Although it is true that your body can't distinguish between the added sugar in a candy bar and the sugar found naturally in fruit, how these sugars are *packaged* makes all the difference. The sugar in fruit is packaged alongside another carbohydrate type—my second-favorite f-word—FIBER. Fiber helps slow the absorption of the sugar in the fruit into the bloodstream, so it lessens the blood sugar impact, providing you with a steadier supply of energy. Fruits do vary in their fiber and sugar content—for example, berries have less sugar and more fiber than many other fruits—but there's no need to deprive yourself of your favorite fruits just because they are more sugar-dense. Variety is key! Plus, there is a simple and tasty way to lessen the blood sugar response of higher sugar fruits even more: pair your fruit with some protein and/or healthy fat. Apple slices with peanut butter, anyone? How about a fruit and yogurt parfait? Sprinkle on some cinnamon, and you'll be adding another ingredient thought to help with blood sugar control (although the evidence on this is mixed, it can't hurt, right?).

"If I were a betting woman, I'd bet that the reason you aren't meeting your health and wellness goals isn't that you're eating too much fruit."

And don't forget, fruit is an excellent source of disease-fighting vitamins, minerals, and phytochemicals, too. In fact, these phytochemicals may be partly responsible for the anti-obesity effects of fruit, along with fiber.

So now that you know that it's a myth that you need to avoid fruit to lose weight, you might be thinking, "Okay, so how much fruit can and should I eat per day?" A general recommendation is to enjoy two to three servings of fruit per day. If you're more active and/or have higher energy needs, you may want to stick to the higher end of that range. And of course, prioritize variety. Bananas are great for you, but that does not mean you should eat three a day. A better option, for example, would be to enjoy berries with breakfast and a banana with peanut butter as an afternoon snack.

Fresh Is Always Better Than Frozen

 MYTH: Frozen food has gotten a bad rap over the years for being highly processed and unhealthy—a largely undeserved reputation, especially when it comes to frozen produce. Freezing is one of the easiest and most effective food preservation methods. Frozen produce is often picked at peak ripeness and frozen within a few hours to lock in the nutrient content; however, it may lose some nutrients during the blanching and freezing process. Fresh produce is often picked before it's fully ripe, giving it less time to develop a full range of nutrients. It's also more likely to sustain some nutrient loss during transport and storage. That said, studies have found that frozen fruits and vegetables are—for the most part—comparable nutritionally to their fresh counterparts.

In the fresh versus frozen produce debate, it's pretty much a tie, so which should you choose? Both! Nothing beats the taste and nutrient content of in-season and locally grown fresh produce if you can easily get your hands on some (like, say, by hitting up the local farmers' market). On the other hand, frozen produce is usually cheaper, more convenient, and lasts longer than fresh, which means less waste and more produce intake.

Although I don't think you need to buy all of your produce from the freezer section, I also don't want the controversy surrounding frozen food to deter you from taking advantage of it and enjoying more produce. Some of my favorite frozen produce items to keep on hand are mixed berries, chopped fruit, and chopped spinach or kale for smoothies, as well as vegetable stir-fry blends and riced cauliflower for easy weeknight meals.

...and Definitely Better Than Canned

MYTH: Like fruits and vegetables picked for freezing, those picked for canning are often harvested at peak ripeness and canned within hours. And they, too, hold their own when it comes to nutrient levels—macronutrient (carbohydrate, protein, and fat), mineral, and fat-soluble vitamin levels do not significantly change in the canning process. Some water-soluble vitamins, like B vitamins and vitamin C, are sensitive to heat and can be damaged by the high-heat canning process, resulting in lower amounts. That said, this process can also *release* other nutrients and antioxidants, which makes them more available. Canned tomatoes, for example, are a better source of the cancer-fighting phytonutrient lycopene than their fresh counterpart. Protein-rich beans, chickpeas, and lentils form the basis of many meals in the plant-forward solution repertoire, and buying them canned is a great time-saving option. Canned products can be a cost-effective and convenient option, but keep in mind that they can be nutritionally compromising if they have high levels of added sugar or sodium, so look for no-salt-added or reduced/low sodium beans and vegetables, no sugar added tomato sauces, and fruits canned in their own juice (often labeled as 100% juice) or water.

And be sure to check the expiration date and look for deep dents, dents on the seam, leaks, or a bulging can. Those abnormalities may be signs of spoilage.

Everyone Should Avoid Gluten

 MYTH: Chances are there's at least one person in your life who's given up gluten—maybe you've even given it up yourself. But is ditching gluten really necessary to avoid inflammation, lose weight, and improve your health? Gluten is a protein found in wheat, barley, and rye that must be avoided by individuals with celiac disease—a disorder affecting approximately 1 percent of the population in which eating gluten triggers a harmful immune response in the body. Therefore, it's an absolute necessity that these individuals avoid it. Some people test negative for celiac disease yet experience similar unpleasant symptoms whenever they eat gluten-containing foods—a condition that is now being referred to as "non-celiac gluten sensitivity." (Although it's unclear whether gluten is the true culprit or other compounds in wheat are to blame—hence why more health experts are now calling it "non-celiac *wheat* sensitivity.")

And what about non-celiac individuals who tolerate gluten-containing foods just fine? Well, if that's you, you're in luck. There is no compelling human evidence that gluten produces inflammation or contributes to chronic disease in this population. In fact, consuming gluten-containing foods likely has the opposite effect, as suggested by a large prospective cohort study that found a lower risk of heart disease with higher gluten intake, likely owing to increased intake of whole grains. Whole grains are not only cardioprotective but also provide prebiotic benefit. And because the gluten-containing grains (e.g., wheat, barley, and rye) are in many whole-grain products, unnecessarily going gluten-free could cause your gut microbiota to suffer, too. Indeed, a month-long gluten-free diet was shown to deplete beneficial bacteria species in favor of the less-friendly fellas in healthy, non-celiac individuals.

But not all grains contain gluten. So, if—for whatever reason—you have chosen to avoid gluten, be sure to incorporate a variety of non-gluten-containing grains in your diet, like quinoa, rice, and gluten-free oats. That said, if gluten has never been a problem for you, don't let the media make it one for you now!

NOTE

If consuming wheat and/or gluten causes you to feel unwell, I encourage you to meet with a qualified healthcare professional who can assist you with diagnostic testing and/or making dietary changes, if necessary.

Lectins Are "Disease Causing," and You Should Avoid Them at All Costs

 MYTH: What's the deal with lectins? Lectins are a family of carbohydrate-binding proteins found naturally in all plant foods, but the greatest amounts are in legumes, whole grains, and certain nightshade vegetables (e.g., tomatoes, eggplant). They serve as a defense mechanism for these plants to help them survive and thrive in nature. But according to a very popular book that shall not be named, these proteins are at the root of chronic disease in humans. Their binding abilities allow them to latch on to the gut lining and wreak havoc, causing increased intestinal permeability (i.e., "leaky gut") and widespread inflammation…or so they say. As if we needed another excuse for people not to eat more plant foods.

To give the anti-lectin brigade the benefit of the doubt here, I will say their claims, albeit extremely misleading, aren't *completely* unfounded. One food is known to cause severe digestive side effects when ingested, all thanks to its lectin content. Raw kidney beans contain a high amount of a certain type of problematic lectin found in beans that can cause food-poisoning-like effects. But who eats kidney beans—or any beans, for that matter—raw? You'd break a tooth! So, it's no wonder that rats fed *high* doses of *isolated* bean lectins were shown to have intestinal damage, but that's not how we (humans) consume lectins in the context of food.

> "The typical Western diet—which is strongly linked to inflammation and chronic disease—lacks many of these lectin-associated foods that are supposedly at the root of these health issues."

Fortunately, most lectins are nontoxic, and all lectins, even the ones that can produce toxic effects, are virtually destroyed in the cooking process. In fact, it's very rare to eat a food with a high amount of active lectins (toxic or not), as many of the lectin-rich foods we consume aren't consumed raw.

It's unfortunate how the hype around lectins has left many convinced that some of the planet's healthiest foods are somehow dangerous. If you think about it, the typical Western diet—which is strongly linked to inflammation and chronic disease—*lacks* many of these lectin-associated foods that are supposedly at the root of these health issues. For most people, the health benefits of these foods far outweigh any unsubstantiated risks. Not only are they not harmful, but the research overwhelmingly supports the exact opposite: legumes, whole grains, and other plant foods are incredibly healthy and *reduce* your risk of chronic disease and inflammation, thanks to their fiber, vitamin, mineral, and phytochemical content. But you already knew that because you meticulously read and highlighted Chapter 2, right? Eat these foods without fear, but of course, be sure to avoid eating raw or undercooked beans (and canned = cooked).

——————— PLANT-POWERED FACT ———————

Certain lectins, like those in mushrooms, have been found to have strong anti-cancer effects and have shown great potential for use in cancer therapeutics.

Stay Away from Soy

 MYTH: What's the scoop on soy? Soy is near the top of the list of most controversial nutrition topics, sitting somewhere between carbs and red meat. Because some popular plant proteins are made from soy (e.g., miso, tofu, tempeh, soy milk, edamame, and some meat alternatives), you may be thinking, "Is soy safe for me to consume?"

Well, why did soy get such a bad rap in the first place? Soy contains polyphenols called isoflavones, which are unique in that they are structurally similar to human estrogen. Increased estrogen has been linked to certain types of breast cancer; however, these plant estrogens bind to estrogen receptors differently and function differently than our own estrogen. In fact, consumption of soy foods has been associated with lower risk of certain cancers (and even the American Cancer Society considers them healthy and safe). And thanks to their high content of polyunsaturated fats, fiber, vitamins, and minerals and low content of saturated fat, soy foods may even be cardioprotective and help lower LDL cholesterol levels, especially when they replace red and processed meats in the diet. As a bonus, some of us may harbor certain beneficial gut bacteria that metabolize the isoflavones in soy into the health-promoting metabolite *equol,* which has powerful anti-inflammatory and antioxidant activity. For these reasons, I've chosen to incorporate soy foods into the meal plan and some of the recipes. When shopping for soy products, I recommend choosing minimally processed products most of the time (bonus points if they are fermented). More processed soy foods, like meatless burgers, are best enjoyed on occasion. Speaking of which...

Meatless Meats Are a Healthy Choice.
Wait, No, They Aren't...

 MYTH/FACT: With sustainability and plant-based eating on the rise, meatless meat has gone mainstream. Although some of these products can indeed be more nutritious and environmentally friendly than their meat-based counterparts, there appears to be a "health halo" effect surrounding all meatless products, which may not be entirely justified. Just because something is labeled "meatless" doesn't always make it a more nutritious choice.

For example, some products attempt to imitate meat as closely as possible. Although this gives you a taste, texture, and even a red "bleeding" center comparable to that of a beef burger, it can come with the calorie and saturated fat content of one, too (usually from added tropical oils like coconut or palm oil). These products— let's call them "imitation burgers"—are often highly processed, meaning they are likely stripped of many of the antioxidants, vitamins, and minerals from the plants they came from and therefore much less nutritious than them. Yes, there is an environmental benefit to these products (although some may be more environmentally friendly than others), but I wouldn't consider them a health food per se. If you crave a burger every once in a while and think you're picking the far more nutritious option by going with one of these imitation burgers, you may want to think again. On the other hand, if you enjoy the taste, prefer to get all your protein from plants and not from meat, and/or appreciate their environmental advantage, there's no reason you can't enjoy them in moderation (essentially treating them as you would a real burger).

And what about the OGs of meatless products: *veggie* burgers—the ones that taste more like plants, a lot less like meat, and occasionally more or less like flavorless hockey pucks. Veggie burgers are made primarily from legumes, veggies, and/or grains. They're typically lower in protein than imitation and real beef burgers, but they're often higher in fiber and lower in saturated fat and calories. They also tend to include less-processed, more "whole" versions of the plant ingredients they're made from compared to imitation burgers—for example, cooked brown rice instead of rice protein—which means they retain more of the natural vitamin, mineral, and phytonutrient content of these plant foods (although this isn't always the case). Some veggie burgers can be a nutritious and convenient option for meatless meals and, jokes aside, can be extremely flavorful. But buyer beware; sodium content can be an issue here. Here's what I recommend looking for when purchasing veggie burgers:

- Whole foods—beans, lentils, quinoa, brown rice, oats, mushrooms, greens, nuts and seeds—emphasized at the top of the ingredient list.

- At least 5 to 10 grams of protein and a few grams of fiber to help satiate you. And you can easily up the protein and/or fiber content of your veggie burger meal when you dress 'em up with toppings, like avocado, sliced veggies, hummus, and cheese.

- Less than 400 mg sodium per patty.

Or make your own! It's not as hard as you'd think. That way, you have total control over what goes in them. Try my easy recipe for Black Bean Quinoa Burgers (page 216).

You'll Develop Nutrient Deficiencies If You Go Plant-Forward

 MYTH: Animal products are the best (and in some cases only) source of a handful of key nutrients, so it is true that a plant-*exclusive* diet can result in nutrient deficiencies if not well-planned (and supplemented). Seeing as how the plant-forward approach does not eliminate these foods, nutrient deficiencies are less of a concern. I could leave it at that, but I'm a firm believer in "better safe than sorry," and so, I do think it's important for you—the plant-*forward* eater—to suffer through (I mean enjoy) some more science-heavy*ish* text to ensure you're getting adequate amounts of these nutrients, especially if you decide to eliminate animal foods in the future.

Omega-3s

Oh my omegas... Omega-3 and omega-6 fatty acids are the two major classes of *polyunsaturated* fats. But while we get more than enough omega-6s from the diet (primarily from vegetable oils), it can be a challenge to get enough omega-3s—especially for plant-predominant eaters—which can greatly skew the ratio of omega-6 to omega-3 intake in favor of the former. To balance the ratio for better health, it's important to make omega-3s a priority. Research shows that omega-3s are critical for brain development and function and healthy aging, and they can positively impact cardiovascular health by lowering triglyceride levels, blood pressure, and inflammation.

Several different omega-3s exist, but the benefits I just listed are tied to two extremely important ones in particular: eicosapentaenoic acid (EPA) and docosahexaenoic acid (DHA). Here's where things can get a little fishy for plant-only eaters—EPA and DHA are found primarily in fatty fish, like salmon, mackerel, and tuna, and fish oils. A third important omega-3 fatty acid, alpha-linoleic acid (ALA), is found in plant-based foods (which is why it's often called the "plant-based omega-3") and can be converted to EPA and DHA in the body. However, this process is inefficient, and only a small percentage is converted—about 5 to 10 percent for EPA and 2 to 5 percent for DHA—which is why it's recommended to include direct sources of EPA and DHA in the diet (the American Heart Association recommends two servings of fatty fish per week).

Luckily, going plant-forward doesn't mean you have to give up fish or other seafood. In fact, I recommend prioritizing them when including animal proteins in some of your meals. But ultimately, it is your diet and your choice. If you choose to not include them in your diet for whatever reason, it's especially important you prioritize ALA-rich plant foods (e.g., flax seed, flax seed oil, chia seeds, hemp hearts [shelled hemp seeds], walnuts, and soy foods) to maximize conversion to EPA and DHA. You'll also want to reduce your intake of omega-6s, which can inhibit conversion, by limiting omega-6-rich vegetable oils, such as grapeseed, safflower, soybean, sunflower, and corn oils. And you may even want to consider a quality DHA supplement (fish oil or algae-based).

Vitamin B12

Of the nutrients of concern for anyone following a plant-exclusive diet, vitamin B12 is typically the first to be mentioned. That's because the only reliable dietary sources of vitamin B12 are animal-derived products. But animals cannot synthesize it themselves (nor can plants); in fact, vitamin B12 is the only vitamin produced exclusively by *microorganisms*. Ruminant animals (cattle and sheep), for example, get vitamin B12 from their very own gut bacteria! These animals have a four-chamber stomach that harbors bacteria that can synthesize vitamin B12, which is then absorbed when it reaches their small intestine.

We harbor some of these same bacteria; however, we absorb little of the vitamin B12 they produce due to a case of "bad plumbing." Our vitamin B12 receptors are in the small intestine, which comes before the location of our vitamin B12-producing bacteria (in the large intestine), and so much of that B12 ends up in the toilet. And no, I'm not suggesting you rummage the toilet for your vitamin B12 (although poo is a source of the vitamin for some animals). But you do have to include animal products, like eggs, dairy products, fish and shellfish, and meat, in your diet or take a supplement to meet your vitamin B12 needs, seeing as how fortified plant-based foods (like nutritional yeast, breakfast cereals, meatless meats, and some nondairy milks) likely aren't enough on their own.

Vitamin B12 has a laundry list of responsibilities—it helps the body synthesize new DNA and is crucial for normal nerve functioning and maintaining healthy red blood cells. Deficiency can manifest as a form of anemia and thus present with symptoms similar to iron deficiency anemia, like fatigue and pale skin. And severe deficiency, if left untreated, can lead to irreversible nerve and brain damage. Deficiency is most common in those who follow strict vegetarian and vegan diets, are over the age of fifty, have been taking antacid drugs long term, have a gastrointestinal disorder (such as celiac or Crohn's disease), or have undergone bowel resection.

On the plant-forward diet, regularly including fortified plant-based products and smaller amounts of animal products in the diet should be enough to meet your needs. However, if you plan on eliminating animal foods or are at risk of deficiency, I recommend considering a supplement (speak with your healthcare provider).

NOTE ─────────────────────────

You may be thinking, "I heard mushrooms are a source of vitamin B12—is that true?" Yes, that's true. Certain mushrooms contain small amounts of vitamin B12 that they've absorbed from the manure-containing compost they're grown in or B12-synthesizing bacteria on the mushroom surface. However, their content is highly variable, so relying on mushrooms for vitamin B12 is risky.

Vitamin D

Funnily enough, vitamin D isn't technically a vitamin. It functions more like a hormone than a vitamin because of its ability to be produced by the body when you're exposed to sunlight. In fact, that's how we get most of our vitamin D—the sun! Yes, you read that correctly. Your skin generates vitamin D from a cholesterol compound when it's hit with UV rays from the sun.

Vitamin D is vital to a healthy body because it aids with calcium absorption to promote bone stability and plays an important role in immune system function. Vitamin D deficiency is common and has been associated with several chronic diseases. Plant-only eaters are at greater risk of deficiency because, of the few foods that are naturally good sources of vitamin D, most are animal-based. The most concentrated sources are fatty fish, like salmon, mackerel, and tuna. Egg yolks, beef liver, and some wild mushrooms contain smaller amounts. (Some foods are fortified with vitamin D, notably dairy and nondairy milks. However, fortified foods rarely provide enough vitamin D to meet the needs of someone with limited sun exposure and little to no intake of the foods just mentioned.)

If you follow current recommendations by getting 10 to 30 minutes of sun exposure to large areas of the body (without sunscreen) between 10 a.m. and 4 p.m. at least a few times per week, you may be maintaining healthy vitamin D levels (although this can vary greatly based on latitude and time of year). But if you dream of the sun more than you actually see it, consider getting your vitamin D levels checked by your healthcare provider to find out whether a vitamin D supplement is warranted. If so, I recommend looking for one with vitamin D3 (cholecalciferol), the form of vitamin D that is most effective at increasing blood levels.

Calcium

Calcium is the most abundant mineral in the body, and 99 percent is stored in your bones and teeth. So, no surprise here, we need it to build and maintain strong bones and reduce the risk of brittle bones (osteoporosis) as we age. The remaining 1 percent of calcium can be found in the blood, muscles, and other tissues where it supports cardiovascular, muscle, and nerve function.

When you think calcium, you probably picture a tall glass of milk. Indeed, dairy products, like milk, cheese, and yogurt, are the best sources of calcium, but many nondairy foods are rich sources of the mineral, too. However, calcium absorption can be reduced by oxalates in plant foods, which can bind to calcium and prevent it from being absorbed. Spinach, for example, is both calcium- and oxalate-rich, so we only absorb about 5 percent of the calcium in it compared to the 30 percent we absorb from milk. To be clear, this doesn't mean you shouldn't eat spinach—you definitely should—just don't rely on it as a *significant* source of calcium. Spinach really is an outlier in this case, as there are many high-calcium, low-oxalate plant foods you can rely on, including kale, bok choy, broccoli rabe, broccoli, okra, tofu, soybeans, edamame, kidney and white beans, tahini, and chia seeds. Nondairy milks are also almost always fortified with a significant amount of calcium. Of course, you can also get calcium from modest amounts of dairy in the diet, should you choose to. And remember, vitamin D helps your body absorb calcium, so be sure to (safely) soak up some sun!

Iron

Iron performs many important functions in the body—its key function as a central part of hemoglobin is to facilitate oxygen transport in the blood. Low iron intake and deficiency can be extremely problematic, leaving you fatigued from not having enough healthy red blood cells to carry oxygen throughout the body (also known as anemia) and vulnerable to health issues. But on the flip side, high intake of iron, specifically *heme* iron—the rapidly absorbed form of iron found in animal proteins—has been implicated as a contributing factor in the link between high red meat intake and heart disease. (The irony of *heme* iron is that its excellent bioavailability also makes it a potential health threat because iron is a pro-oxidant, and too much of it can promote oxidative stress and inflammation.)

For those who limit animal foods, the concern is more about getting enough iron (although it is very much doable on a plant-forward diet) because *non-heme* iron—the form of iron found in plant foods—is absorbed less efficiently. Moreover, phytates (see note) in some iron-rich plant foods can decrease iron absorption further. Therefore, you'll want to include plenty of iron-rich plant foods in your diet, like dark leafy greens, nuts, seeds, quinoa, oats, and legumes (specifically lentils, beans, and soy foods like tofu and edamame). When possible, you may want to consider getting your caffeine fixes between meals—at least an hour before or after—rather than with them because certain polyphenols (called "tannins") in coffee and tea can block iron absorption. And here's a little party trick: to enhance the absorption of iron from your plant foods, add some vitamin C!

Here are some examples:

- Kale salad (iron) + citrus-based salad dressing (vitamin C)

- Black bean burrito bowl (iron) + sliced bell pepper (vitamin C)

- Lentils (iron) + tomato sauce (vitamin C)

- Smoothie with a handful of spinach (iron) + mango or papaya (vitamin C)

- Dark chocolate (iron) + strawberries (vitamin C)

Phytates (phytic acid) are natural, harmless compounds found in plant foods, primarily whole grains and beans. Like lectins, they're often referred to as "antinutrients"—so named because they can bind to some minerals, like iron and zinc, and reduce their absorption. But don't worry, these foods are still good sources of these minerals, and their phytate content shouldn't prevent you from getting enough of them on a varied plant-forward diet. Sprouting or fermenting these foods, although not necessary, can reduce phytate content should you be so inclined to try these preparation techniques. You can also find fermented (sourdough) and sprouted breads in many grocery stores.

Zinc

Although we require only small amounts of zinc, it supports a number of functions in the body, like protein and DNA synthesis, but you likely know it for its role in immune function (which is why you'll often see it in cold lozenges and supplements). Like iron, zinc is found in many plant-based foods but is less bioavailable than zinc from animal foods (like oysters, red meat, and poultry), largely due to the presence of phytates. Studies have found little difference in zinc status when comparing vegetarians and nonvegetarians, so, of the nutrients included on this list, I'm the least concerned with a zinc deficiency when going plant-forward. For good measure, eat plenty of zinc-rich plant sources, such as beans, tofu, tempeh, whole grains, nuts, and seeds (hemp and pumpkin seeds are particularly rich).

You Won't Get Enough Protein If You Go Plant-Forward

 MYTH: We are so used to animal foods being front and center of every plate that it's only natural to question whether you'll get enough protein now that these foods will be playing a smaller role in your diet. But worry not. Per capita meat consumption in the United States is about three times the global average, so it's safe to assume we can survive on less. For adults, the Recommended Dietary Allowance (RDA) for protein is 0.8g/kg body weight, which translates to about 55 grams protein for a 150-pound person or around half of what the average American consumes per day. Let's face it, our recent obsession with "getting enough protein" is a bit unfounded. Even when we consider that the RDA is a *minimum* recommended amount and that many health professionals (myself included) recommend protein intakes closer to 1.0g to 1.2g/kg body weight (which translates to 68g to 82g for a 150-pound person), this is still easily achievable on the plant-forward approach.

To be clear, this isn't to say you shouldn't make it a priority to get protein on your plate. You 100 percent should. Every cell in the human body contains protein, and therefore, it is a crucial component of any diet.

Dietary proteins supply amino acids (i.e., "building blocks") for the growth and maintenance of all of our cells and tissues—like muscles, bones, cartilage, and skin. Amino acids also support the production of hemoglobin (the protein that transports oxygen throughout the body) and many hormones and enzymes (like the digestive enzymes that help break down the food you eat). And I know I've talked up fiber for its fill-you-up-without-filling-you-out abilities, but the satiating effects of protein are well-established. Together, fiber *and* protein make quite the filling duo (which is why fiber-rich plant protein sources can be quite advantageous).

So yes, protein is extremely important, and, yes, you need to make sure you get enough of it. But you don't have to rely solely on animal foods to do so. Legumes (e.g., beans, chickpeas, and soy-based foods like tofu), nuts, and seeds are the first to come to mind when we think of plant-based proteins, but whole-grain foods, like quinoa, oats, and sprouted bread, can be a good source of protein, too. Even fruits and vegetables contain small amounts of protein. For example, a cup of broccoli contains 3 grams protein, and an avocado has 4. This may not seem like a lot, but every little bit counts, and it adds up when you include a lot of produce in your diet.

A plant-heavy burrito bowl made up of black beans, quinoa, bell pepper, and avocado can easily pack at least 20 grams of protein. And because this is the plant-*forward* solution and not the plant-*only* solution, you can up the protein a little more by adding a sprinkle of cheese or a dollop of Greek yogurt—if you want to (I usually want to).

Protein Showdown: Animal Versus Plant

Animal proteins are often hailed as the superior protein source because they are typically more protein-dense and are considered "complete proteins"—meaning all nine essential amino acids are present in adequate amounts. Since most plant proteins technically aren't "complete," it was once commonly believed that plant-based eaters had to strategically pair plant protein sources at each meal to form complete proteins. We now know this isn't necessary—as long as you include a variety of plant-based protein sources in your diet, missing amino acids in one meal are likely to be made up in a meal later. There is also concern over the digestibility of plant proteins. The presence of fiber and other compounds in plant protein sources impacts their digestibility and can slightly reduce the amount of protein we absorb from these sources, some more so than others. But rest assured, you can still meet, and even exceed, your protein needs with plant-based sources when you prioritize variety. Studies support that vegetarian diets supply more than adequate protein and amino acids, provided energy needs are being met. Furthermore, there's the misconception that you'll lose or be incapable of building muscle when you rely on plant proteins over animal ones. Once again, this is simply not true; you can effectively maintain and build muscle mass relying on plant proteins alone. Just take a look at some of the elite athletes who adhere to a plant-based diet, like U.S. soccer star Alex Morgan, tennis legend Venus Williams, Formula 1 champion Lewis Hamilton, and the current number one tennis player in the world, Novak Djokovic. But ultimately, these issues are even less of a concern when going plant-forward because animal proteins can still have a place in the diet, should you want them to.

In the animal protein versus plant protein showdown, there is no denying that both have distinct advantages. However, there is some compelling evidence that supports giving plant proteins the starring role in your diet, thanks to their unique characteristics as outlined in the illustration.

ANIMAL PROTEINS

Examples: **poultry, red meat, seafood, eggs, dairy**

PLANT PROTEINS

Examples: **pulses, soy products, nuts, seeds, some whole grains**

CARBS

Lower in total carbs (dairy is highest) but provide no fiber.

Higher in total carbs but most are a good source of fiber.

PROTEIN QUANTITY

Typically provide the highest amount of protein per gram.

Less protein-dense (except for soy products).

PROTEIN QUALITY

Complete proteins and highly digestible.

Most are incomplete proteins and are less digestible (but still a good source of protein).

FAT

Many can be high in saturated fat. Fatty fish are the best source of important omega-3s, EPA and DHA.

Contain little saturated fat and are rich in healthy unsaturated fats, including the omega-3 ALA (nuts, seeds, and soy products, specifically).

MICRO-NUTRIENTS

Best (and pretty much only) source of vitamin B12.

Heme iron: Better absorbed but absorption is not well regulated by the body. High intake could lead to excess iron absorption and negative health effects.

Rich in disease-fighting phytonutrients (aka "plant nutrients").

Non-heme iron: Less well-absorbed but absorption is strongly regulated by the body.

GUT MICROBIOME

Diet rich in high-fat animal proteins may reduce beneficial bacteria counts and fuel the production of pro-inflammatory metabolites (like secondary bile acids).

Fiber-rich plant proteins fuel the growth of beneficial gut bacteria and their production of anti-inflammatory, health-promoting metabolites (like short-chain fatty acids).

DISEASE

High intake of red meat, especially processed red meat, is associated with increased risk of CVD, diabetes, certain cancers, and all-cause and CVD mortality.

Higher plant protein intake is associated with lower blood pressure and LDL cholesterol levels and lower risk of CVD, diabetes, and all-cause and CVD mortality.

You Should Only Buy Organic and Non-GMO Foods

 MYTH: In all honesty, this is not a topic I wanted to discuss in this book because I know many people have strong, unwavering opinions about it. But I feel it's necessary to address. Is organic produce worth the extra cost? Maybe a better question is whether conventional produce is more harmful and/or less nutritious than organic. According to many a self-proclaimed health guru on social media, the answer is "Yes." According to science, the answer is "Nope."

From a nutritional perspective, certain organic crops have been shown to have slightly higher antioxidant content; on average, they are no more nutritious than their conventional counterparts. But maybe it's not about what organic fruits and veggies *do have* in them; it's what they *don't*. After all, organic equals pesticide-free, right? That's a common misconception—and one that understandably leaves many consumers afraid to buy conventional produce. Although organic crops must be grown without conventional pesticides (*conventional* being the operative word here), that doesn't mean *natural* ones can't be used. Unfortunately, the word *natural* can be misleading and does not mean safe or nontoxic. Virtually all pesticides, synthetic or natural, can be dangerous at the right dose. Yep, like with everything—even water— the dose makes the poison.

But I Should Buy Organic for the Dirty Dozen, Right?

In case you're unfamiliar with the Dirty Dozen, it's a list the Environmental Working Group (EWG) put together of the conventionally grown fruits and vegetables with the highest pesticide residues. The list is updated each year using data from the USDA Pesticide Data Program (PDP), and, year after year, scientists discredit the list—for good reason. The list doesn't consider which pesticides were detected, at what level each pesticide was detected, or how the level compares to the safety level set by the Environmental Protection Agency (EPA). Plus, these lists fail to acknowledge that the USDA PDP finds year after year that around 99 percent of conventional produce tested had pesticide residues well below the EPA safety levels. And more than 40 percent of samples tested had no detectable pesticide residues whatsoever. So, take the Dirty Dozen list with a grain of salt and don't let it influence your overall produce consumption.

Unfortunately, the organic versus conventional debate often detracts from the real issue at hand, which is that only one in ten adults gets enough fruits and vegetables in their diet. And studies have found that fear-based, inaccurate messaging about pesticides and the Dirty Dozen list plays a part here by dissuading people from buying and eating produce altogether (both conventional AND organic). The bottom line is, eating more fruits and vegetables—*organic or not*—is better than eating less. Perhaps you prefer to buy organic, and grocery money is easy peasy organic lemon squeezy—then go for it! Or maybe you—and your wallet—would prefer to buy a mix of organic and conventional. In that case, stick to organic for in-season fruits and veggies (which are usually cheaper) or only go for organic when it's on sale. But if your budget says that buying organic means buying less produce, rest assured that conventional produce is both nutritious and safe. So, for the love of fruits and veggies, please eat more of them!

Above all, it's important that you wash all fruits and veggies, whether conventional or organic, before peeling, cutting, or eating them. Washing helps reduce pesticides loosely attached to the surface but, more importantly, helps remove pathogenic

> "Unfortunately, the organic versus conventional debate often detracts from the real issue at hand, which is that only one in ten adults gets enough fruits and vegetables in their diet."

bacteria that could lead to foodborne illness. No fancy produce washes necessary—simply wash under cool running water using clean hands. Produce with firm skin or a peel can benefit from being scrubbed with a vegetable brush as you wash it.

Are "GMOs" a Reason to Buy Organic?

A proper discussion on genetically modified organisms (GMOs) warrants more than the short paragraph I can dedicate to it. The use of GMOs is prohibited in organic farming; therefore, all organic crops are non-GMO. According to major health groups, including the World Health Organization and the National Academies of Science, Engineering, and Medicine, genetically modified foods are safe, and there is no data to indicate that consumption of them poses a risk to human health. I only mention this because—as with organic—I don't want the fear of GMOs to prevent you from getting more healthful plant-based foods in the diet. And if you are genuinely concerned about GMOs, keep in mind that there are only ten crops approved by the USDA and grown in the United States that *can* be genetically modified: apples, potatoes, corn, canola, alfalfa, soybeans, rainbow papaya, cotton, sugar beet, and summer squash. So, foods like quinoa, kale, tomatoes, grapes, popcorn (which *doesn't* come from field or sweet corn), etc., are always "non-GMO."

What About Organic Animal Products?

One might argue that because you'll be eating fewer animal products and therefore spending less money on them, why not splurge on organic when you do buy them? Unfortunately, organic is but one of numerous labels animal proteins can carry that are anything but intuitive. Organic, grass-fed, pasture-raised—the list goes on. From a nutritional perspective, eggs from pasture-raised hens and some organic and grass-fed meat and dairy products may contain slightly higher amounts of omega-3s than their conventional counterparts (due to longer time spent pasture grazing). However, it's unlikely that these small differences translate into meaningful health benefits, considering that the omega-3 content of beef in general—whether grass-fed or conventional—is fairly small, especially when compared to other sources like fish. From an animal welfare perspective, the organic label may imply some measure of animal welfare, but, in reality, it does not guarantee humane treatment. So, if you're looking to support animal welfare, you're better off looking for third-party certification seals like Animal Welfare Approved and Certified Humane.

Perhaps the most controversial issue on the matter is antibiotic use. Although all conventional meat is required to be free of antibiotic residues (there is a strict withdrawal period after giving antibiotics before an animal can be processed), there is growing concern over the transmission of antibiotic-resistant bacteria to the environment and the food supply chain from the misuse and overuse of antibiotics in conventionally raised livestock. For this reason, the World Health Organization (WHO) advocates preparing meat hygienically and cooking it thoroughly (which is a given) and choosing animal proteins that have been produced without the use of antibiotics for growth promotion or disease prevention when possible. If you value purchasing animal proteins raised without the routine use of antibiotics, look for the organic label (organic livestock must be raised without the use of antibiotics) or the American Grassfed seal. You can also look for meat labeled with *no antibiotics ever*, *never given antibiotics*, or *raised without antibiotics*, as long as they are accompanied by the USDA Process Verified Seal.

As you can see, there's a lot to unpack on this topic, and I've just barely scratched the surface here. Ultimately, choosing conventional or organic (or grass-fed, pasture-raised, etc.) is a personal decision in which both your values and your budget should be factors. Keep in mind, labels like organic and animal welfare certifications put a dent in not only consumers' pockets but also the pockets of the farmers that have to pay a significant chunk of change to use them. Hence, many conventional farms operate with things like animal welfare and sustainability in mind but do not carry any labels simply because they can't or choose not to pay the hefty fee required to do so. So, you may want to consider getting to know your local farmers by checking out your local farmers' market or looking into a local community supported agriculture (CSA) operation. (Google is a big help here.)

PART 2:

HOW TO GO PLANT-FORWARD

CHAPTER 4:
TIME TO PUT PLANTS FORWARD

———

You're on board and ready to get going. You understand the "why" of going plant-forward, and I've debunked some concerns that may have held you back from doing so. Now, let's tackle the "how" of going plant-forward. Contrary to restrictive diets, the plant-forward approach has no hard and fast rules (well, besides *eat more plants*). Instead, it serves as a flexible framework to fit you and your lifestyle rather than the other way around. That said, making any significant dietary change with "no rules" can feel tricky at first, so I've put together the following six general "guidelines" for going plant-forward. There will be no macro or calorie counting and no eliminating anything cold turkey (or should I say, "cold tofu"?). Phew. Pass the plants, please!

Prioritize Prebiotics and Probiotics

Love on Legumes

Aim for less Animals (and more plants)

Nosh on Nuts (and seeds)

Try for Thirty plants per week

Stick with Slow-carb over low-carb

What a coincidence—the guidelines spell *PLANTS*!

Prioritize Prebiotics and Probiotics

Recall from Chapter 2 that our small but mighty gut bugs have a large impact on our health, and to get the most out of going plant-forward, it's important we make them a priority. *So, just feed them a lot of plant-based foods, right?* Well, yes, but if you want to give them Four Seasons–level hospitality, you want to make sure *probiotic-* and *prebiotic-rich* foods are a regular part of your routine. And yes, there's a difference between the two—and it's more than just the prefix.

Probiotics

You've likely heard of "probiotics"—you may even have a probiotic supplement lying around your house somewhere. Probiotics are live microorganisms (like bacteria) that, when ingested, confer a health benefit to the host (aka you). They are often the same as or similar to those that naturally live in your body, which is why you'll often hear people refer to the good bacteria native to the gut as "probiotics," too.

Here's the thing: Most ingested probiotics don't manage to colonize the gut permanently. They're more like tourists passing through, some staying longer than others, but that doesn't mean they can't deliver health benefits. As they travel along, they can interact with your existing bacteria, stimulating the growth of beneficial ones and their production of short-chain fatty acids and crowding out pathogenic bacteria to help keep the peace. They can also interact with your immune cells, improve gut barrier function, and more to deliver benefits. *So, what you're saying is I should run to CVS ASAP and grab a probiotic supplement?* Well, not necessarily. Although evidence suggests probiotic supplements may help treat some gastrointestinal conditions, like irritable bowel syndrome (IBS), for most, the better (and cheaper) option for ingesting living microbes on the reg is food. Fermented foods, to be exact.

> "As the bacteria work their fermentation magic, they're essentially getting a head start on digestion for you, making these foods easier for you to digest than their unfermented counterparts and unlocking their full nutrient potential."

Fermentation for the Win

The process of fermenting foods essentially replicates what happens right inside your gut. Under the right conditions, live friendly bacteria and yeasts already present on a food (or added to it via a starter culture) feast on the carbohydrates in that food for their own energy. And in doing so, they release—you guessed it—metabolites, some of which are responsible for the underappreciated tart or sour taste characteristic of fermented foods. Milk turns to yogurt, cabbage to kimchi, sweet tea to kombucha—you get the point. So, in consuming these foods, you're getting the benefit of both the live microorganisms that hang around—many of which are identical to or share traits with known probiotic species, even if they haven't reached true probiotic status—and their health-promoting by-products, too (which you don't get from a supplement). Lactic acid, for example, a major fermentation end product giving foods like yogurt and kimchi their sour taste, has been shown to have potent anti-inflammatory effects.

But wait, there's more. As the bacteria work their fermentation magic, they're essentially getting a head start on digestion for you, making these foods easier for you to digest than their unfermented counterparts and unlocking their full nutrient potential. Vitamin and antioxidant content increases, and compounds like phytates are reduced, making the minerals they bind to like iron and zinc more available to you. It's truly fascinating and also unfortunate that so many of us (myself once included) don't take advantage of these impressive yet relatively cheap foods that are so readily available to us. (Seriously, you can buy quality kimchi at Target.) Now that you are aware of all they have to offer, I encourage you to incorporate them into your meals at least a few times a week. (Don't worry, I'll show you how in the meal plan.)

Fermented Foods

These fermented foods often retain live microorganisms. You usually can find them in the refrigerated section of the grocery store.

PLANT-BASED (look for words like *unpasteurized, probiotic,* or *raw* on the label):

Apple cider vinegar (with the "mother")

Kimchi

Kombucha*

Miso paste

Natto

Sauerkraut

Other fermented veggies (e.g., some pickles, fermented beets—make sure they are fermented and not just soaked in vinegar)

*Consume in moderation; can be rich in added sugar

CULTURED DAIRY PRODUCTS:

Kefir

Yogurt, including many nondairy yogurts

Some types of cheese

Cultured cottage cheeses

Spotlight on Sourdough: Sourdough bread is another fermented food that, like many of the foods on the preceding list, undergoes fermentation by lactic acid bacteria and yeasts. Unfortunately, these friendly fellas don't stick around because they are killed off in the baking process (bummer), but their hard work fermenting the dough and the lactic acid they produce as a result gives the bread distinct advantages compared to regular bread. Not only does it give it that irresistible sour taste (hence the name), but also improves mineral bioavailability and lowers the bread's glycemic index, meaning it causes less of a blood sugar response. Plus, the fermentation process makes the bread easier to digest and decreases the amount of gluten, which is why it may be a suitable option for some gluten-*sensitive* individuals.

Prebiotics

Prebiotics need no introduction at this point, but, by definition, they are "a substrate that is selectively utilized by host microorganisms conferring a health benefit." All living things need food to function, and gut bacteria are no exception. The word *prebiotics* translates to "before life"—because they essentially give life to our friendly gut bacteria, allowing them to multiply, flourish, and produce loads of health-promoting metabolites. Simply put, prebiotics are food for our good gut bacteria.

You might be wondering whether "prebiotics" is just a fancy way of saying *fiber*. Yes and no. Although most prebiotics are indeed fiber, not all fiber functions as a prebiotic. Without overcomplicating things, some fiber simply cannot be consumed (i.e., fermented) by our gut bacteria, the "bulk" of which serves an important role by quite literally adding "bulk" to your stool, which promotes bowel health and regularity. Although it's good to be aware of this distinction, there's no need to stress too much over it because a) most fiber-rich foods contain a mix of fiber types, and b) consuming a *variety* of fiber-rich food sources will help you get a good mix of them all. If you do want to go the extra mile for your good gut bugs, some food sources are particularly rich in prebiotic fibers, and it certainly can't hurt to know what they are.

Most prebiotics are considered to be a form of soluble fiber, and the main ones include fructans (inulin and fructo-oligosaccharides (FOS)), galacto-oligosaccharides (GOS), and beta-glucans. Quite the mouthful, but don't worry; I won't be quizzing you, so no need to remember them. There is also resistant starch—a form of starch that acts just like fiber (so much so that many classify it as one) in that it "resists" digestion in the small intestine and ends up in the colon, where it can nourish and promote the growth of beneficial gut bacteria. As with probiotics, you can obtain prebiotics from supplements and powders. But again, I encourage you to take a food-first approach here because the grocery store isn't short on prebiotics.

NOTE

If you're currently struggling with or have struggled with irritable bowel syndrome (IBS), then you're likely familiar with the acronym FODMAP—which represents a group of problematic carbohydrates for those with IBS. Fructans and GOS, the prebiotic fibers I just mentioned, represent the "O" part of FODMAP—they are fermentable oligosaccharides. Unfortunately, this means that the prebiotic-rich foods that help strengthen and support a diverse and resilient gut microbiome are the same foods that can also cause digestive distress (e.g., gas and bloat) in some individuals with IBS, which can lead to unnecessary restriction of these foods long term to avoid discomfort. This can make things worse by further reducing microbial diversity and counts of beneficial bacteria. Therefore, if you find yourself really struggling with many of these foods, I recommend working one on one with a digestive health registered dietitian to develop an individualized plan.

Foods Rich in Prebiotic Fibers

Veggies: artichokes, asparagus, beetroot, Brussels sprouts, chicory root, dandelion greens, fennel bulb, garlic, green peas, leek, mushrooms, onion, savoy cabbage, seaweed, shallots, snow peas

Fruits: apples, bananas, dates, figs, grapefruit, nectarines, persimmon, watermelon

Legumes: beans, chickpeas, lentils, soybeans, and soy products

Nuts and seeds: almonds, cashews, flax seed, pistachios, walnuts

Grains: barley, oats, rye, wheat bran

Foods Rich in Resistant Starch

Resistant starch is special because the amount can change depending on how foods are prepared. Green bananas and plantains lose some of their resistant starch when they ripen or are cooked. There's also a type of resistant starch that can be formed in the cooking and cooling process of certain starchy foods.

- Beans and lentils

- Cooked then cooled rice, potatoes, and pasta

- Green or just-ripe bananas

- Green plantains

- Oats and barley

Plant Pigment Power of Polyphenols

Although most prebiotics are some type of fiber, recent evidence suggests nonfiber compounds abundantly found in plants may express prebiotic properties as well. These protective phytonutrients called polyphenols are often associated with the bright and vibrant colors and flavors of the plants they are found in—think the blue of a wild blueberry or the deep purple of an eggplant. Since the vast majority of them (about 95 percent) are poorly absorbed in their natural form, they end up in the colon (like fiber), where the magic happens. Here, the polyphenols can exert a prebiotic effect by fueling the growth and abundance of certain beneficial bacteria, which then metabolize the polyphenols to their bioactive, health-promoting form. And if that doesn't get you excited, this surely will: Even the polyphenols in red wine and cocoa (aka chocolate) have been shown to shift the gut microbiota toward a more health-promoting profile. Lucky for us, polyphenols and fiber like to hang out in the same foods (well, besides wine)!

> "Legumes, especially pulses, are the ultimate package, packing in plenty of fiber—and prebiotic fiber at that—and plant protein, all at a pretty low price point."

Love on Legumes

There is a lot to love about legumes. Legumes are your pulses (e.g., beans, chickpeas, and lentils), soy products (e.g., tofu and tempeh), and *technically* peanuts and peas, too (although I usually group peanuts with nuts and peas with vegetables to simplify things). You'll be showing legumes a lot of love going forward—plant-forward, that is—and I promise they will love you right back.

Legumes, especially pulses, are the ultimate package, packing in plenty of fiber—and prebiotic fiber at that—and plant protein, all at a pretty low price point. We often praise animal proteins as the end-all-be-all solution to our satiety woes, but plant proteins like beans, with less protein but more fiber, can be just as filling. When researchers compared the satiating effects of two different patties with similar energy content but made from different protein sources, the bean-based patties—which were higher in fiber but lower in protein—were as satiating as the meat-based ones. But beans, and other legumes, come with no saturated fat and the bonus of anti-inflammatory, disease-fighting phytonutrients—so named because they are found only in plants.

Beans and other legumes are some of the most underrated and undervalued foods out there; the science agrees—everyone should be taking advantage of all that legumes have to offer. Regular legume consumption has been associated with lower risks of CVD, diabetes, and colorectal cancer. It's also been shown to reduce blood pressure and total and LDL cholesterol levels, improve blood sugar control, and help with weight management. Unfortunately, many people have been led to believe that these powerful foods are somehow inflammatory (no thanks to the Paleo and anti-lectin movements) when, in reality, legumes can help you fight inflammation and have been shown to lower blood C-reactive protein (CRP) levels—a proinflammatory marker—when consumed several times per week, if not daily.

The incredible benefits associated with these dirt-cheap pantry superstars become a lot less shocking when you consider that legumes happen to be the cornerstone of all the diets of the Blue Zones (the regions known for their exceptional health and longevity). In fact, these populations average a full cup a day—whether it be black beans in Costa Rica, chickpeas in Sardinia, or soybeans in Okinawa. Legumes deserve a starring role in your diet, too.

Make It a Half-Cup Habit

Making legumes a part of your daily routine will not only improve your overall health but may also be one of the most effective strategies for weight management. One study found that this simple strategy was as effective at slimming waistlines as following a calorie-restricted diet. (Remember the "eat more but lose weight" concept of energy density from Chapter 2?) So, make it a habit to get in at least a half-cup (or one serving) of legumes (particularly pulses) most days of the week. You can enjoy them all in one meal or throughout the day—say a scoop at lunch and another with dinner. Pulses are so versatile that you can even mix them into sweet treats for an extra fiber and protein boost. Ever heard of black bean brownies or chickpea cookie dough?! Scan the pasta aisles at your local grocery stores and you'll notice a wide range of legume-based pastas popping up. Beyond chickpea pasta, you can now buy lentil penne, black bean spaghetti, edamame fettuccine, mung bean rotini, and more!

Beans, Beans, the Magical Fruit, the More You Eat...

...the better you feel, so eat beans at every meal, right? Yes, true! But that middle "more you toot" part I purposefully skipped can unfortunately hold true, too, especially if you have IBS or aren't used to consuming legumes regularly. You may need to go low and slow when adding them to your diet, but don't be afraid of some gas and wind, which should decrease over time as your gut microbiome adapts. In my opinion, the adage should really go "...the more you eat, the *less* you toot...eventually." Seriously, a study comparing three feeding trials to assess flatulence from increased bean consumption found that although upping bean intake can (unsurprisingly) result in more flatulence initially, it often dissipates after a few weeks of daily consumption. So unless they cause you severe symptoms, don't let a bit of (possibly smelly) flatulence get in the way of you giving these truly magical foods a permanent spot in your diet.

Canned pulses tend to be better tolerated than those cooked from scratch, and lentils seem to be the best tolerated of them all. If you're using canned beans, drain and rinse them first (this helps lower the sodium, too). And if you're working with dried pulses, soaking them overnight and discarding the soaking liquid before cooking them (in fresh water) can help reduce their gassiness. Lastly, be sure to drink plenty of water throughout the day when upping bean intake.

"You may need to go low and slow when adding beans to your diet, but don't be afraid of some gas and wind, which should decrease over time as your gut microbiome adapts."

Aim for Less Animals (and More Plants)

The average American consumes more than two hundred pounds of chicken, pork, and beef a year—which comes out to over half a pound per day, every day. For many people, animal proteins play a starring role in most meals, likely at least two out of three meals a day. It's time for a protein flip—instead of eating more animal proteins than plant, enjoy more plant proteins than animal. Of course, the journey to getting there could look a lot different for you than for another reader, depending on where you're starting. If you are used to eating meat, poultry, and/or seafood at most meals, it might take a little longer to make the flip, and that's A-OK. Studies suggest shifting as little as 3 percent of calories from animal proteins to plant proteins could have a large effect on longevity.

Serve Less Meat, Less Often

Try limiting red meat, poultry, and seafood to one meal a day and aim for the other two meals to be meatless (i.e., vegetarian). And when you do include these animal proteins on your plate...

- **Keep portion sizes in check.** The typical portion size for meat and poultry these days is (at least) double the recommended serving size of approximately 3 to 4 ounces, about the size of your palm or a deck of cards. Try to stay closer to that amount...

- **Or go 50/50!** Animal and plant proteins are not sworn enemies. In fact, they can complement each other quite nicely in meals. So, it doesn't have to be an either/ or situation when picking your protein for a meal—you can have a little of both! A good rule of thumb is to sub 1 or 2 ounces of meat for about ¼ cup of pulses. For example, try a burrito bowl made with 2 ounces of shredded chicken and a big scoop of black beans.

- **Prioritize.** Make fatty omega-3-rich fish like salmon, mackerel, tuna, and so on, your first priority and red meat your last priority. This isn't to say you can't or shouldn't have red meat, but limiting your unprocessed red meat intake to one to two times per week (or less) is optimal. (Limit *processed* red meat intake as much possible.) And be sure to opt for leaner cuts when doing so.

If or once you feel comfortable with scaling back on meat, you can challenge yourself to one or more meatless days per week. Maybe you hop on the "Meatless Monday" bandwagon to start, and then add a day or two from there (or don't).

And Where Do Dairy and Eggs Fit In?

Incorporating more meatless meals into your routine is enough of a daunting task as is, so don't feel pressured to make all (or any) of your meals vegan unless you want to. The Dietary Guidelines have long recommended three servings of dairy per day, but not without controversy because it seems the science behind this recommendation is thin. Dairy products, especially fermented ones like yogurt, kefir, and some cheeses, can be a nutritious addition to your day, providing probiotics and vitamins and minerals, like calcium and vitamin B12, in addition to protein, of course. So, although there's no need for dairy overkill, there's also no need to cut ties with it if you enjoy it and tolerate it well. If you do opt to eat dairy, I recommend enjoying it as part of a snack or using it to accessorize meals instead of as a main ingredient—think a sprinkle of feta on a Mediterranean quinoa salad, some kefir or yogurt mixed into overnight oats, or a dollop of Greek yogurt on a black bean burrito bowl. And choose no-sugar-added versions when possible.

As for eggs, for years they were considered unhealthy because of their cholesterol content. We now know that this dietary cholesterol has much less of an effect on our blood cholesterol levels than our saturated fat and refined carbohydrate intake. Eggs provide protein as well as several vitamins and minerals (which are mostly concentrated in the yolk), including vitamin B12, which is hard to come by on plant-centric diets. However, the American Heart Association still recommends most people limit consumption to one egg a day (or up to seven per week). So, as with dairy, instead of daily multi-egg omelets, treat eggs more as a meal "accessory," like topping a salad or avocado toast with a hard-boiled egg.

Nosh on Nuts (and Seeds)

Nuts were once considered high-fat villains, the consumption of which would be a sure-fire recipe for weight gain. Nuts are indeed rich in fat and therefore calorically dense, so the logic makes sense at face value. But nuts have been shown to be incredibly satiating, thanks in large part to their plant protein and fiber content. Numerous studies have found that consumption of nuts can suppress hunger and decrease subsequent food intake, therefore offsetting some of their calories. Plus, studies have estimated that up to 20 percent of the calories in nuts aren't even absorbed because of how the fat in them is stored in their cell walls, which don't easily break down during digestion.

You can rest assured; the weight of the evidence does not indicate that nuts pose a threat to your waistline. In fact, noshing on them regularly may make you less likely to gain weight.

And despite their high-fat content—most of which is our favorite *unsaturated* kind—nuts are consistently linked with good health outcomes, including significantly lowering your risk of heart disease. It's these very fats along with an array of powerful phytonutrients found in nuts that work together to fight inflammation and offer protection against disease, which may even translate to greater longevity. Seriously, enjoying a handful of nuts a day has been associated with keeping both the doctor and the undertaker away.

> "The weight of the evidence does not indicate that nuts pose a threat to your waistline. In fact, noshing on them regularly may make you less likely to gain weight."

As for seeds, these nutritional powerhouses are equally as health-promoting for similar reasons yet they're even more versatile. So, aim for one serving of nuts and/or seeds daily. Serving sizes vary depending on the nut or seed. In general, a serving is roughly equivalent to one ounce of nuts or seeds, which translates to about ¼ cup of nuts, 2 to 3 tablespoons of seeds, or 2 tablespoons of nut or seed butter. Opt for unsalted raw or dry roasted nuts and nut butters without added sugar or oils, if possible.

The Virtues of Variety

Each nut and seed has its own nutritional virtues, which is why variety is key (yet again).

ALMONDS: Among the nuts, almonds offer the most fiber, calcium, and vitamin E. A 1-ounce portion provides nearly half of the recommended daily amount of vitamin E for adults. Vitamin E is a fat-soluble vitamin that acts as an antioxidant, helping to protect cells from free radical damage.

CASHEWS: If you're looking for a nut that's a tad lower in fat content, look no further than cashews. (Interestingly, despite their lower fat content, they make for the best dairy-free cream, ricotta, and cheese sauces when blended.) Plus, they're a great source of copper and magnesium, the latter of which is involved in more than 300 chemical reactions in the body.

MACADAMIA NUTS: More than 75 percent of the fat in macadamia nuts is the *monounsaturated* kind. The predominant monounsaturated fatty acid in them is oleic acid, the same fatty acid found in olive oil that's responsible for its beneficial effects on heart health and inflammation.

PEANUTS: At 7 grams protein per 1-ounce serving, peanuts have the highest protein content of all the nuts, even though they're *technically* a legume. The humble peanut may be considered inferior to its pricey tree nut friends, but research shows peanuts yield similar health benefits.

PECANS: Although their pronunciation is still up for debate, the power of pecans to support a healthy heart isn't. A recent intervention trial found that when adults at risk for cardiovascular disease ate a little more than two ounces of the unsaturated fat- and fiber-rich nut per day for eight weeks, they dramatically improved their cholesterol and apolipoprotein B levels—both risk factors for CVD.

PISTACHIOS: Pistachios are one of the lowest calorie nuts, with only 160 calories per serving (which is forty-nine nuts!). They contain the highest amount of vitamin B6—important for energy production—of all the nuts. In fact, they are one of the most vitamin B6–rich foods around.

WALNUTS: Walnuts are well-known for their high omega-3 and antioxidant content, but recent research has them making waves as a potent prebiotic, too. Consumption of walnuts was shown to increase the abundance of beneficial bacteria, including butyrate-producing species, and to decrease production of pro-inflammatory bacterial metabolites (specifically, secondary bile acids that may play a role in colon cancer).

CHIA SEEDS: Chia seeds take the cake for most fiber, with 10 grams of fiber per 2-tablespoon serving. They are also a good source of ALA, iron, and, interestingly, calcium (one serving provides 13 percent of the recommended daily amount for calcium).

FLAX SEEDS: Along with walnuts, flax seeds are one of the best sources of the plant-based omega-3 ALA. They are also known for being particularly rich in lignans—phytonutrients that may have a protective effect against hormone-related cancers—and have a well-documented cholesterol-lowering effect thanks to their soluble fiber content. Whole flax seeds don't fully break down in your gut, so it's best to eat ground flax seeds (i.e., flax seed meal) to reap their benefits.

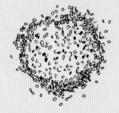

HEMP SEEDS/HEMP HEARTS: Of all the seeds, hemp seeds are the most protein-packed, providing a whopping 10 grams of protein per 3-tablespoon serving (plus about 20 percent of your recommended daily amount for iron). Like flax seeds and chia seeds, they are also a good source of the plant-based omega-3 ALA. Hemp hearts are simply shelled, or hulled, hemp seeds; they are what I use in my cooking for ease of use and digestion.

SESAME SEEDS: When sesame seeds are ground into a paste, you get tahini—a key ingredient in hummus. Two tablespoons of tahini provides more than half of the recommended daily amount of copper, which helps the body absorb iron and works with iron to help the body make red blood cells. Speaking of iron, sesame seeds and tahini are also an excellent source of that, too.

SUNFLOWER SEEDS: Sunflower seed butter is a popular, protein-packed alternative to nut butters for those who have peanut or tree nut allergies (and those without, too). Like almonds, sunflower seeds are rich in the free-radical-fighting, antioxidant vitamin, vitamin E.

Try for Thirty Plants per Week

We know that gut health is the key to overall health and that plant-based foods are the best fuel for a thriving gut microbiome. Although this may tempt you to crush a bag of spinach a day, limiting your diet to the same few plant foods every day isn't the best way to set up your gut for success. Recall from Chapter 2 that a more diverse gut microbiome is associated with health, whereas an imbalanced, less diverse one has been linked to numerous chronic health conditions, such as diabetes, obesity, IBD, and more. Why might this be? Well, a diverse microbiome tends to be more stable and resilient, meaning it's better able to adjust to or recover from a disturbance or stressor—like antibiotics, dietary and environmental stressors, etc.—and fend off potential pathogens.

So, how can you increase microbial diversity? You diversify your diet! Yes—quantity is important when it comes to your intake of plant-based foods. But diversity is equally important. Bacteria differ in their nutritional requirements for successful growth. Put very (and I mean very) simply, if beneficial bacteria X thrives on bananas and friendly bacteria Y thrives on apples, eat bananas and apples, and you'll support both. But eat mostly bananas, and you could be leaving bacteria Y high and dry.

> "Yes—quantity is important when it comes to your intake of plant-based foods. But diversity is equally important."

The More the Merrier

The American Gut Project I mentioned earlier found that those who included at least thirty different plant foods in the diet per week had gut microbiomes that were more diverse than those who included ten or fewer per week, regardless of their overall dietary pattern (i.e., vegetarian, vegan, nonvegetarian, etc.). So, eating (at least) thirty different plant foods per week is our goal! I know that sounds overwhelming and borderline impossible but trust me—it's very doable. And eventually, you'll be exceeding thirty without even trying.

Take a deep breath—it's not just fruits and veggies that count! Think pulses, soy foods, nuts, seeds, and whole grains, and even fresh herbs, and the different varieties within each of these groups, too! Now, something like French fries could technically count as a plant food—they are made from potatoes, a plant, after all. But if you try to cheat the system, you're only cheating yourself. So, let's only count the *less* processed, more whole versions. (This includes oils, too.)

To see how easy—and dare I say, fun—this can be, I'll use breakfast as an example. A bowl of overnight oats with chia seeds, apple, and a dollop of almond butter— that's four different plant foods right there (and I didn't even try hard on that one). Alternate between the oats and a smoothie—with spinach, banana, frozen triple berry mix, flax seed, and peanut butter—for a week's worth of breakfasts, and that's eleven out of your thirty plant foods covered for that week, and it's well before noon each day. See, easy!

Color Me Healthy

There's a reason that "eat the rainbow" cliché from your childhood exists. The different colors you'll find in the produce section represent different antioxidants and phytonutrients within the major classes (i.e., polyphenols and carotenoids) that have unique health benefits—no one color is superior to another; all are important. So, use color as your guide as you diversify your produce intake. Getting the most phytonutrients also means enjoying the colorful skins, where they are often most concentrated. Try to avoid peeling fruits and veggies if you can.

COLOR	PHYTONUTRIENTS	EXAMPLES	HEALTH BENEFITS
Red	Anthocyanins, ellagic acid, lycopene	Beets, cherries, cranberries, raspberries, tomatoes, watermelon	Protect against certain cancers (especially prostate), support heart, prostate, and urinary tract health
Orange/yellow	Beta-carotene, lutein	Apricots, bell peppers, carrots, oranges, pumpkin, squash	Support immune and heart health and may reduce risk of cataracts and age-related macular degeneration
Green	Chlorophyll, indoles, lutein, sulforaphane	Avocado, broccoli, Brussels sprouts, kale, kiwi, parsley, spinach	Protect against certain cancers, support brain and eye health, and promote healthy estrogen metabolism
Blue/purple	Anthocyanins, flavonoids, resveratrol	Blackberries, blueberries, eggplants, plums, purple cabbage, purple grapes	Support brain and heart health, healthy aging, and protect against certain cancers and inflammation
White	Allicin, quercetin	Cauliflower, garlic, onions	Regulate blood pressure, lower cholesterol, and provide anti-inflammatory and antihistamine benefits

Stick with Slow-Carb Over Low-Carb

It's a low-carb world, and we're just living in it. But if I didn't make it abundantly clear in Chapter 2, carbs are friend, not foe! To be clear, that doesn't mean you should treat all carbohydrate-rich food sources the same. Common sense tells us that oats and frosted corn flakes—two carbohydrate-rich breakfast foods—are not equal. Remember, by focusing on carb quality, you can stress less over carb quantity. The quality, carbohydrate-rich foods you want to choose *most* of the time (like oats) have little to no added sugar and retain their fiber (and may even be a good source of protein), which helps slow digestion and the release of glucose into the bloodstream—hence the name "slow carbs."

On the other hand, quick carb sources (like many breakfast cereals) lack fiber and often are rich in added sugar, causing glucose to be rapidly absorbed into the bloodstream and giving you a quick—but not sustained—burst of energy. Eating for balanced blood sugar is a helpful strategy for anyone looking to lose weight and/or improve/maintain overall health, not just individuals with diabetes. Choosing slow carbs over quick carbs most of the time—but not necessarily all of the time—can help you do just that.

SLOW CARBS	QUICK CARBS
EXAMPLES: Lentils, beans, and chickpeas Roasted sweet potatoes with skin Whole and sprouted grains, like oats, quinoa, and whole-wheat products Whole fruits Winter squash (like acorn and butternut)	**EXAMPLES:** Breakfast cereals Cookies, candies, and pastries Many energy and granola bars Fried potato products Fruit juices Refined wheat bread and pasta
Less processed, more whole, so they retain fiber and other valuable nutrients	Often stripped of fiber and other valuable nutrients in processing, and rich in added sugar
Slow to digest	Quick to digest
Steadier, gradual rise in blood sugar levels for sustained energy	Rapid rise in blood sugar levels give a quick—but not sustained—burst of energy
Support the growth and activity of "good" gut microbes that promote good health	In excess, can impede the growth of "good" gut microbes in favor of promoting the growth of "bad" ones linked to disease

No carbs stand alone is a good rule of thumb when enjoying any carb-rich food—even a "slow" one. Protein and/or healthy fat can act as a buffer, helping to slow digestion and dampen the blood sugar response even further.

Don't Give Up on Grains

Over the years, grains have developed a bad reputation. Their carbohydrate content has put them at the top of the "avoid" lists of most weight-loss plans, and the misguided fear of gluten and lectins has many convinced that grains cause inflammation to run amok (which I debunk in Chapter 3). I'd be lying if I said I didn't once fall victim to the vendetta against grains, too.

There's no arguing that refined grains should play a limited role in the diet, but whole grains are a *whole* different story. Most of the goodness in grains is in the outer bran layer and the nutrient-rich core of the kernel, which are removed during the refining process. So, when you choose whole grains over refined ones, you'll get around two to three times more of most nutrients, like fiber, vitamin E, magnesium, and antioxidants and other phytonutrients, and up to 25 percent more protein, too. Plus, this whole-kernel structure takes longer to digest, which slows the release of glucose from the starch in the grain into the bloodstream and gives you a gentler rise in blood sugar levels.

Can't I Get My Nutrients from Other Foods?

Team Give-Up-Grains commonly argues that you can get the nutrients found in whole grains from other sources. (And I once preached this myself.) It is true—you don't *need* grains, and you could get everything you need from other foods, if you wanted to. But the evidence says the whole grain package has a whole lot to offer. The macro-, micro-, and phytonutrients in whole grains synergistically contribute to their beneficial effects, so living against the grain could be doing your health and waistline a disservice. In fact, an average intake of three servings of whole grains per day has been linked to a lower BMI, smaller waist size, and less belly fat. And this same intake has been associated with a nearly 20 percent lower risk of colorectal cancer. But the good news doesn't stop there. Regularly consuming whole grains at around two to three servings per day was found to reduce risk of CVD and diabetes by about 20 to 30 percent. And our gut friends love whole grains, too—they can fuel a diverse and healthy gut microbiome that fights inflammation and supports the health benefits just mentioned.

> "An average intake of three servings of whole grains per day has been linked to a lower BMI, smaller waist size, and less belly fat."

Shopping for Whole Grains

I know this is exciting news—you can finally enjoy oats and bread without guilt!—but before you drop everything and run to the grocery store, let's talk *shopping* for whole grains. Oats, brown rice, and ancient grains like quinoa, barley, and others are virtually always whole grains, even if the word *whole* isn't used (for example, some oat brands list the oats as "whole-grain rolled oats," and others just say "rolled oats"). But that's definitely not the case for *wheat* and wheat-containing products. You'll have to do a little extra investigating here because labels can be extremely deceptive, especially when it comes to bread and bread products. Here are some tips:

- Front-of-package labels you shouldn't rely on include "made with whole grains," "contains whole grains," "multigrain," and "#-grain" (e.g., 12-grain bread). These labels do not indicate that the product is made entirely of whole grains—a mix of whole *and* refined grains could have been used.

- If you see "100% whole wheat" or "100% whole grain" on the packaging, then you can be sure the product is made up entirely of whole grains.

- Take a peek at the ingredient list. If wheat flour is used, you'll want to see the word *whole* in front of it (e.g., "whole wheat flour" instead of just "wheat flour" or "enriched wheat flour") or *sprouted*. Sprouted grains are by necessity whole grains because you can't sprout a refined grain.

- Look for a 10:1 ratio (or less) of total carbs to fiber on the nutrition label of grain products in general (for example, if a product has 20 grams total carbs, you want *at least* 2 grams of fiber). With breads specifically, I recommend looking for closer to a 5:1 ratio (for example, if a slice of bread has 15 grams carbs, look for at least 3 grams fiber).

A final word on carbs: While there is no doubt that whole foods are healthier than their refined counterparts, we are human. Yes, food is fuel, but it has evolved into so much more for us. We have personal, social, and emotional ties to it (hence why many of us can't quit meat, either). Although you do want to stick with the less processed, more whole versions *most* of the time, some baguette at happy hour, a slice of your favorite chocolate cake on date night, or a meal at home with white spaghetti rather than whole-wheat pasta won't ruin your health or progress unless you let it. In fact, by going plant forward and mostly following the PLANTS acronym, you'll build a resilient, health-promoting gut microbiome that can handle the occasional less nutritious but "good-for-the-soul" stuff. Being too rigid in any aspect of your diet will set you up for failure. Why not set yourself up for success starting today?

———————

"Although you do want to stick with the less processed, more whole versions most of the time, some baguette at happy hour, a slice of your favorite chocolate cake on date night, or a meal at home with white spaghetti rather than whole-wheat pasta won't ruin your health or progress unless you let it."

———————

Your Plant-Forward Plate

Now, let's put it all together! Consider this your "cheat sheet" for building balanced, plant-forward meals. You'll get plenty of plant-forward recipe ideas in this book and lots of practice putting them together during the 28-day reset, but you may find it helpful to have a visual representation of what a balanced plate looks like as you put together some of your own plant-forward plates. They should include lean protein, slow carbs, (lots of) nonstarchy veggies, and healthy fat. And as you build these plates, keep PLANTS top of mind.

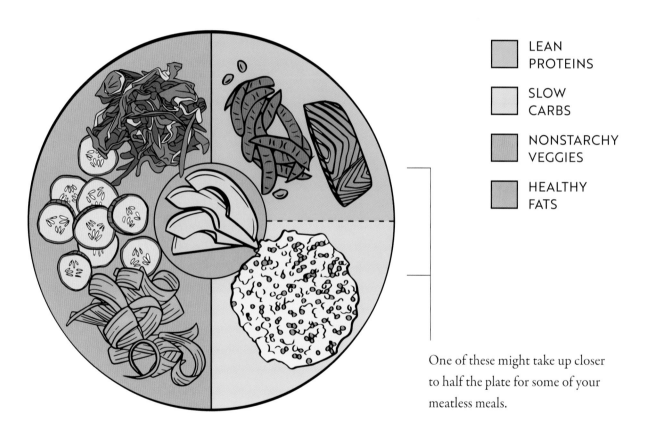

LEAN PROTEINS

SLOW CARBS

NONSTARCHY VEGGIES

HEALTHY FATS

One of these might take up closer to half the plate for some of your meatless meals.

(P) Prioritize Prebiotic and Probiotic-rich foods

Consume a variety of fiber-rich foods to feed your good gut bacteria and add fermented/cultured foods to your weekly rotation.

(L) Love on Legumes

Especially pulses. Make it a habit to get at least a half-cup of them most days of the week.

(A) Aim for less Animals (and more plants)

Give your plate a protein flip. Give plant proteins a starring role and serve less meat, less often.

(N) Nosh on Nuts (and seeds)

Enjoy a serving of nuts and/or seeds daily as a snack or as part of a meal.

(T) Try for Thirty plants per week

Every different fruit, vegetable, legume (pulses and soy products), grain, nut, seed, and fresh herb counts!

(S) Stick with Slow carb over low carb

Carb-rich foods have a place on your plate, but choose "slow" ones for the most part.

LEAN PROTEINS	SLOW CARBS	NONSTARCHY VEGGIES	HEALTHY FATS
(½ to ¾ cup cooked pulses or 3 to 4 ounces cooked soy foods or animal proteins)	(½ to 1 cup cooked)	(unlimited but aim for 1 to 2 cups)	(varies)

PLANT PROTEINS

- Pulses (beans, chickpeas, lentils, split peas, etc.)—canned, cooked from dried, or pasta versions

- Soy foods (edamame, tempeh, tofu, etc.)

ANIMAL PROTEINS

- Cultured dairy products (i.e., yogurt and cultured cottage cheese) and other dairy
- Eggs
- Fish and other seafood
- Poultry
- Lean red meat

STARCHY VEGGIES

Corn, green peas, potatoes (sweet, colored, and white—skin on if possible), winter squash

WHOLE GRAINS

- Ancient grains (quinoa, farro, barley, buckwheat, etc.)
- Brown or wild rice
- Oats (rolled, quick, steel-cut)
- Sprouted or whole-grain breads and pastas
- Whole-grain (wheat- or corn-based) tortillas
- Grain-free alternatives (cassava pasta, grain-free tortillas, etc.)

FRUITS

Apples, bananas, berries, tropical fruits, etc.

LEAFY GREENS

Arugula, kale, spinach, spring greens, Swiss chard, etc.

FERMENTED VEGGIES

Kimchi, sauerkraut, other fermented veggies

EVERYTHING ELSE

Bell peppers, bok choy, broccoli, Brussels sprouts, cabbage, cauliflower, eggplant, mushrooms, spaghetti squash, tomatoes, zucchini, etc.

AVOCADO

OILS (olive, avocado, walnut, flax seed, sesame)

OLIVES

PROTEIN-PACKED HEALTHY FATS (add to meals for a protein boost):

- Hummus
- Nuts and unsweetened nut butters
- Seeds and unsweetened seed butters (like tahini)

When referencing this chart, keep in mind that rarely is a food made up of just one macronutrient—with the exception of sugar (100 percent carbohydrate) and oils (100 percent fat). Most foods contain a mixture of macros but are often classified by the predominant macro.

LEAN PROTEINS: Not only does protein help build and maintain lean muscle mass but it also curbs hunger. Plus, incorporating protein into a carb-rich meal (or snack) helps dampen the blood sugar response. Make plant proteins a priority on your plate. Also try limiting seafood, poultry, and red meat to one plate per day and make the other meals meatless.

SLOW CARBS: These fiber-rich, quality carb sources give you the energy you need while also filling you (and your gut friends) up. Some, like farro, quinoa, oats, whole-wheat pasta, and sprouted and whole-grain breads, contribute a good chunk of protein, too. Enjoy a variety of starchy veggies, fruits, and grains—sticking with whole, less-processed versions of these foods when possible. Fruits can also make up some of the fiber-rich carbs on your plate (or off to the side).

NONSTARCHY VEGGIES: These veggies provide you with fiber and add volume and phytonutrients to your meals without adding many calories, giving you the most bang for your calorie buck. Fill half your plate with them or strive for at least five servings a day (one serving equals 1 cup raw leafy greens or ½ cup everything else).

HEALTHY FATS: Fat is critical to the structure and function of the body and should have a place on your plate. In fact, fat will help you absorb the fat-soluble vitamins—A, D, E, and K—on your plate. (And no, eating fat does not make you fat.) Because plant proteins are generally low in fat, incorporate small amounts of healthy fat sources into most of your meals, putting extra emphasis on the whole-food healthy fat sources that come with the added bonus of protein and/or fiber, like avocado, olives, nuts, seeds, and nut/seed butters.

Meatless/Vegetarian Meal Ideas

This book is full of meatless recipes built with the plant-forward plate in mind, but here are some quick meatless meal ideas to get your brain juices flowing. And, as you can see, the possibilities are endless!

🌱	PROTEIN	SLOW CARBS	NONSTARCHY VEGGIES	HEALTHY FATS	EXTRAS
AVOCADO EGG SALAD SANDWICH	Hard-boiled egg	Whole-grain or sprouted bread	Celery, lettuce, red onion	Avocado	Lemon juice, dry ranch seasoning
SOUTHWESTERN QUINOA SALAD	Black beans	Quinoa, canned corn	Bell pepper, cherry tomatoes, canned green chiles	Extra-virgin olive oil	Cilantro, lime juice, taco seasoning
MEDITERRANEAN PASTA SALAD	Chickpea pasta (plus optional sprinkle of feta)		Arugula, cucumber, red onion, sun-dried tomatoes	Pesto, olives	Lemon juice
PEANUTTY TOFU	Extra-firm tofu	Brown or wild rice	Broccoli	Unsweetened peanut or almond butter, sesame oil	Honey, rice vinegar, soy sauce or tamari
SIMPLE STUFFED SWEET POTATO	Black beans (plus optional dollop of Greek yogurt)	Sweet potato, canned corn	Bell pepper, green onion	Guacamole	Salsa, taco seasoning
ROASTED VEGGIE & GRAIN BOWL	Quinoa and butternut squash		Brussels sprouts, kale	Hemp hearts (shelled hemp seeds), tahini	Cumin, lemon juice, paprika
FALL SALAD	Chickpeas (plus optional sprinkle of goat cheese)	Apple	Romaine lettuce, red onion, spinach	Walnuts, extra-virgin olive oil	Apple cider vinegar, Dijon mustard
BEAN TOSTADAS	Pinto beans	Corn tortillas	Pickled onions, slaw mix, tomatoes	Avocado	Apple cider vinegar, chili powder, cumin
HUMMUS 'DILLAS	Whole wheat tortilla		Onion, spinach, sun-dried tomatoes	Roasted red pepper hummus (for protein, too)	Basil
VEGGIE LOADED FRIED RICE	Scrambled egg and/or edamame	Brown rice	Cauliflower rice (mixed in with the rice), carrot, red bell pepper	Olive or sesame oil	Soy sauce or tamari

CHAPTER 5:
THE 28-DAY PLANT-FORWARD RESET

———

And now, the part you've been anxiously flipping page after page for—your 28-day plant-forward reset. Remember, adding more plants to your plate is *not* an all-or-nothing proposition. *Any* movement in the direction of adding nutrient-dense plant foods into your routine is a win for your health—and I'm a firm believer in the "your health is a marathon, not a sprint" mantra. That said—there was only enough room in this book to include 28 days, and I wanted to pack those days with as much plant goodness as possible. So, if you find that you need more animal protein in your diet to start with than what the meal plan calls for, you can tweak it to fit your needs without guilt. Consider this meal plan a flexible blueprint!

Before you dive in, there are a few things I want you to keep in mind:

- Energy needs vary greatly from person to person and are influenced by factors such as age, activity level, body size and composition, and goals. So, while the recipes were designed to maximize satiety with the plant-forward plate in mind, you may find that the meal plan (plus whatever snacks you choose from the snacks lists) isn't enough for you. If this is the case, you may need to serve yourself a larger portion at meals and adjust the recipes accordingly, or you may want to make a little extra of the main protein and/or slow carb in each recipe to serve along with it (e.g., extra quinoa for a quinoa salad or more chickpeas in a chickpea curry). Remember, this meal plan is meant as a flexible blueprint, a starting point that can be tailored to fit your needs. You are not restricted to a certain number of calories here—so, let your hunger cues be your guide. And if they're telling you you're hungry, *then eat*!

- The meal plan is designed to feed two people, but you'll notice many of the recipes yield four servings. This sets you up to cook once and eat twice with leftovers.

- If a recipe in the meal plan doesn't tickle your fancy, feel free to swap it out for a different one from the recipe section. (Some of the Smaller Fare recipes can serve as a light meal or can be easily made into a larger meal with the addition of some protein and/or slow carb.) And if you decide to create some of your own recipes, use the plant-forward plate and chart at the end of Chapter 4 as your guide.

One last thing—this isn't your average, run-of-the-mill meal plan. Each week has a "focus" that I developed with the PLANTS acronym (page 102) in mind.

Here's a little snapshot:

- Week 1: Get comfortable cooking with less meat (and more plants)

- Week 2: Expand your plant protein repertoire

- Week 3: Prioritize prebiotic- and probiotic-rich (i.e., fermented) foods

- Week 4: Diversify your diet

WEEK 1: Get Comfortable Cooking with Less Meat (and More Plants)

Welcome to your first week of the reset, your initiation into the plant-forward approach. Get excited—you're about to dive headfirst into plant-forward cooking, which will open up a whole new world of flavors, textures, and colors for you. And you'll finally get to experience firsthand just how satisfying and nourishing these plant-centric meals can be.

This week is all about getting comfortable cooking with less meat (and more plants, obviously). You'll start loving on legumes and be introduced to Pick-Your-Protein (PYP) recipes, which give you the option of adding some animal protein or keeping it plant-powered.

Should you choose to create some of your own less-meat or meatless recipes, here are some tips for creating something hearty, tasty, and satisfying that won't leave you missing meat. *(I used these very same tips to create the recipes for this week and the following weeks, too.)*

- **Add "meaty" veggies to your dishes.** Mushrooms, eggplant, and jackfruit can add a meaty texture to your stir-fries, sandwiches, soups, stews, and more. They can also add a meaty flavor because they...

- **Up the umami.** Umami is one of the five basic tastes alongside sweet, sour, bitter, and salty. It's described as a savory, meaty taste typically detected in—no surprise here—meats and other animal proteins. However, the umami-eliciting substances (notably the amino acid glutamate) can also be found in several plant-based foods, specifically mushrooms; tomatoes; onions; seaweed; soy sauce, tamari, or coconut aminos; and miso. And roasting, sautéing, caramelizing, or grilling can boost the umami flavor. Incorporating umami elements in your meatless meals can give you some of that mouthwatering savory sensation you get from meat. You can also find umami seasoning blends made from dried mushroom powder. Speaking of which...

- **Spice it up.** You don't usually serve beef or chicken without seasonings, so why would you do so with plant proteins? In fact, you can even use steak and poultry seasoning blends in your meatless dishes (despite their names, these seasonings don't contain any meat). If you want to add a little smokiness to your meal, give chipotle chili powder or smoked paprika a try. (Smoked paprika is my absolute favorite, and I use it often.) And everything bagel seasoning truly makes anything and *everything* taste better, even veggies.

- **Explore recipes from cultures that put less focus on animal products.** Think Middle Eastern, Indian, and Thai cuisine. You can find many recipes packed with hearty vegetables and filling plant proteins that are bursting with flavor from spices and herbs. Curries are a great example of a flavorful dish that tastes as good (if not better) without animal proteins as it does with them.

- **Give recipes a 50/50 makeover.** You can easily lower the meat content of your favorite dishes without sacrificing satiety or flavor by going 50/50 and swapping legumes for about half of the red meat or poultry called for. Turn pork tacos into pork and pinto bean tacos, a steak burrito bowl into a steak and black bean burrito bowl, chicken noodle soup into chicken and chickpea noodle soup, a pork pad thai into a pork tofu pad thai. You get the picture. In general, swap ¼ cup of pulses or an ounce of tofu for every ounce or two of meat.

- **Don't forget the fat.** You know that mouth-coating richness you get from meaty dishes? Yeah—that's fat! Fat from animal protein gives meals a juicy richness that can make meatless meals seem lackluster. The solution? Don't forget to add some healthy fat! Plus, fat carries flavor, so it can make veggies taste better, too. And what's great about meatless cooking is you have control over *how much* and *what kind* of fat you add. Healthy fats like avocado, extra-virgin olive oil, nuts, nut butter, olives, and tahini are my go-tos.

Before You Dive In

As you introduce more plant foods—and therefore, fiber—into your diet this week, be sure to drink up (water, not margaritas)! It's very important to hydrate throughout the day to help fiber pass smoothly and do its thing and to prevent constipation.

And speaking of fiber, you'll notice pulses show up in several of the recipes this week and the remaining weeks. After all, they are one of the MVPs (most valuable proteins) of the plant-forward approach. If you know you have trouble tolerating them, keep in mind that they vary in their fermentable carbohydrate content, so you may tolerate some better than others. (Lentils tend to be the best tolerated.) You may also find a ½-cup portion of most pulses bothersome at first but do fine with a smaller ¼-cup portion. If this is the case, try cutting the amount called for in the recipes in half to start—and adding some tofu, tempeh, protein-rich whole grains like quinoa or buckwheat (which are generally well-tolerated), or a little animal protein—then gradually increase the pulse quantity over time as you train and strengthen your gut microbiome. Also, you may want to stick to mostly canned (and well-rinsed) pulses because they are generally better tolerated than those cooked from scratch.

WEEK 1 MEAL PLAN

This menu is for two people.

	Breakfast	Lunch	Dinner
Monday	182 Wild Blueberry Muffin Superseed Overnight Oats	196 Strawberry & Feta Quinoa Salad	228 "Meaty" Bolognese over spaghetti squash (PYP: 50/50)
Tuesday	182 Wild Blueberry Muffin Superseed Overnight Oats *leftover*	196 Strawberry & Feta Quinoa Salad *leftover*	228 "Meaty" Bolognese over spaghetti squash (PYP: 50/50) *leftover*
Wednesday	182 Wild Blueberry Muffin Superseed Overnight Oats *leftover*	218 Hummus Power Sandwich + 1 clementine	220 Portobello Pitas + side of Mixed Root Veggie Fries (optional)
Thursday	173 Chocolate Cherry Smoothie	220 Portobello Pitas + side of Mixed Root Veggie Fries (optional) *leftover*	208 Tuscan Red Pepper, Tomato & White Bean Soup
Friday	173 Chocolate Cherry Smoothie	EBTKS Salad (see sidebar)	208 Tuscan Red Pepper, Tomato & White Bean Soup *leftover*
Saturday	173 Chocolate Cherry Smoothie	224 Farmers' Market Quiche + handful of grapes	238 One-Pot Chickpea & Cauliflower Curry (PYP: 50/50)
Sunday	173 Chocolate Cherry Smoothie	224 Farmers' Market Quiche + handful of grapes *leftover*	238 One-Pot Chickpea & Cauliflower Curry (PYP: 50/50) *leftover*

Everything-but-the-Kitchen-Sink Salad

As the name implies, for this salad, you essentially throw together whatever you have in your kitchen—anything and everything (but the kitchen sink). I've incorporated an EBTKS salad toward the end of each week's meal plan because it's a great way to use up whatever odd leftovers you have before they go to waste. Use the plant-forward plate (page 101) as your guide or stick with this simple formula: about 2 cups of leafy greens + 1 cup of other produce (like crunchy veggies, fruit, or starchy veggies) + 1 serving of lean protein (plant, animal, or 50/50) + 1 to 2 tablespoons of healthy, whole fats (like avocado, nuts, or seeds) + 1 to 2 tablespoons of dressing.

NOTE ————

PYP indicates a Pick-Your-Protein recipe. I've noted which protein option I think you should choose for each PYP recipe in the meal plan, but feel free to go with a different option (and adjust the grocery list accordingly).

Snack ideas for this week:

The meal plan does not include snacks, so be sure to add some. You'll want to prioritize protein and fiber for your snacks to help you feel full and satisfied until your next meal.

- Sliced veggies or baby carrots, whole-grain or grain-free (e.g., almond flour) crackers, and hummus

- Piece of fruit and spoonful of nut or seed butter

- Handful of grapes or a clementine and an ounce of raw or dry-roasted nuts (pistachios make for the perfect snacking nut)

- Popcorn trail mix: Sea salt popcorn + raw or dry-roasted nuts and seeds + dried or freeze-dried fruit + dark chocolate chips (optional)

WEEK 1 PREP PLAN

Weekend before:

- Grocery shop! Take inventory of what you already have in your kitchen and comb through the grocery list. Determine what substitutions are necessary for a dietary need (e.g., dairy- or nut-free). Take a look at the substitutions noted in the recipes for the week and adjust your grocery list accordingly.

- On Sunday: Prep the Strawberry & Feta Quinoa Salad (page 196) and a double batch of the Wild Blueberry Muffin Superseed Overnight Oats (page 182). Slice and freeze four bananas to be used in the smoothies. I recommend roasting your own red bell peppers for the Hummus Power Sandwich (page 218) and Tuscan Red Pepper, Tomato & White Bean Soup (page 208). You can do that ahead of time (today) and store them in the fridge or wait until day of.

Throughout the week:

- On Saturday: Use spinach, Roma tomato, and zucchini (or you can use whatever veggies you'd like) for the Farmers' Market Quiche.

- Don't throw anything out! Even the tomato paste—you use it more than once. Same goes for fresh herbs. And you should use any leftover produce or other foods for the EBTKS Salad.

Homemade Versus Store-Bought

I suppose in an ideal world, we'd all be milking our own almonds and making everything from scratch, but in our fast-paced world, that's simply unrealistic for most. Luckily, you can find quality premade versions of basic pantry/fridge items like beans, hummus, salsa, pesto, tomato sauce, vegetable broth, and so on at most grocery stores. If you enjoy making most of these items from scratch, then more power to ya! But if relying on premade versions of some of these items works better for your lifestyle, makes plant-forward cooking less daunting and more enjoyable, and ultimately helps you sustain this plant-forward lifestyle, then that's A-OK, too. I do, however, encourage you to try some of the Basics recipes in this book. (The Easy Salsa Verde on page 156 is one of my favorites and is, as the name implies, very *easy*.)

Pantry Basics

These items will be used throughout the four weeks and won't be listed in each week's grocery list:

- Apple cider vinegar, raw, unfiltered
- Baking powder
- Balsamic vinegar
- Bay leaves
- Chili powder
- Crushed red pepper
- Dijon mustard
- Dried oregano leaves
- Extra-virgin olive oil
- Garlic powder
- Ground cinnamon
- Ground cumin
- Honey
- Maple syrup (100% pure, not the pancake kind)
- Olive oil cooking spray
- Rice vinegar
- Salt and black pepper (I typically use sea salt or table salt)
- Smoked paprika
- Soy sauce or tamari (low-sodium)
- Sweet paprika (typically labeled as just paprika)
- Vanilla extract

WEEK 1 GROCERY LIST

Fresh produce:

- Arugula, 5 ounces
- Avocado, 1 medium
- Baby spinach, 10 ounces
- Bananas, 4 medium
- Basil, 1 small bunch
- Bell peppers, red, 4 large
- Carrot, 1 medium
- Cauliflower, 1 small head
- Clementines, 2
- Cucumbers, 1 large, 2 medium
- Dill, 1 small bunch
- Garlic, 1 head
- Ginger, 1 (1-inch) piece
- Grapes, 1 bunch
- Green onions or scallions, 1 bunch
- Lemons, 2
- Lime, 1
- Microgreens or sprouts, 1 small container (if available)
- Mint, 1 small bunch
- Mushrooms, cremini or shiitake, 8 ounces
- Onion, red, 1 small
- Onions, yellow, 2 medium
- Parsley, 1 small bunch
- Parsnip, 1 large
- Portobello mushroom caps, 4 large
- Rosemary, 1 small bunch
- Shallot, 1
- Spaghetti squash, 1 medium
- Strawberries, 1 pound
- Sweet potatoes, 2 large
- Tomato, beefsteak, 1
- Tomato, Roma, 1
- Zucchini, 1 medium

Frozen:

- Cherries, 1 (16-ounce) bag
- Wild blueberries, 1 (16-ounce) bag

Dairy, nondairy & eggs:

- Nondairy milk, unsweetened, ½ gallon
- Greek yogurt, plain, 1 (24-ounce) container
- Feta cheese, crumbled, 4 ounces
- Goat cheese, crumbled, 4 ounces
- Eggs, large, 1 dozen

Meat, poultry & seafood:

- Beef or turkey, lean, ground, 8 to 10 ounces
- Chicken breast, boneless and skinless, 10 ounces, or 1 plain rotisserie chicken

Bread, grains & pulses:

- Beans, cannellini, 2 (15-ounce) cans or 1 (16-ounce) bag dried beans
- Beans, chickpeas, 1 (15-ounce) can or 1 (16-ounce) bag dried beans
- Corn or arrowroot starch, 1 (16-ounce) bag/container
- Lentils, green or brown, 1 (15-ounce) can or 1 (16-ounce) bag dried lentils
- Pita bread, 100% whole-wheat (or gluten-free pita), 1 package
- Quinoa, 1 (16-ounce) bag
- Rolled or old-fashioned oats (gluten-free if necessary), 1 (42-ounce) container
- Sprouted or 100% whole-grain bread (or gluten-free bread if necessary), 1 loaf

Canned & jarred goods:

- Broth, low-sodium vegetable, 1 (32-ounce) carton
- Coconut milk, light, 2 (14-ounce) cans
- Pesto, 1 (6-ounce) jar
- Tomato paste, 1 (6-ounce) can
- Tomatoes, crushed, 1 (15-ounce) can
- Tomatoes, whole peeled, 1 (28-ounce) can

Condiments:

- Thai red curry paste, 1 (4-ounce) jar

Nuts & seeds:

- Almond butter, 1 (12-ounce) jar
- Almonds, sliced, 1 ounce
- Chia seeds, 1 (12-ounce) bag
- Flax seed, ground, 1 (16-ounce) bag
- Hemp hearts (shelled hemp seeds), 1 (8-ounce) bag

Miscellaneous:

- Hummus, 1 (10-ounce) container*
- Plant-based protein powder, vanilla, 1 (2-pound) container
- Red wine, 1 bottle (or sub 100% pomegranate juice)
- Unsweetened cocoa powder, 1 (8-ounce) container

*If you prefer to make Basic Hummus (page 164), add the necessary ingredients to your list.

Don't forget to add ingredients for your snacks of choice to your list!

WEEK 2: Expand your plant protein repertoire

Now that you've gotten your feet wet, it's time to expand your plant protein repertoire. Remember, eating less meat does not mean sacrificing protein because there are plenty of protein-packed plant foods. I'm not just talking about your beans, chickpeas, and lentils. Have you ever had tofu? How about tempeh? Don't knock 'em till you try 'em! Protein hides in many plant foods you wouldn't expect beyond legumes, like in whole grains and even vegetables, too.

Protein Power of Plants

LEGUMES		WHOLE GRAINS (1 cup cooked)	NUTS (1 ounce)
Pulses (½ cup cooked/ canned)	Soy foods	Amaranth (9g)	Almonds (6g)
		Buckwheat (6g)	Cashews (5g)
		Farro (9g)	Hazelnuts (4g)
Black beans (8g)	Edamame (1 cup, shelled = 17g)	Oats (6g)	Peanuts (7g)
Black-eyed peas (7g)		Pearled barley (4g)	Pistachios (6g)
Cannellini beans (7g)	Tempeh (3 ounces = 17g)	Quinoa (8g)	Walnuts (4g)
Chickpeas (7g)	Tofu (3 ounces = 9g)	Sprouted bread (4 to 5g/slice)	
Lentils (9g)		Whole-wheat pasta (7.5g)	

SEEDS (2 tablespoons)	VEGGIES (1 cup cooked)	OTHER (1 tablespoon)
Chia seeds (4g)	Broccoli (3g)	Nutritional yeast (2g)
Ground flax seed (3g)	Brussels sprouts (4g)	Spirulina (4g)
Hemp hearts (6g)	Green peas (9g)	
Pepitas (5g)	Spinach (5g)	
Sunflower seeds (4g)		
Tahini/sesame seed butter (6g)		

So, give at least one new-to-you plant protein source a try this week and continue expanding your plant protein repertoire beyond the reset. (I've incorporated some new plant proteins into this week's meal plan, too.) Here are some ideas for a quick-and-easy plant-based protein boost for your meals:

- Add a generous spread of hummus to (pretty much) any sandwich. Hummus may be rich in healthy fats from olive oil and tahini, but let's not forget the star ingredient is protein-rich chickpeas (and you'll get some protein from the tahini, too).

- Nuts aren't just for snacking—they can add a boost of healthy fat and protein to your meals. Try toasted walnuts on a salad or chopped cashews in a stir-fry.

- Hemp hearts are the most protein-dense of the small seeds, and they're super versatile. Add a tablespoon to a smoothie or your morning oats or sprinkle some on avocado toast or salads.

- Nutritional yeast is quite popular among plant-based eaters thanks to its cheesy and nutty flavor. Add a sprinkle to pasta dishes, roasted vegetables, and even popcorn!

Hempesan: The Nondairy "Parmesan"

If, for whatever reason, you avoid dairy or you simply want to give some dairy alternatives a try, this simple protein-packed "hempesan" is great for topping your pastas, avocado toasts, and more: ½ cup hemp hearts + 2 to 3 tablespoons nutritional yeast + ¼ to ½ teaspoon salt + ¼ teaspoon garlic powder. Place all of the ingredients in a mason jar, secure the lid, and shake! Alternatively, you can place the ingredients in a blender or food processor and pulse a few times for a finer consistency.

WEEK 2 MEAL PLAN

This menu is for two people.

	Breakfast	Lunch	Dinner
Monday	186 — Peaches & Cream Quinoa Porridge	218 — Hummus Power Sandwich + 1 pear	198 — Spring Niçoise Salad (PYP: salmon)
Tuesday	186 — Peaches & Cream Quinoa Porridge (leftover)	198 — Spring Niçoise Salad (PYP: salmon) (leftover)	232 — Lasagna Roll-Ups with Plant Ricotta
Wednesday	174 — The Green Machine Smoothie	232 — Lasagna Roll-Ups with Plant Ricotta (leftover)	202 — Less Kale Caesar (PYP: tempeh)
Thursday	174 — The Green Machine Smoothie	202 — Less Kale Caesar (PYP: tempeh) (leftover)	230 — Creamy Caulifredo
Friday	174 — The Green Machine Smoothie	230 — Creamy Caulifredo (leftover)	260 — Takeout Tofu Lettuce Wraps + ½ cup cooked brown rice per serving
Saturday	174 — The Green Machine Smoothie	260 — Takeout Tofu Lettuce Wraps + ½ cup cooked brown rice per serving (leftover)	242 — Mean Green Enchilada Skillet (PYP: 50/50)
Sunday	188 — Banana Buckwheat Blender Pancakes	EBTKS Salad	242 — Mean Green Enchilada Skillet (PYP: 50/50) (leftover)

Here are the possibly new-to-you plant proteins and plant protein combos in this week's meal plan:

- Tofu and cashews to make the plant ricotta in the Lasagna Roll-Ups with Plant Ricotta (page 232)

- Tempeh in the Less Kale Caesar (page 202)

- Hemp hearts, nutritional yeast (optional), and peas in the Creamy Caulifredo (page 230)

- Tofu in the Takeout Tofu Lettuce Wraps (page 260)

Snack ideas for this week:

The meal plan does not include snacks, so be sure to add some. You'll want to prioritize protein and fiber for your snacks to help you feel full and satisfied until your next meal.

- Sliced veggies or baby carrots, whole-grain or grain-free (e.g., almond flour) crackers, and hummus

- Piece of fruit and spoonful of nut or seed butter

- Handful of grapes or a clementine and an ounce of raw or dry-roasted nuts

- Creamy Chia Pudding (page 286)

- Chickpea Poppers (page 274)

WEEK 2 PREP PLAN

Weekend before:

- Grocery shop! Take inventory of what you already have in your kitchen and comb through the grocery list. Determine what substitutions are necessary for a dietary need (e.g., dairy- or nut-free). Take a look at the substitutions noted in the recipes for the week and adjust your grocery list accordingly.

- On Sunday: Prep the Peaches & Cream Quinoa Porridge (page 186) and Hummus Power Sandwich (page 218). Also, slice and freeze two zucchini to be used in the smoothies.

Throughout the week:

- On Wednesday night: Prep a full batch of Chickpea Poppers (page 274); use half for the Less Kale Caesar (page 202) and save the other half to enjoy as a snack.

- On Sunday: You can freeze any leftover Banana Buckwheat Blender Pancakes (page 188) for another day.

- Don't throw anything out—including any leftover fresh herbs! Any leftover produce or other foods should be used for the EBTKS Salad at the end of the week.

WEEK 2 GROCERY LIST

Double-check the Pantry Basics list on page 114 for any items that you may need to replenish. You may still have these items from Week 1:

- Bread, whole-grain or sprouted
- Corn or arrowroot starch
- Eggs, large, 5
- Ground flax seed or flax seed meal
- Hemp hearts (shelled hemp seeds)
- Microgreens or sprouts
- Parsley
- Pesto
- Protein powder
- Quinoa
- Rolled, or old-fashioned, oats (gluten-free if necessary)

Frozen:

- Mango chunks, 1 (16-ounce) bag
- Peas, 1 (10-ounce) bag
- Pineapple chunks, 1 (16-ounce) bag
- Spinach, chopped, 1 (10-ounce) bag

Meat, poultry & seafood:

- Chicken breast, boneless and skinless, 10 ounces, or 1 plain rotisserie chicken (and use leftover in beginning of Week 3)
- Salmon, 2 (6-ounce) fillets

Dairy, nondairy & eggs:

- Greek yogurt, plain, full-fat or 2%, 1 (5-ounce) container
- Monterey Jack or Mexican blend cheese, shredded, 8 ounces
- Mozzarella cheese, shredded, 4 ounces
- Nondairy milk of choice, unsweetened, ½ gallon
- Parmesan cheese, 1 ounce (optional, or use nutritional yeast)

Nuts & seeds:

- Cashews, raw, 8 ounces
- Peanut butter, 1 (16-ounce) jar
- Pecans or walnuts, chopped, 1 ounce
- Tahini, 1 (16-ounce) jar

Fresh produce:

- Asparagus, 8 ounces
- Avocados, 3 medium
- Baby spinach, 5 ounces
- Bananas, 2 small
- Basil, 1 small bunch
- Bell pepper, red, 1
- Carrots, 2 medium, or 1 (10-ounce) bag shredded carrots
- Cauliflower, 1 medium head
- Cilantro, 1 small bunch
- Cucumber, 1 medium
- Garlic, 1 head
- Ginger, 1 (1-inch) piece
- Green beans, 8 ounces
- Green onions, 1 bunch
- Kale, 1 large bunch
- Lemons, 4
- Lettuce, butter, 2 heads
- Lettuce, chopped romaine, 10 ounces
- Lime, 1
- Medjool dates, pitted, 12 ounces
- Onion, white, 1 medium
- Orange, 1 medium
- Peaches, 2 medium
- Pears, 2 medium
- Pepper, poblano, 1
- Pepper, serrano or jalapeño, 1
- Potatoes, baby, 1 pound
- Radishes, small, 1 bunch
- Shallot, 1
- Tomatillos, 1 pound (about 8 medium)
- Zucchini, 3 large

Condiments:

- Sriracha or sambal oelek, 1 bottle/jar

Canned & jarred goods:

- Capers, 1 (3-ounce) jar
- Coconut milk, light, 1 (14-ounce) can
- Marinara sauce, 1 (16-ounce) jar
- Olives, niçoise or Kalamata, 1 (6-ounce) jar

Bread, grains & pulses:

- Beans, black, 1 (15-ounce) can or 1 (16-ounce) bag dried beans
- Beans, chickpeas, 2 (15-ounce) cans
- Brown rice, 1 (32-ounce) bag
- Buckwheat flour, 1 (16-ounce) bag
- Lasagna noodles, whole-grain, 1 (12-ounce) box
- Pasta of choice, legume-based, 1 (8-ounce) box
- Tortillas, corn, 6 (6-inch)

Miscellaneous:

- Hummus, 1 (10-ounce) container*
- Nutritional yeast, 1 (5-ounce) container or bag
- Spirulina or matcha powder (optional)
- Tempeh (gluten-free, if necessary), 1 (8-ounce) package
- Tofu, extra-firm, 1 (14-ounce) block
- Tofu, firm, 1 (14-ounce) block

*If you prefer to make Basic Hummus (page 164), add the necessary ingredients to your list.

Don't forget to add ingredients for your snacks of choice!

Storing Fresh Herbs 101

You'll notice several fresh herbs used throughout the reset, some used from one week to the next. It can be tempting to toss the rest of the bunch after one use, especially if you won't be using it again for several days or longer. After all, fresh herbs go limp after a few days, right? Well, if you toss them into your fridge haphazardly, that could be the case. But in a few quick steps, you can greatly extend their life, some to even the full length of this 28-day reset. So, don't throw out those precious phytonutrient-rich flavor-enhancers prematurely. Instead, give the following methods a go!

First, wash the herbs under cool water (you should really do this before using them the first time) and thoroughly dry using a salad spinner and/or paper towels.

Wrap hard herbs (like chives, rosemary, sage, and thyme) loosely in a damp paper towel and store in an airtight resealable bag or container in the fridge. For tender herbs (like basil, cilantro, dill, mint, and parsley), treat them as if they were a bouquet of flowers. Trim the bases of their stems, place in a large mason jar or glass with an inch or two of water, and change out that water every few days. Store basil at room temperature and out of direct sunlight. For all other tender herbs, cover them loosely with a plastic bag (I use a resealable one that I rinse and reuse) and store in the fridge.

WEEK 3: Prioritize Prebiotic- and Probiotic-rich Foods

Prebiotics and probiotics need no introduction at this point, but it's time you make them a priority in your diet. Guess what? If you've been following the meal plan for the most part up to this point, then you've been getting plenty of prebiotics already! So, for this week, I want to introduce a few more particularly prebiotic-rich food sources to your diet, like barley in the Miso Mushroom & Barley Stew (page 212) and resistant starch–rich day-old rice in the Kimchi Fried Rice (page 240), and throw some fermented foods into the mix, too. I also give you full permission to enjoy a glass (or three) of red wine this week while you're at it. After all, our good gut bugs do love those red wine polyphenols!

NOTE

Mandatory disclaimer: Overdoing it on alcohol—no matter the source—has the opposite effect on our gut friends. So please enjoy responsibly and in moderation!

I want you to keep your passion for pre- and probiotics alive once the reset is over. So, here are some easy ways to continue incorporating them into your diet beyond the 28 days:

- **Start with breakfast.** Oats are jam-packed with prebiotic fiber and resistant starch. Make a batch of overnight oats on the weekend for easy grab-and-go, gut-friendly breakfasts throughout the week. Use some Greek yogurt, probiotic dairy-free yogurt, kefir, and/or cultured cottage cheese in them to add a probiotic punch. And for extra credit, top with some not-fully-ripe sliced banana, which is rich in resistant starch. (But if you can't stomach the taste—I get it. Adding ripened banana will still provide you with prebiotics.)

- **Sip on soup.** Soups are the perfect vessel for a variety of gut-health-promoting foods. Whipping up a hearty plant-based soup filled with veggies, whole grains, and pulses (white beans and lentils are particularly rich in resistant starch) is an easy way to provide lots of grub to your good gut guys. Add some miso to the broth and seaweed for a Japanese-inspired sip that offers both the "biotics."

- **Repurpose leftovers.** Rice and potatoes that have been cooked, cooled, and reheated are full of resistant starch. Prep extra during dinner time, refrigerate the leftovers, and turn them into tomorrow's prebiotic-filled lunch or dinner.

- **Top off your meals.** Fermented foods like kimchi and sauerkraut are great toppings for sandwiches, stir-fries, soups, salads, and more. Even foods like pizza, avocado toast, and stuffed baked potatoes can benefit from a spoonful of these fermented foods.

- **Whip up some energy bites.** No need to awaken your inner Betty Crocker to whip up some gut-friendly treats. No-bake energy bites are tasty, customizable, and pack a prebiotic punch, giving both you and your gut bugs an energy boost. They're typically made from a combination of gut-boosting ingredients, like dried fruit (especially dates), oats, and/or nuts and seeds. Try the Omega Energy Bites (page 284) in this book.

- **Dress up your salads.** Although both raw and cooked alliums (e.g., garlic and onions) are a good source of prebiotic fiber, enjoying them raw increases their prebiotic potential. One of the few appetizing ways to enjoy them raw is in salads! You can add raw onion as a salad topper or make dressings with raw garlic, onion, and/or shallots blended in. Just be sure to have a breath mint afterward.

WEEK 3 MEAL PLAN

This menu is for two people.

	Breakfast	Lunch	Dinner
Monday	173 Happy Belly Smoothie	222 Green Goddess Smashed Bean Sammies with Quick Pickled Onions + 1 peach	210 Lemony Greek-Style Soup (PYP: 50/50)
Tuesday	173 Happy Belly Smoothie	210 Lemony Greek-Style Soup (PYP: 50/50) *leftover*	200 10-Minute Lentil-Walnut Taco Salad with Quick Pickled Onions
Wednesday	182 Morning Glory Superseed Overnight Oats	200 10-Minute Lentil-Walnut Taco Salad with Quick Pickled Onions *leftover*	246 Spicy Roll "Sushi" Bowl (PYP: salmon)
Thursday	182 Morning Glory Superseed Overnight Oats *leftover*	246 Spicy Roll "Sushi" Bowl (PYP: salmon) *leftover*	204 Spiced Green Tahini Salad
Friday	182 Morning Glory Superseed Overnight Oats *leftover*	204 Spiced Green Tahini Salad *leftover*	240 Kimchi Fried Rice
Saturday	173 Happy Belly Smoothie	240 Kimchi Fried Rice *leftover*	212 Miso Mushroom & Barley Stew + 1 Sweet Potato Tahini Brownie
Sunday	173 Happy Belly Smoothie	EBTKS Salad	212 Miso Mushroom & Barley Stew + 1 Sweet Potato Tahini Brownie *leftover*

This week's meal plan includes the following prebiotic and fermented foods that you may be unfamiliar with:

- **Apple cider vinegar:** Let me be clear: Apple cider vinegar is not the solution to all (or any) of your health woes that social media has made it out to be. Yes, that cloudy mass hanging out at the bottom of the bottle (the "mother") contains the living bacteria that fermented it but likely not enough to provide a significant health benefit when you're consuming so little of it at a time. That said, the *by-product* of fermentation—acetic acid—that gives the vinegar its pungent taste has been shown to have small but favorable effects on the post-meal blood sugar response. But please, skip the vinegar tonics and gummies, and stick to using it as it's intended to be used, like to make a zesty salad dressing or to pickle veggies, like you'll be doing this week.

- **Kefir:** Kefir is a fermented yogurtlike beverage cultured by both bacteria and yeasts. It often contains more of these friendly microorganisms (and a wider variety) than its cultured cousin yogurt, but it also has a more tangy, sour taste. (If you prefer to avoid dairy products, no problem—you can easily swap out the kefir in this week's smoothie recipe.)

- **Kimchi:** Kimchi is a traditional Korean food consisting of salted and chili pepper–spiced vegetables, often including napa cabbage and garlic, that are fermented by lactic acid bacteria (the same bacteria involved in the fermentation of yogurt and other cultured dairy products). By adding this mildly sour and pleasantly spicy food to your dishes, you get the benefits of both the beneficial bacteria and the phytonutrient-rich vegetables they are fermenting.

- **Miso:** Miso is a traditional Japanese paste made from fermented soybeans that adds a salty umami flavor (along with living microorganisms) to your dishes. Although it is high in sodium, research suggests it doesn't cause the negative effects associated with high-salt consumption, possibly because they are counteracted by the health-promoting compounds found in soy. So, where can you find miso? In the refrigerator section, often near the tofu.

- **Seaweed:** Seaweeds provide a wide array of minerals and phytonutrients, like the green-pigmented chlorophyll, and they function as powerful prebiotics. There are numerous seaweed varieties, but the one you'll be using this week is nori—the dried seaweed sheets often used in making sushi.

Snack ideas for this week:

The meal plan does not include snacks, so be sure to add some. You'll want to prioritize protein and fiber for your snacks to help you feel full and satisfied until your next meal.

- Sliced veggies or baby carrots, whole-grain or grain-free (e.g., almond flour) crackers, and hummus

- Piece of fruit and spoonful of nut or seed butter

- Cultured cottage cheese, plain Greek yogurt, or dairy-free yogurt (unsweetened) topped with warmed berries and cinnamon (and nuts or seeds for protein if using dairy-free yogurt)

- Omega Energy Bites (page 284)

WEEK 3 PREP PLAN

Weekend before:

- Grocery shop! Take inventory of what you already have in your kitchen and comb through the grocery list. Determine what substitutions are necessary for a dietary need (e.g., dairy- or nut-free). Take a look at the substitutions noted in the recipes for the week and adjust your grocery list accordingly.

- On Saturday night: Make your own oat flour to use in the Sweet Potato Tahini Brownies (page 290) by processing a little more than ½ cup rolled oats in a blender or food processor until you get a flourlike consistency.

- On Sunday: Make the Quick Pickled Onions to be used for the Green Goddess Smashed Bean Sammies (page 222) and the 10-Minute Lentil-Walnut Taco Salad (page 200). Slice and freeze four bananas to be used in the smoothies.

Throughout the week:

- On Tuesday night: Prep a double batch of the Morning Glory Superseed Overnight Oats (page 182).

- On Wednesday night: When you make the Spicy Roll "Sushi" Bowls (page 246), double the amount of rice called for in the recipe and save half of it for the Kimchi Fried Rice (page 240) on Friday (I explain why later).

- Remember, don't throw anything out, including the chipotle peppers and adobo sauce—you'll use them next week!

WEEK 3 GROCERY LIST

Double-check the Pantry Basics list on page 114 for any items that you may need to replenish. You may still have these items from the previous weeks:

- Almond butter
- Brown rice
- Chia seeds
- Cilantro
- Ground flax seed or flax seed meal
- Hemp hearts (shelled hemp seeds)
- Medjool dates
- Rolled or old-fashioned oats
- Sriracha sauce
- Tahini
- Unsweetened cocoa powder

Frozen:

- Peas & carrots, 1 (10-ounce) bag
- Pineapple chunks, 1 (16-ounce) bag
- Riced cauliflower, 1 (10-ounce) bag

Dairy, nondairy & eggs:

- Eggs, large, 1 dozen
- Greek yogurt, plain, 24 ounces
- Kefir, plain, unsweetened, 1 (32-ounce) bottle
- Nondairy milk of choice, unsweetened, ½ gallon

Meat, poultry & seafood:

- Chicken breast, boneless and skinless, 10 ounces (unless you have leftover rotisserie chicken from Week 2)
- Salmon, 2 (6-ounce) fillets

Fresh produce:

- Apples (any kind), 2 small
- Avocados, 4 small
- Baby spinach, 10 ounces
- Bananas, 4 medium
- Basil, 1 small bunch
- Carrots, 6 medium
- Cauliflower, 1 medium head
- Chives, 1 small bunch
- Cucumbers, Persian, 3
- Dill, 1 small bunch
- Garlic, 1 head
- Green onions or scallions, 1 bunch
- Kale, 1 large bunch
- Lemons, 4
- Lettuce, mixed greens or chopped romaine, 6 ounces
- Limes, 2
- Mushrooms, assorted (such as oyster, cremini, and/or shiitake), 16 ounces
- Onion, red, 1 medium
- Onion, sweet, 1 medium
- Orange, 1
- Parsley, 1 small bunch
- Peaches, 2 medium
- Pepper, jalapeño, 1
- Shallots, 2
- Sweet potato, 1 medium
- Thyme, 1 small bunch
- Tomatoes, cherry, 1 pint

Bread, grains & pulses:

- Beans, cannellini or navy, 1 (15-ounce) can or 1 (16-ounce) bag dried beans
- Beans, chickpeas, 2 (15-ounce) cans or 1 (16-ounce) bag dried chickpeas
- Bread, sprouted or 100% whole-grain (or gluten-free bread if necessary), 1 loaf
- Lentils, any kind, 1 (15-ounce) can
- Orzo, whole-wheat, 1 (16-ounce) bag/box
- Pearled barley, 1 (16-ounce) bag
- Pita bread, 100% whole-wheat (or gluten-free pita), 1 package

Canned & jarred goods:

- Broth, vegetable, low-sodium, 3 (32-ounce) cartons
- Chipotle peppers in adobo sauce, 1 (7-ounce) can
- Coconut oil, 1 (14-ounce) jar
- Corn, fire-roasted, 1 (15-ounce) can
- Salsa, mild, 1 (16-ounce) jar

Condiments:

- Olive or avocado oil–based mayonnaise
- Toasted sesame oil (optional)

Nuts & seeds:

- Cashews, 4 ounces
- Walnuts, chopped, 4 ounces

Miscellaneous:

- Dark chocolate chips, 1 (10-ounce) bag
- Kimchi, 1 (14-ounce) jar
- Miso paste, white, 1 (8-ounce) container
- Roasted seaweed snacks, 1 package

Don't forget to add ingredients for your snacks of choice!

WEEK 4: Diversify Your Diet

You've made it to the last and final week of the plant-forward reset. This week, *diversity is the name of the glowing gut game,* and I want you to strive for those thirty different plant foods. This might sound overwhelming, but I want to let you in on a little secret: in the first three weeks of this meal plan, you were already averaging well over thirty plants per week! So, this week's plan continues to maximize plant diversity in the recipes—think a rainbow salad, a triple-berry smoothie, and a three-bean chili. I certainly don't expect you to treat every meal after the reset with this same oomph (to be honest, I love an easy weekday two-ingredient chickpea pasta and marinara sauce dinner), I simply want to show you just how easy it can be to up the plant diversity in some of your meals.

Once you transition out of the meal plan, keep these tips for increasing diet diversity in mind:

- Look for mixed blends in the freezer section. Triple berry, tropical fruit, and chopped kale and spinach blends are all great for smoothies. And stir-fry veggie blends are great for, well, stir-fries.

- Speaking of blends, you can also find them elsewhere in the grocery store. Canned three-bean blends are great for soups, stews, and chilis, and quinoa and rice blends are great as a bowl base.

- Keep at least two different seeds on hand to incorporate into your meals. For example, add flax seeds to your smoothies and sprinkle hemp hearts on your avocado toast, soup, salad, etc.

- On that note, keep more than one nut and/or seed butter on hand, too. Peanut butter is great and all (I mean, really really great) but don't forget about cashew, almond, walnut, pecan, hazelnut, and sunflower seed butters (and tahini, too).

- Rotate your pastas. Maybe it's whole-wheat spaghetti on Monday and lentil penne on Wednesday...and have you ever tried edamame pasta?!

- Go 50/50 with some of your noodle and rice dishes just like you would with your proteins. Try whole-wheat spaghetti mixed with zucchini noodles (as in the Zoodles & Noodles Primavera, page 234) and brown rice or quinoa mixed with riced cauliflower (as in the Kimchi Fried Rice, page 240).

- Include muesli in your morning routine. Muesli is essentially raw granola without the sweetener and oil. It's usually a blend of rolled oats and other whole grains plus nuts, seeds, and dried fruit; so, it's up there on the plant diversity scale. You can enjoy it hot—essentially cooking it as you would oatmeal—or treat it as a cereal and enjoy it in a bowl of milk or with yogurt.

- Consider joining a Community Supported Agriculture (CSA) program or a produce delivery service. They usually include a mystery box option in which they choose the produce you receive for each delivery, therefore exposing you to a variety of produce! As a bonus, their top priorities are often affordability, sustainability, and fighting food waste.

- Use more than one leafy green in your salads. A kale and romaine Caesar salad (sound familiar?), a spinach and iceberg chopped salad—the possibilities are endless! Or use a spring mix for your salad base.

- Try to work fresh herbs into your meals more often. These fragrant leaves—basil, cilantro, dill, mint, parsley, and the like—not only enhance the flavor and aroma of your dishes but are also chock-full of health-promoting phytonutrients.

Here's an example of how you can easily *double* the number of different plant foods in your day.

	BEFORE	AFTER
BREAKFAST	Smoothie made with yogurt + spinach + strawberries (2)	Smoothie made with yogurt + spinach + triple berry blend + ground flax seed (5)
LUNCH	Salad with romaine + chicken + cucumber + tomato (3)	Salad with romaine + kale + chickpeas + cucumber + tomato + red onion (6)
SNACK	Baby carrots + hummus made from chickpeas and tahini (3)	Baby carrots + sliced bell pepper + hummus made from chickpeas and tahini (4)
DINNER	Salmon served over quinoa + broccoli (2)	Salmon served over quinoa + cauliflower rice, topped with salsa made from avocado + tomato + cilantro (5)
TOTAL PLANTS	10	20

WEEK 4 MEAL PLAN

This menu is for two people.

	Breakfast	Lunch	Dinner
Monday	192 Make Your Own Muesli (served with yogurt, optional)	206 Rainbow Soba Salad	248 Harvest Nourish Bowl
Tuesday	192 Make Your Own Muesli (served with yogurt, optional) *leftover*	248 Harvest Nourish Bowl *leftover*	214 Smoky Butternut Squash Three-Bean Chili (PYP: 50/50)
Wednesday	192 Make Your Own Muesli (served with yogurt, optional) *leftover*	206 Rainbow Soba Salad + 1 pear *leftover*	226 Sheet Pan Pesto Gnocchi, Sausage & Veggies (PYP: poultry sausage)
Thursday	192 Make Your Own Muesli (served with yogurt, optional) *leftover*	226 Sheet Pan Pesto Gnocchi, Sausage & Veggies (PYP: poultry sausage) + 1 apple *leftover*	244 Chipotle Pineapple Mushroom Tacos
Friday	172 Berry Bliss Smoothie	214 Smoky Butternut Squash Three-Bean Chili (PYP: 50/50) *leftover*	244 Chipotle Pineapple Mushroom Tacos *leftover*
Saturday	172 Berry Bliss Smoothie	EBTKS Salad	236 Roasted Ratatouille Rigatoni
Sunday	172 Berry Bliss Smoothie	236 Roasted Ratatouille Rigatoni *leftover*	Plant-centric dinner out!

Snack ideas for this week:

The meal plan does not include snacks, so be sure to add some. You'll want to prioritize protein and fiber for your snacks to help you feel full and satisfied until your next meal.

- Sliced veggies or baby carrots, whole-grain or grain-free (e.g., almond flour) crackers), and hummus

- Piece of fruit and spoonful of nut or seed butter

- Plant-Powered Chipotle "Queso" (page 166) with sliced veggies

- Chickpea Hazelnut-ella (page 282) on sweet potato toast or with sliced fruit

WEEK 4 PREP PLAN

Weekend before:

- Pick the ingredients you want to use for the Make Your Own Muesli (page 192), then add those ingredients to the grocery list before you grocery shop. The grocery list already includes yogurt for serving, but feel free to change that.

- On Sunday, prep the Make Your Own Muesli (page 192) and Rainbow Soba Salad (page 206). Slice and freeze three bananas to be used in the smoothies.

Throughout the week:

- On Monday night: When you make and use The Perfect Pesto (page 158) for the Harvest Nourish Bowls (page 248), store the remainder for the Sheet Pan Pesto Gnocchi, Sausage & Veggies (page 226) on Wednesday.

WEEK 4 GROCERY LIST

Double-check the Pantry Basics list on page 114 for any items that you may need to replenish. You may still have these items from the previous weeks:

- Chipotle peppers in adobo sauce
- Green onions
- Hemp hearts (shelled hemp seeds)
- Medjool dates
- Peanut butter
- Protein powder
- Thyme

Frozen:

- Edamame, shelled, 1 (10-ounce) bag
- Gnocchi, cauliflower, potato, or sweet potato, 1 (10- to 12-ounce) bag
- Mixed berries or triple berry blend, 1 (32-ounce) bag
- Riced cauliflower, 1 (10-ounce) bag

Dairy, nondairy & eggs:

- Feta, Cotija, or queso fresco cheese, crumbled, 1 ounce
- Greek yogurt, plain, 24 ounces
- Nondairy milk of choice, unsweetened, ½ gallon
- Parmesan cheese, 1 ounce (optional, or use nutritional yeast)

Meat, poultry & seafood:

- Beef or turkey, lean, ground, 8 to 10 ounces
- Turkey or chicken sausage, Italian, cooked, 1 (10-ounce) package

Fresh produce:

- Apples, any kind, 3 medium
- Avocados, 2 medium
- Baby spinach, 5 ounces
- Bananas, 3 medium
- Basil, 1 large bunch
- Bell peppers, 2 red, 2 yellow
- Broccoli, 1 small crown/head
- Brussels sprouts, shaved, 10 to 12 ounces
- Cabbage, red, shredded, 8 ounces
- Carrots, 2 medium
- Cilantro, 1 small bunch
- Cucumber, 1 medium
- Eggplant, 1 medium
- Garlic, 1 head
- Ginger, 1 (1-inch) piece
- Kale, 1 large bunch
- Lemon, 1
- Limes, 3
- Mint, 1 small bunch
- Mushrooms, assorted (shiitake, cremini, and/or oyster), 16 ounces
- Onion, red, 1 small
- Onion, yellow, 1 large
- Orange, 1
- Pears, 2 medium
- Pepper, poblano, 1 medium
- Pineapple, 1 small, or 2 cups frozen or canned
- Squash, butternut, 1 small, or 10-ounce bag frozen cubed
- Squash, yellow, 1 medium
- Sweet potato, 1 large
- Tomatoes, cherry, 1 pint
- Tomatoes, Roma, 1 pound
- Zucchini, 1 medium

Canned & jarred goods:

- Broth, vegetable, low-sodium, 1 (32-ounce) carton
- Tomatoes, fire-roasted, diced, 1 (15-ounce) can
- Tomatoes, sun-dried packed in oil, 1 (7-ounce) jar

Nuts & seeds:

- Pepitas (shelled pumpkin seeds), 1 ounce
- Pine nuts, 1 ounce

Don't forget to add ingredients for your muesli and snacks of choice!

Bread, grains & pulses:

- Beans, black, 1 (15-ounce) can, or 1 (16-ounce) bag dried beans
- Beans, cannellini or navy, 1 (15-ounce) can, or 1 (16-ounce) bag dried beans
- Beans, tri-bean blend (black, kidney, pinto), 1 (15-ounce) can

- Farro, 1 (16-ounce) bag
- Pasta of choice, legume-based, 1 (8-ounce) box
- Soba noodles, 1 (8-ounce) package
- Tortillas, corn, 8 small (5- to 6-inch)

BEYOND 28 DAYS

You came, you cooked, you conquered. Now what? Going plant-forward isn't a 28-days-and-done deal. Remember, it's a "for life" approach. You have set the foundation for long-term optimal health; now you simply need to continue to champion PLANTS—both the acronym and the plants themselves—going forward. Keep in mind, you may find yourself faced with the temptation to revert to old, plant-poor eating habits along the way. So it can't hurt to revisit earlier chapters or even the 28-day reset periodically to remind yourself of all the goodness plants have to offer. And if the perfectionist, all-or-nothing mindset has sabotaged your health efforts in the past as it has for many, be sure to keep your mind alert for any negative, self-sabotaging thoughts creeping in throughout your plant-forward journey.

You shouldn't give the time of day to thoughts like "I barely had any produce this weekend—might as well give up on this whole plant forward-thing" or "I ate way too much meat today—I'm a failure." Whenever you experience a "dietary detour" big or small, don't let it derail you. As I tell my clients, treat every eating opportunity as a metaphorical Monday morning—a fresh start to continue putting plants forward.

PLANT-POWERED KITCHEN TOOLS

The proper kitchen tools can make plant-forward cooking a breeze, and not having the right tools can leave you feeling frustrated. Beyond the basics (pots, saucepans, baking pans, measuring cups/spoons, and mixing bowls), I recommend investing in a few tools. These gadgets have saved me countless hours of frustration in the kitchen and have made cooking a lot more enjoyable and a lot less of a chore. But remember, Rome wasn't built in a day, and your perfectly equipped plant-forward kitchen won't be, either.

Top priorities:

- **Can opener:** You probably already own a can opener, but if you dread using it because it does a poor job of actually opening cans, it's probably time to invest in a new one.

- **Chef's knife:** A good knife is essential in a plant-forward kitchen. No need to shell out hundreds of dollars on a good knife set if you don't want to. Instead, invest in one, good-quality 8-inch chef's knife.

- **Cutting boards:** It helps to have multiple cutting boards in different sizes, so you don't have to take out that large, heavy one every time you want to slice an avocado.

- **Food processor:** You can use this versatile gadget to do everything from chopping veggies to blending frozen bananas into banana "nice cream" and making date-and-nut energy bites, like the Omega Energy Bites (page 284). It also comes in handy for all the recipes that aren't blended or processed successfully in a blender—think pesto or thick dips like hummus.

- **High-powered blender:** Like a food processor, a high-powered blender is equally as versatile and useful in your plant-forward kitchen (maybe even more so). It's not just for smoothies; you'll use it to puree plant-centric soups and break down soaked nuts with ease to make things like cashew cream perfectly smooth.

- **Vegetable peelers:** Although, yes, these can be used to actually *peel* produce, I more often use them for slicing long vegetables, like carrots, cucumber, and zucchini, to be used to top salads or bowls or as makeshift "noodles." A standard vegetable peeler comes in handy for slicing wider ribbons, and a julienne peeler is great for slicing thinner strands.

Not *necessary,* but nice to have:

- **Air fryer:** Tofu cooked in the air fryer > tofu cooked any other way.

- **Citrus squeezer:** Acids like lemon and lime juice can really elevate plant-centric dishes (which is why I use them in many of the recipes), and using a squeezer makes juicing them a cinch (and less messy).

- **Mandoline slicer:** Mandoline slicers are useful for cutting extra-thin, perfectly even slices from your produce, especially firmer items like potatoes.

- **Pressure cooker/multicooker:** A great tool for cooking your beans from scratch, should you choose to.

ABOUT THE RECIPES

When developing the recipes for this book, I tried to keep things simple but interesting to accommodate both the novice and more experienced home chef. I wanted to give you a gentle push out of your comfort zone without requiring you to scale grocery store shelves in search of some fancy-schmancy superfood (that you come to find out isn't actually available at any of your local grocery stores). I developed most of the main dishes with the plant-forward plate in mind—prioritizing fiber-rich carbs (i.e., slow carbs), lots of nonstarchy vegetables, healthy fats, and plant proteins, with some animal proteins sprinkled in here and there. You'll find familiar favorites and dishes inspired by different international cuisines, all with a plant-forward twist. You'll also find that most recipes fit—or can be easily accommodated to fit—several dietary needs, such as gluten- and dairy-free. But should you need to tailor a recipe in this book or outside of this book, use the chart to help you.

SPECIAL DIET	REPLACE THIS	WITH THIS
DAIRY-FREE	Shredded and sliced cheese	Plant-based cheeses (e.g., Daiya, Field Roast, Follow Your Heart, Violife)
	Cream cheese	Plant-based cream cheese (e.g., Kite Hill, Miyoko's)
	Queso	Plant-Powered Chipotle "Queso" (page 166)
	Parmesan cheese	Nutritional yeast Hempesan (page 117)
	Yogurt	Unsweetened plant-based yogurts (e.g., 365 Whole Foods Market, Forager, Kite Hill, Lavva, So Delicious)
	Milk	Plant-based milks, like coconut, nut, oat, pea, or soy milk
EGG-FREE	Eggs (added to a meal for protein)	Crumbled tofu Any other protein
	Eggs (as a binder in baking)	Flax or chia "egg": Stir together 1 tablespoon ground flax seed or chia seed and 2½ tablespoons warm water; let sit for 5 to 10 minutes ¼ cup mashed banana or unsweetened applesauce

SPECIAL DIET	REPLACE THIS	WITH THIS
NUT-FREE	Nuts & nut butter (for snacking and in recipes)	Seeds (e.g., pumpkin, sunflower, etc.) Sunflower seed (or other seed) butter, tahini
	Cashew cream (in soups)	Unsweetened full-fat oat milk or an unsweetened plant-based nut-free creamer (made from oats, coconut, or both) Canned light or full-fat coconut milk or cream
	Almond flour (in baking)	Make your own seed flour (grind sunflower kernels in a blender or coffee grinder until flourlike) Oat flour, but not usually a one-to-one substitution (start with less)
GLUTEN-FREE	Wheat-based breads, pastas, grains	Gluten-free breads Gluten-free grains like brown/wild rice, buckwheat, oats, quinoa Legume-based pastas
	Soy sauce	Coconut aminos (has significantly less sodium than most soy sauces, so you may need to add more) Tamari (usually, but not always, gluten-free, so check the label).
MEAT-FREE	1 to 2 ounces red meat or poultry	~¼ cup beans, chickpeas, or lentils or 1 ounce tofu or tempeh *And vice versa—if you need more animal protein to start, swap some in for some of the plant protein*

Pick-Your-Protein Recipes: You'll find many PYP recipes—mostly in the Mains section—that give you the option of keeping the recipe mostly plant-based or going 50/50 with plant and animal proteins. For example, a soup recipe calls for one can of beans, and gives you the option of adding a second can of beans or adding some shredded chicken. The directions may vary slightly depending on your protein choice, but it's well noted.

WHERE'S THE NUTRITION INFO?!

You may notice that I haven't included nutritional information with the recipes. So, I figured it's in both of our best interests I address it right away!

Unfortunately, several factors make it difficult to provide accurate nutritional information. Similar food products can vary greatly in their nutrient content depending on the brand—even choosing one tomato sauce over another can affect the stats. But what makes it even more challenging is that I've included options for modifications in most of the recipes to accommodate different dietary needs and to allow you to swap animal and plant proteins (as is the case in the pick-your-protein recipes).

Ultimately, I'd rather you not be fixated on the numbers if you don't need to be. You can rest assured that I've designed these recipes with fiber, protein, and your health in mind. That said, if you do like or need to track nutritionals because of a health condition, you can easily obtain them by entering the specific ingredients/products you used for a recipe into one of several user-friendly, free recipe calculator programs (simply do an online search for "recipe calorie calculator").

PART 3:

HOW TO COOK PLANT-FORWARD: THE RECIPES

BASICS

BEST CRISPY TOFU

YIELD: 3 to 4 servings

The qualities of tofu that keep people from buying it—like its flavor, or rather lack thereof, and spongy texture—become its greatest assets once you learn how to prepare and cook it (the right way). It's essentially a blank canvas that soaks up other flavors like a sponge. Press it, cube it, and throw a little starch on it, and you'll end up with tasty little bites of tofu with a crispy exterior and pillowy interior. Tofu is one of the highest plant-based sources of protein. But, much like its taste, its nutritional qualities aren't without controversy because it's a soy-based food (see page 60 for some soy myth-busting).

---

1 (14-ounce) block extra-firm tofu, drained

1 tablespoon low-sodium soy sauce or tamari

2 teaspoons toasted sesame oil or extra-virgin olive oil

1 teaspoon total seasonings of choice: garlic powder, paprika, etc. (optional)

1 tablespoon cornstarch or arrowroot starch

1. Press the tofu (to remove excess liquid): Lay a clean, absorbent dish towel or some paper towels on a cutting board and place the tofu block on top. Wrap the dish towel around it or set more paper towels on top of the block, then set something heavy on top, like a cast-iron skillet or another cutting board topped with books (which is what I like to use). Alternatively, you can buy a handy tofu press on Amazon that eliminates the need for paper towels and heavy objects. Let sit for about 15 minutes. Then cut the tofu into roughly ½-inch cubes.

2. Meanwhile, in a medium bowl, whisk together the soy sauce, oil, and seasonings, if using. Transfer the tofu cubes to the bowl and toss in the oil mixture until all pieces are well coated. Then sprinkle the cornstarch over the tofu and toss again until evenly coated.

3. *To cook in the oven:* Preheat the oven to 425°F and line a sheet pan with parchment paper. Arrange in a single layer on the prepared sheet pan and bake until the tofu is golden and crispy, 25 to 30 minutes, turning halfway through.

To cook in an air fryer: Preheat the air fryer to 400°F. Arrange in a single layer in the air fryer basket and cook until the tofu is golden and crispy, 10 to 15 minutes, turning halfway through.

GLUTEN-FREE: Use gluten-free tamari/soy sauce.

COOKING BEANS 101

YIELD: About 6 cups cooked beans (more or less, depending on the type)

Hopefully, "to bean or not to bean?" is no longer a question in your mind (refer to Chapter 4 if you need a quick refresher on why the answer is a resounding "to bean!"). But at this point, you might be wondering whether to buy them canned (aka already cooked) or dried to be cooked at home. Nothing beats the convenience and ease of canned pulses, period. On the other hand, dried beans are cheaper per serving (we're talking a matter of cents here, but still) and can come out tastier than their canned counterparts. Nutrition-wise, both are great sources of fiber and plant protein, but canned takes the cake for sodium content, and not in a good way. Luckily, most canned brands offer reduced-sodium or no-salt-added varieties, and rinsing them helps reduce their sodium content significantly. So, it ultimately boils down to what works better for you and your lifestyle. Should you choose to cook your beans for some of the recipes in this book, here's how.

16 ounces (about 2 cups) dried beans, chickpeas, or lentils

½ small onion, halved (optional)

1 clove garlic, peeled (optional)

1 bay leaf (optional)

1 teaspoon salt

1 tablespoon extra-virgin olive oil or avocado oil, for pressure cooking method only

NOTE ───────────

Lentils are small with tender skins, cook quickly, and do not need to be soaked.

1. Pick out any small rocks or debris from the dried beans and rinse well.

2. Soak or don't soak. If you plan on cooking the beans on the stovetop, soaking the beans the night before will shorten the cook time and may improve their digestibility and reduce their gas-inducing effects, but it isn't necessary if you forget. (You'll just have to cook them a little longer.) To soak, place the beans in a large pot, cover them with cool water by about 2 inches, cover with a lid, and let sit at room temperature for 8 hours or overnight.

If you plan on cooking the beans in a pressure cooker, soaking them ahead of time really isn't necessary because the cook time is already so short. However, some people find that soaking does ease digestion. If you choose to soak the beans, you can shave at least 10 minutes from the listed cooking times for the pressure cooker.

3. Cook! If you soaked the beans, drain the soaking water and rinse them before you start cooking.

Stovetop Method

Place the beans in a large stockpot and cover with water by about 2 inches. Stir in any of the optional aromatics and the salt. Bring to a boil, then reduce the heat to low and simmer, partially covered, until the beans are tender and done to your liking, adding more water as necessary to keep them submerged.

Depending on the bean variety and whether you soaked them, this will take as little as 15 minutes for red lentils to up to 2 hours (or more) for everything else. I suggest using the timing on the package as a guideline.

Pressure Cooker Method

Place the beans in a 6- or 8-quart pressure cooker and cover with 6 cups of cool water. Stir in any of the optional aromatics, the salt, and the oil (to prevent bean foam from clogging the pressure valve). Secure the lid and set the valve to the sealing position. Cook on high pressure for the time indicated below for the type of beans you're using. When done, allow the pressure to release naturally for 15 minutes.

- Black, cannellini, great Northern, navy, pinto, or red kidney: 25 to 30 minutes

- Black-eyed peas: 14 to 18 minutes

- Lentils (split red or yellow): 1 to 2 minutes

- Lentils (green or brown): 7 to 8 minutes

- Chickpeas: 35 to 40 minutes

Many factors, including the altitude at which you are cooking, the mineral content of your water, and how old your beans are (beans can last a while in the pantry but are best cooked within a year), can significantly affect cook time. These cook times are general guidelines, but you may need to do some experimenting to get it just right.

4. Use immediately or refrigerate for later. If using the beans immediately, drain and discard any aromatics. If storing the beans for later, cool completely and store them in their cooking liquid in an airtight container in the refrigerator for up to 5 days. You can also freeze completely cooled, drained beans. Store in airtight freezer-safe containers or resealable bags in the freezer for up to 6 months (but for best quality, enjoy within 2 to 3 months).

PLANT-POWERED FACT: Kombu is a Japanese dried seaweed that contains an enzyme that helps break down gas-producing components in beans, making them easier to digest. So, if you're extra prone to beans' gas-inducing effects, keep some on hand. (You can find it in the international section of many grocery stores or at an Asian food market.) Simply add a strip to the pot when cooking your dried beans.

TAHINI SAUCE/ DRESSING 5 WAYS

YIELD: 4 to 6 servings, about 2 to 3 tablespoons per serving

Tahini—aka sesame seed butter—serves as the base for these creamy dairy-free sauces. Drizzle them over roasted vegetables or nourish bowls and use them as salad dressings (like for the Spiced Green Tahini Salad on page 204)—you can even use them in sandwiches and wraps! (P.S. The base is great on its own, too!)

BASE:

¼ cup tahini (see note)

1 tablespoon extra-virgin olive oil

2 tablespoons fresh lemon juice

1 to 3 teaspoons pure maple syrup

Salt to taste

FOR GREEN TAHINI, ADD:

¼ cup fresh cilantro leaves

¼ cup fresh parsley leaves

½ jalapeño pepper, seeded

1 clove garlic, roughly chopped

FOR GOLDEN TAHINI, ADD:

½ teaspoon curry powder

¼ teaspoon ground turmeric

1 to 2 teaspoons Sriracha sauce, or a pinch of crushed red pepper or cayenne pepper (optional)

1 clove garlic, roughly chopped

FOR CREAMY CAESAR TAHINI, ADD:

2 teaspoons capers plus 1 teaspoon of the caper brine

1 teaspoon Dijon mustard

1 or 2 cloves garlic, roughly chopped

FOR CREAMY PARM CAESAR TAHINI, ADD:

Ingredients listed for Creamy Caesar Tahini, plus 1 to 2 tablespoons freshly grated Parmesan cheese or nutritional yeast

FOR POPPY SEED TAHINI, ADD:

1 teaspoon Dijon mustard

⅛ teaspoon onion powder

2 teaspoons poppy seeds

For all versions except for the Poppy Seed Tahini: Place all of the ingredients in a blender or food processor (starting with 1 teaspoon maple syrup and adding more to taste); blend until smooth. Add warm water 1 tablespoon at a time to thin the sauce to your liking. Season with salt to taste.

For the Poppy Seed Tahini: Follow the same directions as above except do not add the poppy seeds in with the other ingredients. Once your sauce is at the desired consistency, add the poppy seeds and pulse a few times to incorporate.

Store in an airtight container in the fridge for up to 5 days.

NOTE

A smooth, drippy tahini with just sesame seeds listed on the ingredients list—and a little salt is okay—works best.

ORANGE GINGER PEANUT SAUCE

YIELD: 4 to 6 servings, about 2 to 3 tablespoons per serving

Orange juice adds a dimension of flavor and sweetness to this not-your-average peanut sauce. Honestly, I could eat this sauce with or on just about anything, but it tastes especially delicious in the Takeout Tofu Lettuce Wraps (page 260) and the Rainbow Soba Salad (page 206). You can easily transform it from sauce to dressing consistency by adding a little water or extra OJ.

⅓ cup unsweetened peanut butter

¼ cup fresh orange juice (about 1 medium orange)

1 to 2 soft pitted Medjool dates, roughly chopped (see note), or 2 to 3 teaspoons pure maple syrup or honey

1 to 2 tablespoons low-sodium soy sauce or tamari

1 tablespoon rice vinegar

1 clove garlic, roughly chopped

1 (½-inch) piece ginger, peeled and roughly chopped

1 to 2 teaspoons Sriracha sauce or sambal oelek

1. Place all of the ingredients in a blender or food processor and blend until smooth.

2. If using as a dressing, add water or additional orange juice 1 tablespoon at a time to thin it out to your liking.

3. Store in an airtight container in the fridge for up to 1 week.

NOTE

If your date isn't very soft, place it in a small bowl and cover it with hot water. Let it sit for 5 to 10 minutes to soften, then drain and chop it before adding it to the food processor.

PEANUT-FREE/NUT-FREE: Swap unsweetened almond butter or sunflower butter for the peanut butter.

GLUTEN-FREE: Use gluten-free tamari/soy sauce.

EASY SALSA VERDE

YIELD: 8 servings, about 2 tablespoons per serving

Despite their name and tomato-like appearance, tomatillos are not, in fact, tomatoes—or green tomatoes at that—but more like a distant relative with a brighter, tangier flavor. Turning them into fresh, homemade salsa may seem like a daunting task, but it couldn't be easier or quicker. I'm a big fan of store-bought salsas, but they simply can't compete with the fresh and vibrant flavors in a salsa made from scratch.

1 pound tomatillos (about 8 medium), husked and halved

1 large poblano pepper, halved, stems and seeds removed

1 jalapeño or serrano pepper, halved, stems and seeds removed

2 cloves garlic, peel left on (but papery outer skin removed)

⅓ medium white onion, roughly chopped

¼ cup fresh cilantro leaves, plus more as needed

1 tablespoon fresh lime juice

½ teaspoon salt

FOR CREAMY VERSION (OPTIONAL):

1 small avocado, cut into chunks

1. Move the top rack of the oven 6 inches from the broiler and preheat the oven to the high broil setting. Line a sheet pan with aluminum foil sprayed lightly with cooking spray.

2. Place the tomatillos and poblano and jalapeño halves (cut side down) on the prepared sheet pan and place the garlic cloves among them. Broil until the tomatillos and peppers are charred in spots, 5 to 6 minutes. Remove from the oven, carefully flip the tomatillos and peppers over using tongs, and continue broiling until softened and charred in spots on the other side, 5 to 6 minutes more.

3. Let cool for 5 minutes, then remove the peels from the garlic cloves and carefully transfer them to a food processor along with the tomatillos (with juices) and peppers. Add the remaining ingredients, including the avocado, if using, and pulse to your desired consistency. If the salsa is too thick, add a splash of water or vegetable broth. Taste and add more salt and cilantro as needed.

4. Serve or store in the refrigerator for up to 1 week or up to 3 days if you've included the avocado.

THE PERFECT PESTO

YIELD: 6 servings, about 2 tablespoons per serving

A good pesto can instantly elevate almost any savory dish. And while your basic basil, pine nut, and parm pesto is great and all (I mean *really great*), there are numerous ways to get creative with pesto—which comes in handy when there's a leafy green, fresh herb, or nut you're trying to use up. The flavor combinations are endless! This recipe uses less oil than most recipes you'll find on the internet, but trust me when I say you won't miss it.

2 cups lightly packed fresh basil leaves

¼ cup freshly grated Parmesan cheese

¼ cup pine nuts

2 cloves garlic, roughly chopped

3 to 4 tablespoons extra-virgin olive oil

2 tablespoons fresh lemon juice

Salt

SWITCH IT UP:

Replace 1 cup of the basil with:

2 cups leafy greens, such as arugula, stemmed kale, or spinach

1 cup other fresh herb, such as cilantro, mint, or parsley

Replace the pine nuts with an equal amount of:

Almonds, cashews, or walnuts

Hemp hearts or shelled sunflower seeds (for nut-free)

Replace the Parmesan with:

2 to 3 tablespoons nutritional yeast (for dairy-free)

Replace 2 tablespoons of the olive oil with:

1 small avocado (plus water to thin)

Add some heat:

Jalapeño or serrano pepper, to taste

Crushed red pepper, to taste

1. Place all of the ingredients except for the oil, lemon juice, and salt in a food processor and pulse until chopped. Add the olive oil and lemon juice and process until relatively smooth. If the pesto is too thick, add water 1 tablespoon at a time to thin it out. Season with salt to taste.

2. Store in an airtight container in the refrigerator for up to 1 week. You can also freeze the pesto in an ice cube tray. Once frozen, store the cubes in a freezer-safe resealable bag or container.

TIPS

- *To use the pesto as a pasta sauce, thin it with some of the pasta cooking water.*

- *Add another dimension of flavor by lightly toasting the nuts before blending!*

10-MINUTE ANY BERRY CHIA JAM

YIELD: About 1½ cups

Unfortunately, many store-bought jams are more added sugar than fruit, which is why it's not a bad idea to try making your own jam. Although it may seem like a long and complicated task, with chia jam, you can have a jar up and ready in less time than it would take you to go buy a jar from the store, and it takes only a few simple ingredients you likely already have on hand. Instead of pectin or gelatin, this recipe relies on the speedy gelling power of chia seeds. They may be small, but they can absorb up to ten times their weight in liquid! Choose any berry, or get a little crazy and combine two or more.

---

2 tablespoons chia seeds

¼ cup fresh orange juice (about 1 medium orange)

2 heaping cups frozen or fresh berries of choice

1 to 2 tablespoons pure maple syrup or honey (optional)

NOTE ———————————

I find that frozen berries work particularly well in chia jam, so don't be afraid to use them. If you're concerned that frozen fruit isn't as nutritious as fresh, refer to the myth on page 55 for more information.

1. In a small bowl, stir together the chia seeds and orange juice; set aside to thicken.

2. Meanwhile, heat the berries in a small saucepan over medium heat, stirring occasionally. Crush the berries periodically as you stir, although if the berries are small, you may want to leave some whole for texture. Cook until the berries are mushy and bubbling, 5 to 7 minutes.

3. Stir in the chia mixture and maple syrup, if using, and continue cooking for 2 to 3 minutes.

4. Remove from the heat and allow the jam to cool and thicken in the saucepan before using or storing for later.

5. Store in an airtight container or mason jar in the fridge for up to 1 week.

PLANT-POWERED FACT: Not only do chia seeds serve as a great thickener in recipes, but they also add a boost of fiber, protein, omega-3 fatty acids, minerals (like calcium), and antioxidants. In fact, folklore has it that ancient civilizations relied on these small but mighty, nutrient-dense seeds in their diets for strength and endurance, and the word *chia* is the ancient Mayan word for *strength*.

QUICK PICKLED ONIONS

YIELD: About 1½ cups

Pickled red onions can liven up just about any dish, which is why I always have a batch on hand, and why you'll find them listed as a component of several of the recipes in this book. I put them in and on everything from salads to sandwiches, veggie burgers and burger bowls, nachos, and more!

1 heaping tablespoon granulated sugar, honey, or pure maple syrup

1 teaspoon salt

¾ cup raw, unfiltered apple cider vinegar

1 medium red onion, very thinly sliced

1. Pour ¾ cup of water into a small, microwave-safe bowl and microwave on high for 90 seconds. Whisk in the sugar and salt until the sugar and salt dissolve. Whisk in the vinegar.

2. Place the onion in a pint-sized (16-ounce) mason jar or similar container and pour in the brine. Use a spoon to push the onions down so that they are fully submerged in the liquid. Let the jar sit at room temperature, uncovered, for about 30 minutes.

3. At this point, the pickled onions are ready to be used, or you can seal the jar and store it in the refrigerator for up to 2 weeks.

BEET & WHITE BEAN HUMMUS

YIELD: 6 servings

To be honest, I'm not *in love* with beets (which is a shame because they've been associated with numerous health benefits). In fact, one of the few ways I eat them is by diluting their flavor in a tasty, nutritious hummus. This creamy pink-hued hummus has one other secret ingredient in addition to beets: aquafaba (aka the liquid in a can of beans). It's often used in vegan baking recipes as an egg white substitute, but you can also use it in homemade hummus to yield a smoother and creamier texture.

1 (15-ounce) can cannellini beans plus 2 tablespoons of the aquafaba, remaining liquid drained and beans rinsed

2 small or 1 large precooked beet(s), quartered (see note)

2 tablespoons fresh lemon juice

2 to 3 tablespoons tahini

2 tablespoons extra-virgin olive oil

2 cloves garlic, roughly chopped

½ teaspoon salt

¼ to ½ teaspoon smoked paprika

Pinch of cayenne pepper (optional)

Optional garnishes: Drizzle of extra-virgin olive oil, sprinkle of paprika, chopped fresh parsley, and/or grated lemon zest

TIP

To make a basic hummus, swap chickpeas for the cannellini beans and omit the beets—easy as that!

1. Place all of the ingredients in a food processor and process until smooth and creamy. Periodically pause the blending to scrape down the sides of the food processor.

2. Taste and season with additional salt if necessary. Serve topped with any or all of the optional garnishes.

3. Store in an airtight container in the fridge for up to 1 week.

NOTE

You can use precooked beets (which are usually located in the produce section) or roast the beets yourself. If you want to do the latter, here's how: Preheat the oven to 400°F. Remove the tops and scrub the beets, then wrap them tightly in foil. Transfer the foil-covered beets to a sheet pan and roast until easily pierced with a fork, 45 to 60 minutes. Once cool enough to handle, rub with your fingers to peel off the skins.

PLANT-POWERED FACT: Athletes have long been using beets and beet juice for their energy- and stamina-boosting abilities. Researchers have credited these abilities to the dietary nitrates found naturally in beets. These nitrates are converted to nitric oxide in the body, which relaxes and dilates blood vessels, improves blood flow, and increases oxygen in the blood.

PLANT-POWERED CHIPOTLE "QUESO"

YIELD: 6 servings

This creamy dairy-free chipotle "queso" is made from simple plant-based ingredients, including some veggies and the star of the show: magnesium-rich cashews (my favorite nut and also the name of my dog). Serve it as a dip with sliced veggies and/or tortilla chips, or use a dollop of it on any of the Mexican-inspired dishes in this book, like the Chipotle Pineapple Mushroom Tacos (page 244) or the Fully Loaded Plantain Nachos (page 270). It also wouldn't be unheard of to treat this like soup and eat it by the spoonful.

1 cup raw cashews

1 cup cubed fresh or frozen butternut squash

1½ cups low-sodium vegetable broth

½ cup unsweetened nondairy milk

1 (4-ounce) can green chiles, drained

1 chipotle pepper in adobo sauce

3 to 4 tablespoons nutritional yeast

1 tablespoon raw, unfiltered apple cider vinegar or fresh lemon juice

1 clove garlic, peeled

½ teaspoon salt

1. Place the cashews, squash, and vegetable broth in a medium saucepan. Bring to a boil, then lower the heat to medium and cook, covered, until the squash is fork-tender, 10 to 15 minutes.

2. Transfer the cashews and squash to a high-powered blender using a slotted spoon and reserve the cooking broth. Add the remaining ingredients to the blender along with ½ cup of the reserved broth. Blend until smooth and creamy, stopping periodically to scrape down the sides of the blender and adding additional hot broth as necessary. Taste and season with additional salt as needed.

3. Serve immediately or store leftovers in an airtight jar or container in the refrigerator for up to 1 week. Reheat in a saucepan over medium-low and add a splash of nondairy milk or water if it's too thick.

BREAKFASTS

BUILD A BETTER-BALANCED SMOOTHIE

I'm a big—no, huge—fan of smoothies. I find that for my clients and me, smoothies are one of the easiest ways to get a hefty daily dose of plant foods—especially those dang veggies. But not all smoothies are created equal. For example, smoothies at your local smoothie bar can be packed with sugar from added sweeteners, fruit juices, and even an excessive amount of fruit, but they often lack protein. So, here's my not-so-secret formula for building a better-balanced smoothie in the comfort of your own kitchen.

The Better-Balanced Smoothie Formula
(per serving)

1	**Choose your base liquid.**	6 to 8 ounces unsweetened nondairy milk (nut, soy, pea, coconut) or water
2	**Pick your protein.**	½ to 1 serving plant-based protein powder ⅓ to ½ cup plain Greek yogurt, kefir, or cultured cottage cheese
3	**Get fruity.**	1 cup fruit (apple, banana, berries, mango, papaya, peaches, pineapple, pitaya, etc.)
4	**Add fiber-rich fats.**	1 to 2 tablespoons avocado, unsweetened nut or seed butter, or small seeds such as chia, hemp, or flax
5	**Veg out with a serving of fresh or frozen vegetables.**	1 cup fresh leafy greens (fresh spinach or kale leaves) or ½ cup everything else (frozen chopped spinach or kale, frozen riced cauliflower, raw or frozen zucchini slices or chunks)
6	**Jazz it up with optional extras (to taste).**	Spices (cinnamon, pumpkin pie spice, nutmeg, ginger, turmeric, etc.), fresh herbs (mint, basil, etc.), extracts (mint, vanilla, etc.), unsweetened cocoa powder, adaptogens (ashwagandha, maca, reishi, etc.), matcha, spirulina

TIPS

- *Don't want to use protein powder or yogurt? No problem! Nuts and seeds are packed with protein, so substitute a couple tablespoons of hemp hearts (the most protein-dense of the seeds) and/or some nut/seed butter instead. You can also up the protein by using unsweetened soy or pea milk as your liquid base.*

- *When choosing a protein powder, I recommend choosing one with less than 5 grams of sugar per serving or one sweetened with "natural" low-calorie sweeteners like monkfruit or stevia.*

- *Chocolate protein powder or unsweetened cocoa powder, banana, and pineapple are the best for masking the taste of greens if you really can't stomach them in your smoothie.*

- *To save time, buy small, freezer-safe containers or resealable bags and portion out several servings of smoothie ingredients (except for the liquid) for several servings of smoothies at once. When you're ready to whip up a smoothie, simply dump the contents of one of the containers into your blender, pour in your preferred base liquid, and blend, and you've got yourself a smoothie in 30 seconds.*

- *I often use frozen fruits and/or veggies in my smoothies to help thicken 'em up without adding ice. Plus, frozen fruits are more convenient and last longer, and you can find a variety of "blends" that make it easy to get more plant diversity into your diet!*

- *Feel free to swap things out! Don't have almond butter? Use whatever nut butter you have on hand. Rather use fresh over frozen produce? No problem! You'll just have to add some ice.*

Smoothies Versus Juices

Juicing fruit separates the juice from the pulp, removing the fiber and leaving you with straight sugar. Without fiber, your body more rapidly absorbs that sugar into the bloodstream, and the fruit loses its satiating power. Juices do retain many of the vitamins and minerals from the fruit, but it's still better to choose fruit in whole or smoothie form rather than juice form when possible.

Oh, and speaking of juices, don't get me started on celery juice. It does NOT do any of the magical, disease-fighting things you've read about all over social media.

SMOOTHIE RECIPES

YIELD: 2 servings

Pour the base liquid into the blender, then add the remaining ingredients. Blend until smooth. Add milk, water, or ice as needed to thin or thicken the smoothie to your liking.

BERRY BLISS SMOOTHIE

1½ cups unsweetened nondairy milk

1½ cups frozen mixed or triple berry blend

1 medium banana, sliced and frozen

1 cup frozen riced cauliflower

1 serving vanilla plant-based protein powder

2 tablespoons unsweetened nut or seed butter of choice

NOTE

Cauliflower seems like an odd choice for a smoothie, but trust me on this one. It adds thickness and creaminess yet is virtually tasteless!

CARAMEL APPLE SMOOTHIE

1 to 1½ cups unsweetened nondairy milk

1 large apple, cut into chunks

2 soft pitted Medjool dates

1 serving vanilla plant-based protein powder

1 cup frozen riced cauliflower

2 tablespoons unsweetened cashew or almond butter

2 tablespoons ground flax seed

½ teaspoon ground cinnamon

CHOCOLATE CHERRY SMOOTHIE

1½ cups unsweetened nondairy milk

1 heaping cup frozen cherries

1 medium banana, sliced and frozen

2 cups fresh baby spinach

2 tablespoons unsweetened cocoa powder

1 serving chocolate or vanilla plant-based protein powder

2 tablespoons unsweetened almond butter

HAPPY BELLY SMOOTHIE

½ to 1 cup unsweetened nondairy milk

1 cup frozen pineapple chunks

1 medium banana, sliced and frozen

2 cups fresh baby spinach

1 cup unsweetened plain kefir (see note)

2 tablespoons ground flax seed or chia seeds

2 tablespoons unsweetened almond butter

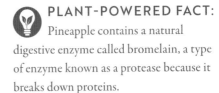 **PLANT-POWERED FACT:** Pineapple contains a natural digestive enzyme called bromelain, a type of enzyme known as a protease because it breaks down proteins.

NOTE

If you can't find kefir or don't want to use it, use ⅔ cup plain Greek or nondairy yogurt and an extra ⅓ cup nondairy milk instead. If you use nondairy yogurt, I recommend adding a serving of protein powder (because nondairy yogurts are often low in protein).

TAHINI DATE SHAKE

1 cup unsweetened nondairy milk

½ cup strong brewed coffee, chilled

1 medium banana, sliced and frozen

1 cup frozen riced cauliflower

2 soft pitted Medjool dates

3 tablespoons tahini

1 serving vanilla or chocolate plant-based protein powder

Pinch of salt

THE GREEN MACHINE SMOOTHIE

1½ cups unsweetened nondairy milk

1 heaping cup frozen pineapple chunks

1 heaping cup frozen mango chunks

1 cup fresh baby spinach or stemmed kale

½ large zucchini, sliced and frozen

½ small avocado

1 serving vanilla plant-based protein powder

2 tablespoons hemp hearts

1 to 2 teaspoons spirulina powder (optional)

PLANT-POWERED FACT: Spirulina is a blue-green algae hailed as a "superfood." Although I'm not a fan of that word, I can't say it isn't deserved in this case, thanks to spirulina's impressive nutritional profile. It's rich in vitamins and minerals, including iron, vitamin A, and certain B vitamins. And just 1 tablespoon provides a whopping 4 grams of protein.

NOT YOUR BASIC BREAKFAST TOAST

YIELD: 2 servings

Toast may seem a little basic, but with so many different nutritious base and topping combinations available, it's anything but. Choose between bread or sweet potato for your base and go sweet or savory with your toppings. If you're new to sweet potato toast, sliced sweet potato functions as a gluten-free, lower-calorie, potassium- and vitamins A and C–rich alternative to bread.

CHOOSE A BASE:

1 large sweet potato, sliced lengthwise into 4 (⅓-inch-thick) slices

2 large slices sourdough, sprouted, or whole-grain bread, toasted

CHOOSE A SPREAD (¼ TO ½ CUP):

Cultured cottage cheese

Hummus (savory or sweet)

Mashed avocado

Dairy or nondairy ricotta cheese

Unsweetened nut or seed butter

ADD TOPPINGS AND GARNISHES:

Savory toppings:

Chickpeas, plain or roasted

Feta or fresh goat cheese crumbles

Sliced hard-boiled egg

Sliced avocado

Sliced or pickled veggies

Sweet toppings:

Chopped or sliced fruit or berries

Chopped nuts, raw or toasted

Granola

Garnishes:

Seasonings, such as cinnamon, crushed red pepper, everything bagel seasoning, salt, etc.

Fresh herbs

Hemp hearts or chia seeds

Drizzle of honey, extra-virgin olive oil, or balsamic vinegar

Citrus juice or grated zest

Unsweetened coconut flakes

Microgreens or sprouts

Roasted cocoa nibs

1. *If using sweet potato:* Preheat the oven to 450°F and lightly grease a sheet pan or line it with parchment paper. Arrange the sweet potato slices on the sheet pan and bake until lightly browned and tender when pierced with a fork, 12 to 15 minutes, flipping halfway through.

2. Top the toast or sweet potato with your desired spread, toppings, and garnishes. Keep it simple with just a few ingredients (and using whatever needs to be used up in your fridge/pantry), or try one of the following tested and approved *gourmet* combinations:

PLANT-POWERED FACT: Avocados may be known for their high monounsaturated fat (aka good fat) content, but did you know that just one medium avocado provides a whopping 12 grams of fiber? That's nearly half the recommended daily amount! This helps explain how, despite their high fat content, avocados have been shown to be a weight loss–friendly food and to have favorable effects on the gut microbiota. No need to go overboard on avocado toast—after all, too much of a good thing is never a good thing—but you can rest assured knowing there is good reason to include avocados in your diet. (As if you needed another reason to eat them...)

SAVORY:

Savory Classic: mashed avocado + chickpeas or hard-boiled egg + fresh lemon juice + crushed red pepper + salt

Everything but the Bagel: cultured cottage cheese or hummus + sliced avocado + sliced cucumber and/or radish + everything bagel seasoning

Feta Bruschetta: mashed avocado + halved cherry tomatoes + crumbled feta cheese + balsamic vinegar + extra-virgin olive oil + chopped fresh basil + salt

Bougie Beet: Beet & White Bean Hummus (page 164) + sliced avocado + Quick Pickled Onions (page 162) + microgreens

SWEET:

Sweet Classic: unsweetened peanut butter + sliced banana + hemp hearts or chia seeds + cinnamon

Feelin' Figgy: dairy or nondairy ricotta cheese + sliced figs + chopped walnuts or pecans + fresh lemon juice + honey + salt

Chocolate-Covered Strawberry: Chickpea Hazelnut-ella (page 282) + chopped or sliced strawberries + unsweetened coconut flakes

Grown-Up AB & J: unsweetened almond butter + 10-Minute Any Berry Chia Jam (page 160) + grated lemon zest

TIP

To meal prep sweet potato toasts for the week ahead, make a batch of two to three sweet potatoes' worth of toasts at once, let cool completely, and store in one or more airtight containers in the fridge. When you're ready for some sweet potato toast, simply toast your piece(s) in a toaster (like bread) or a toaster oven until warmed.

CREAMY CAULI-POWERED STEEL-CUT OATMEAL

YIELD: 2 to 3 servings

Thanks to the low-carb trend, cauliflower somehow managed to sneak its way into yet another meal: breakfast. Although I'm not a fan of a bowl of straight cauliflower masquerading as oats first thing in the morning, I don't mind adding a little to my oatmeal sometimes (emphasis on *sometimes*) as a way of getting a serving of veggies into breakfast. It sounds downright crazy, but trust me when I say you can't taste it! This recipe also uses steel-cut oats, which have a denser and chewier texture than rolled oats and take a little bit longer to cook—but they're well worth it.

1 teaspoon coconut oil, or 1 teaspoon butter

½ cup steel-cut oats

2 cups unsweetened nondairy milk

1 cup frozen riced cauliflower

1 medium ripe banana, mashed

½ teaspoon ground cinnamon

Pinch of salt

Fresh fruit, nuts, seeds, unsweetened coconut flakes, nut/seed butter, and/or pure maple syrup or honey, for topping

1. Heat the coconut oil in a medium saucepan over medium heat. Add the oats and toast for 2 minutes.

2. Pour in the milk, turn the heat to high, and bring to a boil. Reduce the heat to low and simmer for 15 minutes, stirring occasionally to prevent the oats from sticking to the bottom of the pan.

3. Stir in the remaining ingredients and continue simmering until the oatmeal is tender and most of the liquid is absorbed, 5 to 10 minutes.

4. Serve with the toppings of your choice. Store leftovers in an airtight container in the fridge for up to 4 days.

PLANT-POWERED FACT: Oats are a nutritional powerhouse known for being rich in *beta-glucan*, a soluble fiber that functions as a prebiotic fiber and has been shown to be particularly effective at lowering total and LDL cholesterol. Oats are also naturally gluten-free. So, why are some oats labeled "gluten-free" and others aren't? Since many grains are processed in a similar fashion, oats are often processed in facilities that handle other grains, like wheat, and therefore can be contaminated with gluten. Although this small amount may not be problematic for those with nonceliac gluten sensitivity, it can trigger an immune response in those with celiac disease; therefore, oats that are to be sold and labeled as gluten-free must be processed in a facility that doesn't also process gluten-containing grains.

SUPERSEED OVERNIGHT OATS

YIELD: 3 servings

Overnight oats are a stress-free, no-cooking-whatsoever method for making oats—soaking raw oats in a liquid overnight allows them to absorb the liquid and soften, resulting in a texture that's similar to warm cooked oats, only creamier and with less work. And this version takes the plant power (and fiber, protein, omega-3s, and more) up a notch by adding a variety of seeds to the mix. Simply combine the ingredients, refrigerate overnight, and voilà—you'll have a delicious breakfast waiting for you in the morning (and the next couple mornings, too).

FOR THE BASE:

1 cup rolled/old-fashioned oats

1 cup unsweetened nondairy milk, plus more as needed

½ cup plain Greek yogurt

1 tablespoon each chia seeds, ground flax seed, and hemp hearts

1 tablespoon pure maple syrup or honey

1 teaspoon ground cinnamon

½ teaspoon pure vanilla extract

Pinch of salt

ADD-INS:

Morning Glory Flavor:

1 medium carrot, peeled and grated

1 small apple (any kind), diced or grated

2 soft pitted Medjool dates, chopped

¼ cup chopped walnuts, raw or toasted

Juice and zest of ½ medium orange

Strawberry Banana Flavor:

1 medium ripe banana, mashed, plus additional sliced banana for topping (optional)

1 cup strawberries, diced

2 tablespoons unsweetened almond, cashew, or seed butter

Wild Blueberry Muffin Flavor:

1½ cups frozen wild blueberries (see note)

2 tablespoons unsweetened almond, cashew, or seed butter

1 teaspoon grated lemon zest

1. Place all of the base ingredients in a large bowl and mix.

2. Fold in the ingredients for your flavor choice.

3. Divide the mixture among three 12- to 16-ounce mason jars or other airtight containers. Seal the lids and place the jars in the fridge for at least 4 hours or overnight.

4. When ready to eat, remove from the fridge and stir. If the consistency isn't creamy enough, add a splash of milk and stir again. Overnight oats are meant to be eaten cold, but you can also enjoy them warm by microwaving on high in 30-second increments until warmed to your liking.

5. Store in an airtight container in the refrigerator for up to 4 days.

DAIRY-FREE: Swap ½ cup unsweetened nondairy yogurt or nondairy milk for the yogurt in the overnight oats.

NUT-FREE: Swap unsweetened seed butter for the nuts and nut butters.

TIP

You'll get a fair amount of protein from the oats, yogurt, nuts, and seeds, but if you want an extra boost, add ¼ cup of your favorite vanilla or unflavored plant-based protein powder.

NOTE

Wild blueberries are smaller, sweeter, and have a more intense blueberry flavor than their cultivated cousins (aka regular blueberries). No need to thaw the berries ahead of time; they'll thaw as the mixture sits in the fridge.

MAKE-AHEAD BREAKFAST BURRITOS

YIELD: 6 servings

I don't know about you, but I could eat a burrito at any time of day. And these breakfast burritos are sure to scratch your burrito itch morning, noon, or night. The best part? They can be prepped ahead of time and frozen, so all you have to do is reheat them for a few minutes before chowing down. Choose between scrambled tofu or eggs—or, hey, make a batch of each!

¾ pound baby potatoes (any kind, but medley preferred), scrubbed and cut into ½-inch cubes

1 red bell pepper, thinly sliced

1 green bell pepper, thinly sliced

2 teaspoons extra-virgin olive oil

½ teaspoon paprika

½ teaspoon garlic powder

½ teaspoon salt

3 to 4 cups fresh baby spinach, roughly chopped or torn

6 (8-inch) whole-wheat tortillas

1 batch "Unfried" Beans (page 270)

1 medium avocado, sliced

½ cup salsa, homemade (page 156) or store-bought

PICK YOUR PROTEIN:

Plant-Powered: 1 (14-ounce) block firm tofu, drained + 2 teaspoons extra-virgin olive oil + 2 tablespoons nutritional yeast + a few dashes of hot sauce (optional) + salt

50/50: 6 large eggs + 1 tablespoon milk or water + a few dashes of hot sauce (optional) + salt

1. Preheat the oven to 425°F.

2. Arrange the potatoes and bell peppers on a sheet pan. Drizzle with the olive oil and season with the paprika, garlic powder, and salt; toss to coat all of the pieces evenly.

3. Bake until the potatoes are golden brown, 20 to 25 minutes, stirring halfway through.

4. Remove from the oven and immediately scatter the spinach on the pan. Return the pan to the oven and continue baking until slightly wilted, 1 to 2 minutes.

5. Prepare your protein of choice:

If using tofu: Heat the olive oil in a medium skillet over medium heat. Crumble the tofu into the skillet. Cook for 5 minutes, stirring frequently. Stir in the nutritional yeast and hot sauce, if using, and cook for an additional 5 minutes, stirring frequently. Season with salt to taste.

If using eggs: In a small bowl, whisk together the eggs, milk, and hot sauce, if using, until pale yellow. Lightly grease a medium skillet with cooking spray and cook the eggs scrambled-style over medium heat until just set. Season with salt to taste.

6. *To assemble:* Warm the tortillas by covering them in a damp paper towel and microwaving on high for 15 to 20 seconds. Spread a thick layer of beans down the center of each tortilla, leaving a border on each side. Divide the potato mixture, the tofu or eggs, and the remaining fillings evenly among the tortillas. Roll each burrito, first

folding in the sides and holding them while you fold the bottom flap of the tortilla over the filling. Continue to roll up the tortilla as tightly as you can.

7. Serve immediately. Alternatively, heat a skillet over medium heat and cook the burritos, seal side down, for a few minutes, until slightly crispy. Flip and repeat on the other side.

TIP

To freeze these burritos for the week ahead, let them cool completely, then wrap them in foil and place in the freezer. To reheat, remove the foil and microwave on high until warmed through, 2 to 3 minutes.

PEACHES & CREAM QUINOA PORRIDGE

YIELD: 4 servings

Quinoa for breakfast? And a sweet one at that? Yes! This fluffy pseudo-grain isn't exclusive to savory lunches and dinners. In fact, quinoa is the perfect solution when you want to take a break from your morning oatmeal.

¾ cup quinoa, rinsed

1 (14-ounce) can light coconut milk, divided

1 teaspoon pure vanilla extract, seeds scraped from ½ vanilla bean, or 1½ teaspoons vanilla bean paste

½ teaspoon ground cinnamon

Pinch of salt

2 medium peaches, chopped or sliced, divided

2 tablespoons ground flax seed

1 tablespoon honey or pure maple syrup, plus more as needed

¼ cup chopped raw or toasted pecans or walnuts

1. Place the quinoa, 1 cup of the coconut milk, vanilla extract, cinnamon, salt, half of the peaches, and ½ cup water in a medium saucepan. Mix well and bring to a boil over high heat. Reduce the heat to low and simmer, covered, until all of the liquid is absorbed, 17 to 20 minutes.

2. Remove the pan from the heat, cover with a lid, and allow to sit for 5 minutes. Stir in the ground flax seed and honey.

3. Serve the quinoa topped with the nuts and the remaining peaches and coconut milk. Add honey to taste if necessary.

Basic Breakfast Quinoa Porridge

What about a quick, instant-oatmeal-style quinoa porridge for those busy weekday mornings when you have less than 10 minutes to spare for breakfast? I've got you covered! Make a large batch of quinoa on the weekend and store in an airtight container in the fridge. On the mornings you want a warm bowl of quinoa porridge, place ½ cup of the cooked quinoa, ½ cup milk of choice, and a sprinkle of cinnamon in a small saucepan and bring to a simmer over low heat. Cook until just heated through, 2 to 3 minutes. Top with ½ cup berries or chopped or sliced fruit, a drizzle of honey or pure maple syrup, and any optional toppings, such as chopped nuts or coconut flakes.

BANANA BUCKWHEAT BLENDER PANCAKES

YIELD: 4 servings

These are not your average Sunday morning pancakes. These light and fluffy yet hearty pancakes are fiber- and protein-packed and sweetened entirely by bananas (that is, until you top them with a little syrup!). If you aren't familiar with buckwheat flour, it adds a more complex and almost nutty flavor to the pancakes that is balanced out by the addition of oats. (I'm not a huge fan of pancakes made entirely from buckwheat flour because I find them to be a little *too* "healthy" tasting.) Despite having the word wheat in its name, buckwheat flour is naturally gluten-free, like oats, which makes these pancakes entirely gluten-free.

⅔ cup unsweetened nondairy milk

2 teaspoons raw, unfiltered apple cider vinegar

1 cup rolled/old-fashioned oats

½ cup buckwheat flour

2 small, extra-ripe bananas

2 large eggs

2 teaspoons baking powder

1 teaspoon pure vanilla extract

Pinch of salt

Pure maple syrup or honey, fresh fruit, and/or nuts or seeds, for topping

1. Prepare a makeshift buttermilk by pouring the milk and vinegar into a small bowl and stirring; allow to sit while you prep the oats.

2. Place the oats in a high-powered blender and blend until the consistency is flourlike. Add the remaining ingredients and buttermilk and blend until just smooth, about 30 seconds. Let the batter sit while you heat the skillet.

3. Heat a large skillet or griddle over medium heat and lightly grease with cooking spray. Working in batches of 3 pancakes at a time, pour ¼ cup of the batter for each pancake into the skillet, using a spoon to spread it out a bit if necessary to make pancakes about 4 inches in diameter. Cook until the first side is golden brown, 2 to 3 minutes, or until little bubbles start to form, then flip and cook until the other side is golden, about 2 minutes.

4. Serve with your toppings of choice. Store leftovers in an airtight container in the fridge for up to 3 days.

TIP

These pancakes freeze well and make a great reheat-and-go breakfast for busy mornings. To freeze, allow them to cool completely then lay them in a single layer on a parchment-lined baking sheet or cutting board and place in the freezer for an hour. Transfer them to an airtight freezer-safe container or resealable bag and freeze for up to 2 months. Reheat frozen pancakes in a toaster or in 30-second increments in the microwave until hot.

EGGPLANT SHAKSHUKA

YIELD: 4 servings

Originally from North Africa, shakshuka is a one-skillet breakfast, brunch, or breakfast-for-dinner of eggs poached in a spiced tomato sauce. I've added hearty eggplant, which, though not typically used, pairs nicely with the spices and other components in this dish and ups the fiber and phytonutrients. Not a fan of eggplant? The great thing about shakshuka is that it's quite versatile, so try zucchini and/or bell pepper instead.

1 small eggplant, cut into ½-inch cubes

Salt

1 to 1½ tablespoons extra-virgin olive oil, divided

½ small yellow onion, diced

2 cloves garlic, minced

½ teaspoon ground cumin

½ teaspoon sweet or smoked paprika

2 cups chopped fresh greens, such as baby spinach, Swiss chard, or stemmed kale

1 (15-ounce) can crushed tomatoes, preferably fire-roasted

2 tablespoons harissa (see note)

4 large eggs

1 ounce feta cheese, crumbled

For serving (optional):

Chopped fresh cilantro or basil leaves

Toasted sourdough or whole-wheat pita bread

1. Place the eggplant cubes in a colander, sprinkle lightly with salt, and let drain for 15 minutes.

2. Heat 1 tablespoon of the olive oil in a large skillet or Dutch oven over medium heat. Add the onion and the eggplant and cook until the eggplant has started to soften and brown, about 6 to 8 minutes, adding more oil if necessary.

3. Stir in the garlic, cumin, and paprika and cook until fragrant, about 1 minute. Add the greens, tomatoes, harissa, ½ teaspoon of salt, and ½ cup of water, cover, and let simmer for 5 minutes to allow the flavors to meld.

4. Use the back of a spoon to make 4 wells in the vegetable mixture and gently crack an egg into each well; sprinkle with the feta cheese. Cover, reduce the heat to medium-low, and simmer until the egg whites are set but the yolks are still slightly runny, 7 to 10 minutes.

5. Garnish with fresh herbs and serve with the bread, if using.

NOTE

Harissa is a spicy North African red chile paste made of a few simple ingredients. If you don't like too much heat, purchase mild harissa or use less harissa. You should be able to find it in the international section of the grocery store (a popular brand is Mina), but if you can't, you can substitute Sriracha, hot sauce, or crushed red pepper (to taste) when you add the other spices.

DAIRY-FREE: Omit the feta cheese.

PLANT-POWERED FACT: That deep purple eggplant skin isn't just for looks; it's also responsible for some of the key nutritional benefits of eggplants. The purple hue comes from *nasunin*, an anthocyanin (i.e., type of phytonutrient) that functions as a potent antioxidant to protect against damage to the fragile fats that make up our cell membranes. So, keep that skin on!

MAKE YOUR OWN MUESLI

YIELD: 12 servings (scant ½ cup per serving)

Muesli is a granola-esque mix of grains (often including oats), nuts, seeds, and dried fruit. Swiss physician Maximilian Bircher-Benner is credited with creating and prescribing it as a healthy meal for his patients at the end of the nineteenth century. Unlike granola, there's no added oil or sweetener in it, and it's typically enjoyed raw (although I like to lightly toast the grains, nuts, and seeds for flavor) and served cereal-style or soaked overnight oats–style. What started as a basic mixture of a select few ingredients has since evolved into countless ingredient combinations that make for a filling and nutritious make-ahead breakfast. Try my favorite mix or use my basic formula to make it your own—it's easy to customize based on your tastes or what you have in your pantry!

BASIC FORMULA:

3 cups grains + 1½ cups nuts & seeds + 1 cup dried fruit

Grains: Rolled/old-fashioned oats, oat bran, wheat bran, wheat germ, grain flakes (amaranth, barley, quinoa, rye, or sorghum flakes)

Nuts & seeds: Roughly chopped or sliced almonds, cashews, hazelnuts, pecans, pistachios, walnuts; pepitas (shelled pumpkin seeds), shelled sunflower seeds; chia seeds, ground flax seed, hemp hearts; unsweetened coconut flakes

Dried fruit (preferably unsweetened): Apples, apricots, blueberries, cherries, cranberries, dates, goji berries, mango, raisins

CHARLOTTE'S MUESLI MIX:

2½ cups rolled/old-fashioned oats

½ cup wheat bran

½ cup sliced raw almonds

½ cup raw pepitas

½ cup unsweetened coconut flakes

½ cup dried cherries or raisins

½ cup chopped pitted Medjool dates (5 to 6)

½ teaspoon ground cinnamon

Pinch of salt

1. Preheat the oven to 350°F.

2. Place the grains of choice in an even layer on a sheet pan. Bake for 5 minutes.

3. Add the nuts and large seeds of choice (pepitas and/or sunflower seeds, if using) and coconut, if using, to the sheet pan; toss to combine and bake until the nuts and coconut are lightly toasted and fragrant, 5 to 7 minutes.

4. Remove from the oven and let cool for about 10 minutes. Stir in the remaining ingredients until well combined. If using Medjool dates, toss the chopped pieces in ¼ teaspoon cinnamon before adding so that they don't stick to everything.

5. Serve or cool completely and transfer to a large airtight container. Store at room temperature for up to 1 month.

Serving options:

Cold (1 serving): Mix equal parts of the muesli and milk of choice. Let sit for 10 to 15 minutes if enjoying immediately or cover and let sit in the fridge overnight to enjoy the next day. Add some yogurt, fresh fruit, and/or a drizzle of honey or maple syrup before eating, if desired.

DAIRY-FREE: Use unsweetened nondairy milk and yogurt when serving.

GLUTEN-FREE: Use gluten-free grains in your muesli mix: oats, oat bran, or amaranth, quinoa, or sorghum flakes.

NUT-FREE: Use 1 cup large seeds and ½ cup unsweetened coconut flakes and/or small seeds for the 1½ cups nuts and seeds.

Hot (1 serving): Mix equal parts of the muesli and milk of choice and microwave for 1 minute on high or bring to a simmer on the stove and cook for 3 to 4 minutes until the texture is to your liking, then let sit for few minutes. Add some yogurt, fresh fruit, and/or a drizzle of honey or maple syrup before eating, if desired.

Classic Swiss Bircher-Style (2 servings): Mix a scant cup muesli with ¾ cup milk of choice, ½ cup yogurt, and 2 tablespoons fresh orange juice. Let sit for 10 to 15 minutes if enjoying immediately or cover and let sit in the fridge overnight to enjoy the next day. Top with 1 small chopped or grated apple (½ apple per serving) before eating.

MAINS

STRAWBERRY & FETA QUINOA SALAD

YIELD: 4 servings

This "salad" doubles as both a crowd-pleasing potluck side dish and a standalone bring-to-work lunch. You'll get protein from both the quinoa and the feta cheese (or fresh goat cheese, if you prefer), but feel free to top your salad with another protein of choice (it pairs well with most proteins).

---

1 cup quinoa, rinsed

¼ teaspoon salt

3 tablespoons extra-virgin olive oil

Juice of 1 medium lemon (about 3 tablespoons)

3 cups roughly chopped spinach or arugula

Black pepper

½ pound strawberries, quartered (or halved if small)

1 large cucumber, chopped

⅓ cup chopped fresh mint leaves

⅓ cup chopped fresh parsley leaves

2 to 3 green onions, thinly sliced

2 ounces feta cheese, cubed or crumbled

¼ cup chopped walnuts, pistachios, or sliced almonds, toasted (optional)

1. Place the quinoa in a medium saucepan, stir in 2 cups of water and the salt, and bring to a boil over high heat. Reduce the heat to low, cover, and simmer until all of the water is absorbed, 12 to 15 minutes. Remove the pan from the heat, keep covered, and let sit for 5 minutes. Remove the lid and fluff the quinoa with a fork.

2. Transfer the quinoa to a large serving bowl and let cool for a few minutes, just to the point that it's no longer steaming. Stir in the olive oil, lemon juice, and spinach. Season with salt and pepper to taste. Allow to cool completely.

3. Add the remaining ingredients, toss, and serve. Store leftovers in an airtight container in the fridge for up to 5 days.

PLANT-POWERED FACT: Quinoa is considered a "pseudo-grain"—it's categorized as and prepared and eaten like a grain, but technically, it's a seed. It's naturally gluten-free and is a good source of fiber and protein, with 1 cup of cooked quinoa providing about 8 grams of protein and 5 grams of fiber.

SPRING NIÇOISE SALAD

YIELD: 4 servings

The iconic niçoise (pronounced *nee-swaz*) salad originated in the French city of Nice (pronounced like *niece,* not *nice*—although this salad does taste pretty nice, if I do say so myself). It's traditionally made with haricots verts—thin green beans—along with potatoes, hard-boiled eggs, niçoise olives, and canned anchovies or tuna. This Spring take on the classic niçoise salad adds crunchy radishes, bright green asparagus, and spring herbs.

3 tablespoons extra-virgin olive oil, divided

2 tablespoons fresh lemon juice or champagne vinegar, or 1 tablespoon of each

1 tablespoon minced shallot

1 teaspoon Dijon mustard

Salt and black pepper

1 pound baby potatoes, halved (or quartered if large)

½ pound thin green beans, ends trimmed

½ pound asparagus spears, ends trimmed

3 large eggs, hard-boiled, peeled, and quartered

1 head butter lettuce, leaves separated and torn

6 small radishes, trimmed and quartered or sliced

¼ cup pitted niçoise or Kalamata olives

2 tablespoons capers

2 to 3 tablespoons chopped fresh basil or dill

PICK YOUR PROTEIN:

Plant-Powered: 1½ cups cooked chickpeas or white beans (any type), or 1 (15-ounce) can chickpeas or white beans, drained and rinsed

From the Sea: 8 to 10 ounces canned albacore tuna packed in oil or water, drained and flaked (see note), or 2 (5- to 6-ounce) salmon fillets

1. Preheat the oven to 425°F.

2. Make the dressing: In a small bowl, whisk together 2½ tablespoons of the olive oil, the lemon juice, shallot, and mustard. Season with salt and pepper to taste.

3. Toss the potatoes in 1 teaspoon of the oil and arrange in a single layer on a sheet pan; season lightly with salt and pepper; roast for 15 minutes.

4. Push the potatoes to the side of the sheet pan. Toss the asparagus in the remaining ½ teaspoon of oil, season lightly with salt and pepper, and add to the sheet pan with the potatoes. *If using salmon as your protein:* Add the fillets to the sheet pan with the potatoes and asparagus. Season them lightly with salt and pepper and brush with 1 tablespoon of the dressing. Roast until the asparagus is tender and the salmon (if using) is cooked through and flakes easily with a fork, 10 to 12 minutes.

5. Bring a medium saucepan filled with water to a boil. Add the green beans and a heaping teaspoon of salt to the pot and cook until just tender, 3 to 4 minutes. Drain the beans and transfer them to a bowl of ice water for a few minutes, then drain and pat dry.

6. If using chickpeas, white beans, or tuna as your protein, season lightly with salt and pepper and toss in 1 tablespoon of the dressing.

7. Divide the lettuce among 4 plates. Toss the potatoes with 1 tablespoon of the dressing and divide among the plates. Top with the asparagus, eggs, green beans, radishes, olives, capers, and protein of choice. Sprinkle with the fresh herbs and drizzle with the remaining dressing.

NOTE ─────────────────────────────────

You can use tuna packed in water or olive oil or a can of each. The oil-packed tuna is tastier (shocking, I know), but be sure to drain it well before adding it to the salad.

10-MINUTE LENTIL-WALNUT TACO SALAD

YIELD: 4 servings

The highlight of this salad is the quick-to-prepare lentil-walnut taco "meat"—a surprisingly satisfying substitute for ground meat that's rich in both protein and fiber. Even the most skeptical of meat-lovers will enjoy it!

½ cup raw walnut halves or pieces

1 teaspoon extra-virgin olive oil

1 (15-ounce) can lentils (any kind), rinsed and drained

½ cup mild salsa, plus more for serving

1 chipotle pepper in adobo sauce, minced

1 teaspoon ground cumin

Salt

6 cups chopped romaine lettuce or mixed greens

1 pint cherry tomatoes, halved

1 cup canned or frozen fire-roasted corn

1 small avocado, sliced or cubed

½ cup Quick Pickled Onions (page 162) or sliced red onions

FOR THE HONEY-LIME DRESSING:

3 tablespoons fresh lime juice

2 tablespoons extra-virgin olive oil or avocado oil

2 to 3 teaspoons honey or pure maple syrup

1 small clove garlic, minced

Salt and black pepper, to taste

1. Pulse the walnuts in a food processor until finely chopped. Transfer to a large skillet and heat over medium heat until lightly toasted, stirring often, 1 to 2 minutes. Add the olive oil, lentils, salsa, chipotle pepper, and cumin. Reduce the heat to medium-low and cook until the mixture thickens, stirring occasionally, about 5 minutes. Season with salt to taste.

2. Meanwhile, place all of the dressing ingredients in a small bowl and whisk to combine well.

3. Divide the lettuce, lentil-walnut mixture, tomatoes, corn, avocado, and pickled onions among 4 bowls. Top with additional salsa, if desired, and drizzle with the dressing.

TIPS ───────────────────────

- *If you plan on saving some salad for leftovers, store the dressing and taco meat separately from the salad so that the lettuce doesn't get soggy. The lentil-walnut mixture can be stored in an airtight container in the fridge for up to 5 days.*

- *There's a 99.9 percent chance you'll have leftover chipotles and adobo sauce when a recipe calls for them. Don't toss that precious chipotle goodness! If you plan on using it in a meal in the near future, simply store it in an airtight jar in the fridge until you need it. If not, place the remainder in a blender and blend until smooth. Dollop by the spoonful onto a small parchment paper–lined sheet pan or into an ice cube tray and freeze for a few hours. Once hard, transfer the mounds or cubes to a freezer-safe bag.*

NUT-FREE: Omit the walnuts. (It will still taste delicious.)

LESS KALE CAESAR

You're either team kale or you're not. And if you're not, a kale salad probably sounds pretty unappealing. The trick to making raw kale a lot more palatable (and even tasty) is to massage it. Seriously, a nice massage helps remove some of the bitterness and toughness. It also helps if you combine the kale with another leafy green so you get less kale in every bite. Enter this "less kale" salad. Although it is topped with grilled protein, I have provided alternate cooking instructions in case you don't own a grill.

1 tablespoon extra-virgin olive oil, divided

2 tablespoons fresh lemon juice

2 tablespoons low-sodium soy sauce or tamari

2 teaspoons pure maple syrup or honey

½ teaspoon smoked paprika

Salt and black pepper

4 cups stemmed and roughly chopped kale

4 cups roughly chopped romaine lettuce

1 batch Creamy Caesar Tahini Sauce (page 152)

½ batch Chickpea Poppers (page 274)

PICK YOUR PROTEIN:

Plant-Powered: 1 (8-ounce) package tempeh, cut into 8 small triangles

50/50: 12 ounces medium shrimp, peeled and deveined + wooden skewers, soaked in water for 30 minutes

1. Prepare the marinade by combining 2 teaspoons of the olive oil and the lemon juice, soy sauce, maple syrup, and smoked paprika in a large bowl or resealable bag; mix well. Season the tempeh or shrimp with a pinch of salt and pepper, then add to the marinade and toss until well coated. Let marinate in the fridge for 20 to 30 minutes.

2. Preheat a grill to medium heat (see tip for alternate cooking methods) and lightly oil the grill grate.

3. Grill your protein of choice:

   If using tempeh: Remove the tempeh from the marinade and reserve the excess. Place the tempeh on the grill and cook until lightly charred, 5 minutes per side. Brush the excess marinade onto the tempeh after flipping.

   If using shrimp: Remove the shrimp from the marinade and discard the excess. Skewer the shrimp and place it on the grill until just cooked through and opaque, 2 to 3 minutes per side.

4. Place the kale leaves in a large bowl with the remaining 1 teaspoon of olive oil and a pinch of salt. Gently massage the leaves, rubbing them between your fingers until they start to soften, 2 to 3 minutes.

5. Add the romaine, drizzle with a bit of the dressing, and toss to coat. Divide among 4 plates, top with the cooked protein and the chickpea poppers, and drizzle with additional dressing.

GLUTEN-FREE: Use gluten-free tamari/soy sauce and gluten-free tempeh.

NOTE ——

Some people prefer to steam their tempeh for 10 minutes before baking it to remove any bitterness and help the marinade infuse. If you find the tempeh to be bitter, try steaming it first next time.

TIP ——

No grill? No problem.

- *For the tempeh: Cut the tempeh into cubes instead of triangles before adding to the marinade. Preheat the oven to 400°F and line a sheet pan with parchment paper. Arrange the tempeh in a single layer on the prepared sheet pan, reserving the excess marinade, and bake until golden brown, about 20 minutes, flipping halfway through. Brush with the excess marinade after flipping.*

- *For the shrimp: Sauté the shrimp (with the marinade) in a lightly greased medium-sized skillet over medium heat until just cooked through and opaque, 2 to 3 minutes per side.*

PLANT-POWERED FACT: Like its cousin tofu, tempeh is a protein-packed, soy-based food, delivering nearly 20 grams of protein per serving (about double that of tofu). It's made from fermented soybeans along with various grains and seeds, making it rich in fiber, too. Although tempeh is fermented, it's often pasteurized and is typically cooked before eating, which means it retains minimal probiotics. However, eating tempeh has been shown to increase concentrations of good gut bacteria, in large part thanks to its prebiotic fiber content.

SPICED GREEN TAHINI SALAD

YIELD: 4 servings

This salad is one of my all-time favorites, and you're about to find out why. The combination of crispy chickpeas, crunchy pita "croutons," and an herby green tahini dressing is spectacular, and going a little heavy-handed on the spices makes for a salad that delights all the senses.

---

4 cups cauliflower florets (about 1 medium head)

1½ cups cooked chickpeas, or 1 (15-ounce) can chickpeas, drained, rinsed, and patted dry

1 tablespoon extra-virgin olive oil

2 teaspoons ground cumin

2 teaspoons paprika

1 teaspoon garlic powder

Salt and black pepper

2 whole-wheat pita breads, split into 2 layers

6 cups leafy greens of choice, such as arugula, kale (see note), and spinach

1 small avocado, sliced

1 batch Green Tahini Dressing (page 152)

Sliced jalapeño pepper, for garnish (optional)

1. Preheat the oven to 425°F.

2. Place the cauliflower and chickpeas in a large bowl. Add the olive oil, spices, ½ teaspoon of salt, and a pinch of pepper. Arrange in a single layer on a sheet pan. Roast until lightly browned, tossing halfway through, 20 to 25 minutes. Season with additional salt and pepper to taste. Leave the oven on.

3. Toss the pita bread rounds onto a separate sheet pan, spray lightly with olive oil cooking spray, and sprinkle with salt. Bake until golden and crispy, 5 to 7 minutes. Break into 1-inch pieces.

4. Divide the greens, chickpeas, and cauliflower among 4 plates and top with the pita "croutons," avocado, and jalapeño, if desired. Drizzle with the dressing.

TIP

If you plan on saving some salad for leftovers, store the dressing separately from the greens so that they don't get soggy.

NOTE

If you use kale, see the tip on massaging your kale from the Less Kale Caesar recipe on page 202.

RAINBOW SOBA SALAD

YIELD: 4 servings

Soba is a traditional Japanese noodle made from buckwheat flour that's rich in protein with a slightly nutty flavor. You can generally find soba noodles in the international section or health food aisle of the supermarket or at an Asian supermarket. For a protein boost, add some crispy tofu (see page 146).

8 ounces soba noodles

1 cup frozen, shelled edamame

2 medium carrots, peeled

1 medium cucumber

2 cups shredded red cabbage

1 medium yellow bell pepper, thinly sliced

1 batch Orange Ginger Peanut Sauce (page 154)

¼ cup chopped fresh mint and/or basil

2 green onions, thinly sliced

Sesame seeds, for topping (optional)

1 lime, quartered

1. Bring a large pot of water to a boil. Add the soba noodles and edamame and cook according to the package directions for the noodles. Drain and run under cold water; set aside.

2. Meanwhile, use a julienne peeler to slice the carrots and cucumber lengthwise into long, thin strands. (Alternatively, you can use a spiral slicer or slice them into thin ribbons using a vegetable peeler.)

3. Place the noodles, edamame, carrots, cucumber, cabbage, and bell pepper in a large bowl. Add the peanut sauce and fresh herbs and toss to combine.

4. Top with the green onions and a sprinkle of sesame seeds, if using, and serve with the lime wedges.

PEANUT-FREE/NUT-FREE: Refer to the Orange Ginger Peanut Sauce (page 154) recipe for a substitution.

GLUTEN-FREE: Although you can find soba noodles made with 100 percent buckwheat flour (which is naturally gluten-free), many also contain wheat flour (which is not gluten-free). So, use gluten-free 100 percent buckwheat (if available), legume-based, or brown rice noodles. And use gluten-free tamari/soy sauce in the peanut sauce.

TUSCAN RED PEPPER, TOMATO & WHITE BEAN SOUP

YIELD: 4 servings

Want to know the secret to thick and creamy soup without the heavy cream? White beans. Blending them into this soup delivers a delicious richness that comes with fill-you-up fiber and plant protein. This recipe also entails roasting your own red peppers—it's super easy, I promise—but feel free to use good-quality jarred ones if time is short.

3 large red bell peppers, halved, stems and seeds removed, or 1½ (16-ounce) jars roasted red peppers, drained

2½ tablespoons extra-virgin olive oil, divided

½ medium yellow onion, chopped

3 cloves garlic, minced

Leaves from 2 sprigs fresh rosemary, divided

¼ teaspoon crushed red pepper

1 (28-ounce) can whole peeled tomatoes

3 cups cooked cannellini beans, or 2 (15-ounce) cans cannellini beans, drained and rinsed, divided

2 cups low-sodium vegetable broth

2 tablespoons balsamic vinegar

1¼ teaspoons salt, divided

½ teaspoon garlic powder

Black pepper

1. *To roast the red peppers:* Set the oven rack 5 to 6 inches from the top and preheat the broiler to the high setting. Line a sheet pan with aluminum foil sprayed lightly with cooking spray. Place the red bell pepper halves cut side down on the prepared sheet pan. Put the pan on the top rack in the oven and broil on high heat until the skins are charred black, about 10 minutes. Use tongs to carefully transfer the charred peppers to a glass bowl, cover with a lid or a plate, and let sit for 10 minutes. Once cool enough to handle, remove the charred skins and set aside.

2. Heat 2 tablespoons of the olive oil in a large pot over medium heat. Add the onion and sauté until softened, about 5 minutes. Stir in the garlic, half of the rosemary leaves, and the crushed red pepper and cook for 1 minute.

3. Add the roasted red peppers, tomatoes with their juices, 1½ cups of the beans, the broth, vinegar, and 1 teaspoon of the salt. Bring to a boil, then reduce the heat to medium-low and simmer for 15 minutes.

4. Meanwhile, make the topping: Finely chop the remaining rosemary leaves. Heat the remaining 1½ teaspoons of oil in a medium skillet over medium heat. Add the remaining 1½ cups of beans, season with the garlic powder and the remaining ¼ teaspoon of salt, and cook for 5 minutes. Add the rosemary and continue cooking until the beans are lightly browned and crispy, 2 to 3 minutes.

5. Puree the soup with an immersion blender or in batches in a blender or food processor until smooth. (If using a blender, hold a dish towel over the lid and make sure not to cover tightly to allow

air to escape from the top.) Season with salt and pepper to taste. Serve the soup topped with the crispy beans. Store leftovers in an airtight container in the fridge for up to 5 days.

TIP

You can roast a bunch of red peppers to use throughout the week. To store extras, transfer them to an airtight jar or container (as halves or sliced) and store in the refrigerator for up to 1 week. If you want them to last a little longer, pour in enough olive oil to cover them, seal, and store in the refrigerator for 2 to 3 weeks.

LEMONY GREEK-STYLE SOUP

YIELD: 4 servings

Inspired by the popular avgolemono (or egg-lemon) soup, this soup uses tahini and miso instead of egg for creaminess (plus a few friendly bacteria for your gut). You have the option of making it completely plant-based or adding some shredded chicken.

1 tablespoon extra-virgin olive oil

½ medium sweet onion, chopped

2 medium carrots, diced

3 cloves garlic, minced

6 cups low-sodium vegetable broth

¾ cup whole-wheat orzo

1½ cups cooked chickpeas, or 1 (15-ounce) can chickpeas, drained and rinsed

Salt and black pepper

2 tablespoons white miso paste

2 tablespoons tahini

Juice of 2 large lemons, plus extra lemon slices for serving

3 cups stemmed and chopped kale

2 tablespoons chopped fresh dill, plus more for garnish

Salt

PICK YOUR PROTEIN:

Plant-Powered: extra 1½ cups cooked chickpeas, or 1 (15-ounce) can chickpeas, drained and rinsed

50/50: 1½ cups cooked and shredded chicken (about 8 ounces)

1. Heat the olive oil in a large pot over medium-high heat. Add the onion and carrots and sauté until softened, about 5 minutes. Add the garlic and sauté until fragrant, about 30 seconds.

2. Pour the broth into the pot and bring to a boil. Stir in the orzo, chickpeas (including the extra 1½ cups chickpeas if using the plant-powered protein option), ½ teaspoon of salt, and ¼ teaspoon of pepper. Reduce the heat to medium-low and simmer until the orzo is al dente, 7 to 8 minutes. *If using the 50/50 protein option,* stir in the chicken during the last couple of minutes to allow it to warm through.

3. Remove the pot from the heat and transfer ½ cup of hot broth to a small bowl with the miso paste and tahini. Stir until the miso paste has dissolved, then pour the mixture back into the pot along with the lemon juice; stir well.

4. Stir in the kale and dill and allow to rest for a few minutes until the kale wilts. Season with additional salt and pepper to taste.

5. Serve the soup garnished with the dill and lemon slices, if desired. Store leftovers in an airtight container in the fridge for up to 4 days. To reheat leftovers, heat in a pot over medium-low and try not to let it come to a boil.

MISO MUSHROOM & BARLEY STEW

YIELD: 4 servings

This creamy stew is brimming with gut-supporting ingredients, like prebiotic-rich barley and mushrooms and probiotic-rich miso. The miso is added to the soup once it's done cooking so that you don't kill off the beneficial bacteria.

1 cup raw cashews

6 cups low-sodium vegetable broth, divided

1½ tablespoons extra-virgin olive oil

1 pound assorted fresh mushrooms (such as oyster, cremini, and/or shiitake), sliced

2 medium shallots, finely chopped

3 cloves garlic, minced

1 tablespoon fresh thyme leaves or fresh rosemary leaves, chopped

Salt and black pepper

2 tablespoons balsamic vinegar

⅔ cup pearled barley

2 tablespoons white miso paste

1. Place the cashews and 1 cup of the broth in a small microwave-safe bowl and microwave on high for 2 minutes. Alternatively, you can heat the cashews and broth in a small saucepan over high heat until they just come to a boil. Pour into a high-powered blender, cover, and let sit while you make the rest of the soup.

2. Heat the olive oil in a large pot over medium-high heat. Add the mushrooms, shallots, garlic, thyme, ½ teaspoon of salt, and ¼ teaspoon of pepper, and sauté, stirring often, until the mushrooms soften and begin to brown, 5 to 7 minutes. Stir in the vinegar, then add the barley and cook, stirring often, until lightly toasted, 2 to 3 minutes.

3. Pour in the remaining 5 cups of broth and bring to a boil. Reduce the heat to medium-low, cover, and cook, stirring occasionally, until the barley is tender, about 30 minutes. Remove the pot from the heat.

4. Transfer 1 cup of the soup (including some mushrooms and barley) and the miso to the blender with the cashews and blend until very smooth. (Be sure not to cover too tightly to allow the steam to escape.)

5. Stir the cashew mixture into the stew and season with salt and pepper to taste.

6. Store in an airtight container in the fridge for up to 4 days. To reheat leftovers, heat in a pot over medium-low and try not to let it come to a boil.

GLUTEN-FREE: Swap buckwheat groats for barley.

NOTE

Although technically not a whole grain, pearled barley is one of the most nutritious of the technically refined grains. Barley that has been pearled has had some or all of its outer layer removed. But because its fiber is distributed throughout the kernel, barley that has been lightly pearled is still rich in fiber. Look for a pearled barley that has about 5 grams of fiber (or more) per ¼ cup dry serving. (Bob's Red Mill is one of my favorites.) Its whole grain counterpart, hulled barley, which is much harder to find in stores, can be used in this soup, but you'll likely have to use more broth and cook it for a longer time.

SMOKY BUTTERNUT SQUASH THREE-BEAN CHILI

YIELD: 4 servings

This hearty chili is the perfect comforting, warm-you-up meal for a cold day, with an added clear-your-sinuses bonus from fiery chipotle peppers in adobo sauce. Its heartiness comes from vitamins A and C–rich butternut squash and plant protein–packed beans. Using a canned triple-bean blend helps you tackle your weekly thirty-plus plant foods with ease.

1½ tablespoons extra-virgin olive oil

½ large yellow or red onion, chopped

1 medium poblano pepper, seeded and chopped

1 red bell pepper, seeded and chopped

3 cloves garlic, minced

1 to 2 chipotle peppers in adobo sauce, finely chopped

1 tablespoon chili powder

2 teaspoons ground cumin

1 teaspoon smoked paprika

1 teaspoon dried oregano leaves

1 teaspoon salt

2 to 2½ cups cubed butternut squash (1 small squash), or 1 (10-ounce) bag frozen cubed butternut squash

1½ cups low-sodium vegetable broth

1 (15-ounce) can diced fire-roasted tomatoes, with juices

1 (15-ounce) can tri-bean blend (black, kidney, pinto), drained and rinsed (see note)

1 medium avocado, sliced or cubed

PICK YOUR PROTEIN:

Plant-Powered: extra 1 (15-ounce) can tri-bean blend (black, kidney, pinto), drained and rinsed

50/50: add 8 to 10 ounces lean ground turkey or beef

For topping (optional): Squeeze of fresh lime juice, chopped fresh cilantro, dollop of plain Greek yogurt, Plant-Powered Chipotle "Queso" (page 166)

1. Heat the olive oil in a large stockpot or Dutch oven over medium heat. Add the onion and peppers and sauté until softened, about 5 minutes. Stir in the garlic and sauté until fragrant, about 30 seconds. *If using the 50/50 protein option,* add the ground meat to the pot and cook, using a wooden spoon to crumble the meat as it cooks, until browned and just cooked through, 5 to 7 minutes.

2. Stir in the chipotle pepper, spices, oregano, and salt, and cook for 1 minute. Then add the butternut squash, broth, tomatoes, and beans, including the second can if using the plant-powered protein option. Stir to combine and bring to a boil over high heat.

3. Reduce the heat to medium-low, cover, and simmer until the squash is fork-tender, 20 to 25 minutes. If the chili is too thick for your liking, add a splash of vegetable broth.

4. Serve topped with the avocado and any of the optional toppings.

NOTE ———————————————————————————————————————

Canned tri-bean blends can be found at most grocery stores, right in the canned beans section.

TIP ———————————————————————————————————————

Chili is the perfect freezer meal! Make a double batch, allow whatever amount you're freezing to cool completely, divide into freezer-friendly containers or bags (squeeze out any air if using bags), and freeze for up to 3 months. To serve, let thaw in the refrigerator overnight, then warm on the stove over medium heat until heated through.

BLACK BEAN QUINOA BURGERS

YIELD: 4 burgers

Making your own veggie burgers (that don't taste like flavorless hockey pucks) is a cinch! Each of these burgers is packed with 10 grams of protein and is delicious on a bun, in a plant-powered nourish bowl (like the California Burger Bowl, pictured opposite; see page 249), or even on its own.

½ cup rolled/old-fashioned oats

1½ cups cooked black beans, or 1 (15-ounce) can black beans, drained and rinsed

1 cup cooked quinoa

1 large egg or flax/chia egg (see page 138)

¼ cup finely chopped bell pepper (any color)

2 tablespoons finely chopped onion (any kind)

2 cloves garlic, minced

1 tablespoon Worcestershire sauce

1 teaspoon smoked paprika

½ teaspoon salt

1 tablespoon extra-virgin olive oil, for cooking

1. Place the oats in a food processor and pulse until they're the texture of breadcrumbs.

2. Place the beans in a large bowl and mash with a fork or potato masher, leaving some chunks for texture.

3. Add the oats and the remaining ingredients, except for the oil, to the bowl with the beans and mix with a fork or rubber spatula until well combined.

4. Shape the mixture into 4 (¾-inch-thick) patties. Alternatively, you can chill the mixture in the fridge for 20 to 30 minutes to firm up a bit before shaping.

5. Heat the olive oil in a large skillet over medium heat. Cook the patties until golden brown and crispy, 4 to 5 minutes per side.

6. To freeze, let the burgers cool completely, then freeze in an airtight freezer-safe container or resealable bag, separated by parchment paper so that they don't stick together. To reheat them, place in a lightly greased skillet over medium heat until warmed through, 4 to 5 minutes per side.

HUMMUS POWER SANDWICH

YIELD: 2 servings

This quick-to-throw-together plant-powered sandwich is packed with protein, even though there's no animal protein in sight. All thanks to the combo of hummus and sprouted bread...and even the veggies contribute a little protein, too.

½ cup hummus

4 slices sprouted, whole-grain, or gluten-free bread, toasted

2 tablespoons pesto

½ medium cucumber, thinly sliced

½ cup roasted red peppers or thinly sliced red bell pepper

1 medium carrot, shredded or peeled into ribbons

1 cup microgreens, sprouts, or leafy greens

½ medium avocado, thinly sliced

NOTE

You can use store-bought ingredients or use either of the hummus recipes on page 164 and the pesto recipe on page 158. You can buy jarred roasted red peppers at the store as well, or follow the easy roasting instructions from the Tuscan Red Pepper, Tomato & White Bean Soup recipe on page 208.

1. Spread the hummus on 2 slices of the toast and the pesto on the remaining 2 slices of toast.

2. Layer the remaining ingredients evenly on top of the toast with the hummus, top with the pesto toast, and serve.

TIP

You can swap a variety of other veggies—tomato, pickled beets, grilled zucchini, and more—into this sandwich. One of my favorites is roasted eggplant. Preheat the oven to 425°F. Slice 4, ⅓-inch-thick rounds from an eggplant and place onto a parchment-lined sheet pan. In a small bowl, mix 1 tablespoon balsamic vinegar and 1½ teaspoons olive oil, then brush half of this mixture onto the slices. Season lightly with salt and pepper and roast until tender, 17 to 20 minutes, flipping halfway through and brushing with the remaining mixture after flipping. Add to the sandwich in place of (or in addition to) the carrot and cucumber.

PLANT-POWERED FACT: Sprouts and microgreens are tiny, immature versions of vegetables harvested at an early stage of growth—around a few days after germination for sprouts and seven to fourteen days for microgreens. Not only do they add flavor and crunch to any dish, but they also pack quite the nutritional punch in an itty-bitty package. In fact, many have a greater concentration of various vitamins, minerals, and/or antioxidants than their full-grown vegetable counterparts. Broccoli sprouts, for example, are known to be particularly health-promoting, offering anywhere from ten to one hundred times as much sulforaphane—a powerful phytonutrient with anticancer, anti-inflammatory, and neuroprotective effects—as mature broccoli. Once only available at fancy restaurants, you can now find sprouts and microgreens at most grocery stores, usually near the bagged leafy greens. Or you can easily grow them right in your own kitchen with just a mason jar, some sprouting seeds, and water!

PORTOBELLO PITAS

YIELD: 4 servings

Large, meaty portobello mushroom caps stand in for meat in these gyro-inspired pitas topped with tzatziki. The juicy mushrooms cook quickly, soaking up all the flavors of the spices, so you'll have a pita in your hand in no time.

1 tablespoon extra-virgin olive oil

4 large portobello mushroom caps, sliced

2 tablespoons low-sodium soy sauce or tamari

2 tablespoons fresh lemon juice, divided

2 cloves garlic, minced, divided

1 teaspoon dried oregano leaves

½ teaspoon paprika

Salt and black pepper

1 medium cucumber, halved lengthwise

⅔ cup plain Greek yogurt

1 to 2 tablespoons chopped fresh dill, mint, or a combination

4 whole-wheat pita breads

½ cup hummus

2 cups arugula or baby spinach

1 large tomato, sliced, or 1 cup halved cherry tomatoes

¼ small red onion, thinly sliced

1 ounce feta cheese, crumbled, for topping (optional)

1. Heat the olive oil in a large skillet over medium heat. Add the mushrooms, soy sauce, 1 tablespoon of the lemon juice, half of the minced garlic, the oregano, paprika, and a pinch each of salt and pepper and cook, stirring often, until the mushrooms have softened, 5 to 7 minutes.

2. Meanwhile, make the tzatziki: Grate one-half of the cucumber and place in a small bowl with the yogurt, fresh herbs, the remaining 1 tablespoon of lemon juice and clove of minced garlic, and a pinch of salt; mix well. Thinly slice the other half of the cucumber into rounds and set aside.

3. Warm the pitas by covering them with a damp paper towel and microwaving on high for about 20 seconds.

4. To assemble: Spread 2 tablespoons of the hummus down the center of each pita. Divide the mushrooms and raw veggies evenly among the pitas. Top with the tzatziki and a sprinkle of the feta, if using.

NOTE

You can use store-bought hummus or use one of the hummus recipes on page 164.

DAIRY-FREE: Swap unsweetened nondairy yogurt for the Greek yogurt and omit the feta cheese.

GLUTEN-FREE: Use gluten-free pita bread and gluten-free tamari/soy sauce.

SMASHED BEAN SAMMIES OR WRAPS

YIELD: 3 servings

I love a choose-your-own-adventure-style recipe like this one. You start by selecting your bean du jour (aka whatever you happen to have in your pantry) and then pick between two unique, yet equally tasty, flavor combinations. But the fun doesn't end there. I've even given you three options for how to serve it: sandwich, tortilla wrap, or—if you're in the mood for something a little lighter—collard leaf wrap.

BASE INGREDIENTS:

1½ cups cooked or canned chickpeas, or 1 (15-ounce) can chickpeas, drained and rinsed

¼ cup plain Greek yogurt

1 tablespoon fresh lemon or lime juice

Salt and black pepper

FOR THE CURRIED SALAD VERSION:

1 small carrot, grated

1 small red apple, finely diced

1½ teaspoons curry powder

¼ cup chopped walnuts or cashews, toasted

3 to 4 tablespoons raisins or chopped pitted Medjool dates

1½ teaspoons extra-virgin olive oil

DAIRY-FREE: Swap unsweetened nondairy yogurt for the Greek yogurt.

FOR THE GREEN GODDESS VERSION:

1 small avocado, mashed

¼ cup lightly packed fresh basil leaves, finely chopped

¼ cup lightly packed fresh parsley leaves, finely chopped

1 tablespoon finely chopped fresh chives

½ jalapeño pepper, halved lengthwise, seeded, and minced

CHOOSE BREAD OR WRAP:

6 slices sprouted, whole-grain, or gluten-free bread, toasted

3 whole-grain, sprouted, or gluten-free tortillas or wraps

3 large collard green leaves, washed and patted dry

SERVE WITH:

2 cups leafy greens, microgreens, or sprouts

⅓ cup Quick Pickled Onions (page 162) or sliced red onion

1. Place the base ingredients except the salt and pepper in a medium bowl and lightly mash with a fork or potato masher, leaving some chunks for texture.

2. Add the remaining ingredients for the flavor of your choice and mix well. Season with salt and pepper to taste.

3. *For collard wraps:* Cut off the thick stem pieces that protrude past the leaves; then use a knife or vegetable peeler to shave down the thicker part of the remaining stem (to make them easier to roll).

4. Divide the bean mixture evenly among the bread slices, wraps, or collard leaves, then top with the leafy greens and pickled onions. Roll the wraps or collard green leaves (as you would a regular wrap), if using.

PLANT-POWERED FACT: The word *sprouted* just screams unsubstantiated nutrition fad, doesn't it? But there is merit to this ancient method turned modern trend, and I think it's here to stay. Sprouted grains are simply whole-grain seeds that are soaked in water until they begin to germinate and grow a small sprout. This sprouting process begins breaking down some of the starches and phytates, making the grains a little easier to digest and increasing the availability of certain nutrients, like iron, zinc, magnesium, folate, and protein. And sprouted breads (and other sprouted grain products) are often a little higher in protein and fiber than their non-sprouted counterparts. Now widely available, they are one of my go-tos when buying bread for sandwiches.

FARMERS' MARKET QUICHE

YIELD: 4 to 6 servings

Quiche is a French dish consisting of eggs, cream, and a rich pastry crust. This version swaps the pastry for thinly sliced sweet potato that forms a makeshift crust. Sounds like a lot of work, but it's much easier than you'd think! Fill the quiche with whatever veggies you like or have on hand—perhaps some you've picked up at the local farmers' market.

FOR THE CRUST:

1 large, long sweet potato, or 2 small-to-medium sweet potatoes, scrubbed

Salt and black pepper

FOR THE FILLING:

1 tablespoon extra-virgin olive oil

1 shallot, finely chopped

3 to 4 cups chopped or sliced assorted veggies and/or leafy greens, such as asparagus, bell pepper, broccoli, cherry tomatoes, kale, mushrooms, spinach, zucchini, etc.

2 ounces fresh goat or feta cheese, crumbled, divided

6 large eggs

½ cup unsweetened nondairy milk of choice (see note)

1 tablespoon chopped fresh basil (optional)

Salt and black pepper

NOTE ———

If using milk, 2% or whole cow's milk or unsweetened nondairy milk works. My personal favorite for this recipe is nondairy half-and-half.

1. Preheat the oven to 375°F. Lightly grease a 9-inch pie dish.

2. Peel the sweet potato if you'd like or leave the peel on. Cut off the ends of the sweet potato and then carefully slice it into ⅛-inch-thick rounds using a mandoline or sharp knife.

3. Arrange the sweet potato rounds in a spiral with the edges overlapping slightly on the bottom and sides of the prepared pie dish.

4. Spray the potatoes lightly with olive oil cooking spray. (Alternatively, you can toss the sweet potato slices in 1 teaspoon of olive oil before arranging them in the dish.) Season lightly with salt and pepper. Bake for 15 minutes. Remove the dish from the oven and leave the oven on.

5. Meanwhile, prepare the filling: Heat the olive oil in a large skillet over medium heat. Add the shallot, any veggies except tomatoes and greens, and a pinch of salt and cook until tender, 5 to 7 minutes. Add any leafy greens, if using, and cook until just wilted.

6. Top the sweet potato crust with most of the cooked veggies, reserving some, for the top. Evenly sprinkle most of the goat cheese over the veggies, reserving 1 tablespoon for the top.

7. In a large bowl, whisk together the eggs, milk, basil (if using), ½ teaspoon of salt, and a pinch of pepper. Pour the egg mixture over the vegetables. Top with the remaining cooked vegetables, tomatoes, if using, and remaining goat cheese.

8. Bake until the egg mixture sets, 30 to 40 minutes. Let sit for 10 minutes before slicing. Store in an airtight container in the fridge for up to 4 days.

DAIRY-FREE: Swap nondairy cheese for the goat cheese and use nondairy half-and-half or milk.

SHEET PAN PESTO GNOCCHI, SAUSAGE & VEGGIES

YIELD: 4 servings

This sheet pan meal is a favorite simple and low-effort weeknight dinner. Simply add your gnocchi, veggies, and sausages of choice to the pan, bake, and then toss in pesto. The best part—if your gnocchi are frozen, you don't even need to thaw them!

---

1 (10- to 12-ounce) package frozen or fresh cauliflower, potato, or sweet potato gnocchi

3 cups chopped or sliced assorted veggies, such as bell peppers, broccoli, Brussels sprouts, cherry tomatoes, mushrooms, or zucchini

1½ tablespoons extra-virgin olive oil

Salt and black pepper

3 cups fresh baby spinach

⅓ cup The Perfect Pesto (page 158), any variation

PICK YOUR PROTEIN:

Plant-Powered: 2 large Italian-seasoned vegan sausages (see note), sliced into rounds

Poultry: 2 to 3 large Italian-seasoned precooked chicken or turkey sausages, sliced into rounds

1. Preheat the oven to 425°F. Lightly coat a sheet pan with cooking spray.

2. Place the gnocchi and chopped veggies in a large bowl. Add the olive oil and a pinch each of salt and pepper and toss until everything is well coated.

3. Spread in a single layer on the prepared sheet pan. Scatter the sliced sausage evenly around the pan among the other ingredients.

4. Bake until the veggies are tender, 20 to 25 minutes, tossing halfway through. Add the spinach to the pan and continue baking until slightly wilted, 1 to 2 minutes.

5. Dollop with the pesto and toss before serving.

NOTE ————————————————————

Two brands of vegan sausages that I enjoy are Beyond Meat and Field Roast.

"MEATY" BOLOGNESE

YIELD: 4 to 6 servings

Lentils and mushrooms stand in as a full or partial meat replacement in this plant-centric dairy-free Bolognese. You have the option of going 50/50 by adding some ground beef or turkey or going fully plant-powered with no meat at all. And the options don't end there. Serve this over spaghetti squash or zucchini "noodles," or choose wheat-based or legume-based spaghetti noodles—or anything, really! (If, like me, you can't make decisions to save your life, try it as noted in the week 1 meal plan on page 111.)

8 ounces shiitake or cremini mushrooms, quartered

½ medium yellow onion, roughly chopped

3 cloves garlic, peeled

1 tablespoon extra-virgin olive oil

Salt and black pepper

2 tablespoons tomato paste

1½ teaspoons dried oregano leaves

¼ teaspoon crushed red pepper (optional)

½ cup red wine or 100% pomegranate juice (see note)

1 (15-ounce) can crushed tomatoes

1½ cups cooked or 1 (15-ounce) can green, brown, or black lentils

½ cup canned coconut milk (full-fat or light)

1 bay leaf

¼ cup chopped fresh basil

Cooked spaghetti squash (see tip), or zucchini "noodles," or whole-wheat or legume-based spaghetti, for serving

PICK YOUR PROTEIN:

Plant-Powered: extra 1½ cups cooked or 1 (15-ounce) can green, brown, or black lentils

50/50: 8 to 10 ounces lean ground beef or turkey

1. In a food processor, pulse the mushrooms until finely chopped; transfer to a small bowl and set aside. Place the onion and garlic in the processor and pulse until finely chopped; set aside.

2. Heat the olive oil in a large skillet over medium heat. Add the mushrooms, onions, and garlic and ¼ teaspoon each of salt and pepper and sauté until softened, stirring often, 5 to 7 minutes. *If using the 50/50 protein option,* add the ground meat, using a wooden spoon to crumble it as it cooks, until browned and just cooked through, 4 to 6 minutes.

3. Stir in the tomato paste, oregano, and crushed red pepper and cook for 1 minute. Deglaze the pan with the wine, scraping any browned bits on the bottom of the skillet with your spoon. Cook until the liquid is reduced by half, 2 minutes.

4. Add the tomatoes, lentils (including the extra ½ cup if using the plant-powered protein option), coconut milk, bay leaf, and ½ teaspoon of salt.

5. Reduce the heat to medium-low, cover, and simmer to allow the flavors to meld, stirring occasionally, 15 to 20 minutes. Discard the bay leaf, stir in the fresh basil, and season with additional salt to taste. Serve over the noodles of your choice. Store in an airtight container in the fridge for up to 4 days.

NOTE ———————————————

Pomegranate juice mimics the flavor of red wine quite well in this recipe, but it is less acidic. So, you may want to add a splash of balsamic vinegar at the end.

TIP ———————————————

Want to serve this over spaghetti squash, but you've never cooked one before? It's easy! Preheat the oven to 425°F. Cut a medium spaghetti squash in half lengthwise and use a spoon to remove the seeds and stringy pulp. Rub a little extra-virgin olive oil on the inside of each squash half and sprinkle lightly with salt and black pepper. Place the halves facedown on a parchment- or foil-lined baking sheet and bake until just tender, 30 to 40 minutes. Once cool enough to handle, scrape out the spaghetti-like strands with a fork. Voilà—you've got yourself a nutrient-rich, lower-carb pasta substitute!

CREAMY CAULIFREDO

YIELD: 4 servings

Steamed cauliflower stands in for cream and flour in this alfredo-inspired pasta sauce. You might be huffing in disappointment after reading that—and understandably so—but this creamy "caulifredo" is a lightened-up favorite among adults and kids alike. If cauliflower can be pizza and rice, I'm convinced it can be just about anything.

---

8 ounces whole-wheat or legume-based pasta of choice

1 cup frozen green peas

1 tablespoon extra-virgin olive oil, divided

3 cloves garlic, minced

4 cups fresh cauliflower florets (about 1 medium head)

1 tablespoon unsalted butter, melted, or 1 additional tablespoon olive oil

½ cup unsweetened nondairy milk

¼ cup hemp hearts

2 tablespoons fresh lemon juice

¼ cup freshly grated Parmesan cheese, plus more for garnish

½ teaspoon salt

¼ teaspoon black pepper

Fresh parsley, for garnish (optional)

1. Cook the pasta according to the package directions. Add the peas during the last 2 minutes of cooking time. Reserve 1 cup of the pasta cooking water before draining.

2. Meanwhile, heat 1 teaspoon of the olive oil in a large pot over medium heat. Add the garlic and sauté until fragrant, about 30 seconds. Transfer to a high-powered blender.

3. Using the same pot, bring about 4 cups of water to a boil. Add the cauliflower florets, cover with a lid, and cook until the cauliflower is fork-tender, 8 to 10 minutes.

4. Drain the cauliflower and place in the blender. Add the remaining 2 teaspoons of oil, the butter, milk, hemp hearts, lemon juice, Parmesan, salt, and pepper and ½ cup of the reserved pasta water; blend until smooth and creamy. Add more reserved pasta water and salt if necessary.

5. Return the sauce along with the pasta and peas to the pot, toss, and heat on medium-low until heated through, 1 to 2 minutes.

6. Serve garnished with a little more Parmesan and fresh parsley, if using. Store leftovers in an airtight container in the refrigerator for up to 4 days.

DAIRY-FREE: Swap 2 to 3 tablespoons nutritional yeast for the Parmesan. Top with Hempesan (page 117), if desired.

GLUTEN-FREE: Use legume-based pasta.

LASAGNA ROLL-UPS WITH PLANT RICOTTA

YIELD: 6 servings

These lasagna roll-ups are the epitome of plant-forward—they're rich and cheesy but with less dairy and more plant goodness. They're stuffed with a creamy plant-powered ricotta-style filling made with protein-rich tofu and cashews. Don't do dairy? You can omit the mozzarella, and they'll still taste delicious!

---

1 cup raw cashews

9 whole-grain lasagna noodles (see tip)

½ cup fresh basil leaves, plus more for garnish

2 to 3 tablespoons nutritional yeast or freshly grated Parmesan cheese

2 tablespoons fresh lemon juice

1 tablespoon extra-virgin olive oil

3 cloves garlic, roughly chopped

1 teaspoon salt

1 (14-ounce) block firm tofu, drained

1 (10-ounce) package frozen chopped spinach, thawed and squeezed of excess liquid

1 (16-ounce) jar marinara sauce

1 cup shredded mozzarella cheese

DAIRY-FREE: Swap nondairy shredded cheese for the mozzarella (or omit) and use the nutritional yeast.

GLUTEN-FREE: Use gluten-free lasagna noodles, such as brown rice lasagna noodles.

1. Preheat the oven to 350°F.

2. Place the cashews and 1 cup of water in a small microwave-safe bowl and microwave on high for 2 minutes. Alternatively, you can heat the cashews and water in a small pan over high heat until they just come to a boil, then remove from the heat. Cover the bowl or pan with a plate and allow to soak while you cook the noodles.

3. Bring a large pot of water to a boil. Cook the lasagna noodles according to the package directions; drain and rinse under cold water to stop the cooking.

4. Drain the cashews and place in a food processor or high-powered blender with the basil, nutritional yeast, lemon juice, olive oil, garlic, and salt. Use your hands to crumble in the tofu block. Process until smooth.

5. Transfer the cashew mixture to a medium bowl and stir in the spinach. Spread about ¼ cup of the mixture down the center of each noodle and roll. With a sharp knife, carefully slice each roll in half widthwise (without squeezing the filling out of the sides) to create 18 mini rolls.

6. Pour the marinara sauce into the bottom of a 2-quart baking dish. Place the rolls in the dish with the ruffled edges facing up. Sprinkle the mozzarella over the top.

7. Cover with aluminum foil or a lid and bake for 15 minutes. Uncover and bake until hot and bubbly, 10 to 15 more minutes.

TIP ———————————————

I usually cook an extra noodle in case one rips during boiling.

ZOODLES & NOODLES PRIMAVERA

YIELD: 4 servings

When zucchini noodles were in their prime, I would "healthify" my favorite pasta dishes by swapping zucchini noodles for wheat-based noodles. More often than not, I'd end up unsatisfied and hungry (shocking, I know), until I had the thought that it didn't have to be all noodles or no noodles. Enter Zoodles AND Noodles Primavera.

2 medium zucchini

2 medium carrots, peeled

6 ounces whole-wheat spaghetti, linguine, or fettuccine

1 cup frozen peas

2 tablespoons extra-virgin olive oil

1 tablespoon butter

½ pound asparagus spears, ends trimmed and cut into 2-inch pieces

2 cloves garlic, minced

¼ teaspoon crushed red pepper (optional)

Grated zest and juice of ½ medium lemon

½ teaspoon salt

Pinch of black pepper

⅓ cup freshly grated Parmesan cheese, plus more for garnish

¼ cup chopped fresh basil, parsley, or a combination, plus more for garnish

1. Use a spiral slicer or julienne peeler to cut the zucchini and carrots into spaghetti-like noodles or long, thin strands. Set aside.

2. Cook the pasta according to the package directions. Add the peas during the last 2 minutes of cooking time. Reserve ½ cup of the pasta cooking water before draining.

3. Meanwhile, heat the olive oil and butter in a large skillet over medium heat. Add the asparagus and cook until slightly softened, 2 to 3 minutes. Add the carrot and zucchini noodles and cook until just tender and al dente, 2 to 3 minutes. Add the garlic, crushed red pepper, if using, lemon zest, salt, and pepper and cook for 1 minute more.

4. Remove from the heat. Immediately add the pasta and peas, reserved pasta water, and lemon juice and toss. Season with additional salt and pepper to taste. Add the Parmesan and fresh herbs and toss once more.

5. Serve the noodles garnished with a little more Parmesan and fresh herbs. Store leftovers in an airtight container in the refrigerator for up to 4 days.

GLUTEN-FREE: Use legume-based pasta.

ROASTED RATATOUILLE RIGATONI

YIELD: 4 to 6 servings

Ratatouille—a classic, hearty vegetable-heavy dish hailing from the South of France—is one of those dishes that many people are too intimidated by to ever bother attempting. Is it a little time-consuming? Yes. Impossible? No. And this "chop and dump" roasted version cuts the hands-on time in half. Look, if a rat can make it, you can, too.

1 medium eggplant, cut into ½-inch cubes

1 pound Roma tomatoes, chopped into 1-inch pieces

1 medium red bell pepper, chopped into 1-inch pieces

1 medium zucchini, sliced into half moons

1 medium yellow squash, sliced into half moons

½ large yellow onion, chopped

3 tablespoons extra-virgin olive oil

2 tablespoons balsamic vinegar

3 cloves garlic, peeled

2 teaspoons fresh thyme leaves

1 teaspoon salt

¼ teaspoon black pepper

8 ounces legume-based rigatoni or pasta shape of choice

⅓ cup sun-dried tomatoes packed in oil, drained and minced, plus 1 tablespoon oil from the jar

3 to 4 tablespoons chopped fresh basil

1. Preheat the oven to 400°F.

2. Place the eggplant, tomatoes, bell pepper, zucchini, yellow squash, and onion in a 13 by 9-inch baking or casserole dish.

3. In a small bowl, mix together the olive oil, balsamic vinegar, garlic, thyme, salt, and pepper. Drizzle over the veggies and toss until the pieces are well coated.

4. Roast until the vegetables are very soft, 45 minutes to 1 hour, stirring halfway through. Season with additional salt and pepper to taste.

5. Meanwhile, cook the pasta according to the package directions. Reserve ½ cup of the pasta cooking water before draining.

6. Add the pasta, sun-dried tomatoes and oil from the jar, basil, and a small splash of pasta water to the vegetables. Add more pasta water if the pasta seems too dry.

7. Store in an airtight container in the fridge for up to 4 days.

ONE-POT CHICKPEA & CAULIFLOWER CURRY

YIELD: 4 servings

This quick plant-powered curry recipe is a must in your plant-forward cooking repertoire. It's packed with flavor from the curry paste and comes together in about 20 minutes! For this PYP recipe, choose between adding extra chickpeas or some shredded chicken.

1 tablespoon extra-virgin olive oil

½ medium yellow onion, chopped

3 cloves garlic, minced

1 (1-inch) piece ginger, peeled and grated

3 tablespoons red curry paste

2 tablespoons tomato paste

3 cups fresh cauliflower florets (about 1 small head)

1½ cups cooked chickpeas, or 1 (15-ounce) can chickpeas, drained and rinsed

1 (14-ounce) can light coconut milk

½ teaspoon salt

Pinch of black pepper

Juice of 1 lime

For serving (optional):

Chopped fresh cilantro or basil leaves

Toasted whole-wheat naan or pita bread, for serving

PICK YOUR PROTEIN:

Plant-Powered: extra 1½ cups cooked chickpeas, or 1 (15-ounce) can chickpeas, drained and rinsed

50/50: 1½ cups cooked and shredded chicken (about 8 ounces)

1. Heat the olive oil in a large pot or skillet over medium heat. Add the onion and sauté until softened, about 5 minutes. Stir in the garlic and ginger and sauté until fragrant, about 30 seconds.

2. Add the curry paste, tomato paste, and cauliflower, stir to coat, and cook for 2 minutes.

3. Add the chickpeas (including the extra 1½ cups if using the plant-powered protein option), coconut milk, salt, pepper, and ½ cup water and bring to a simmer over medium-low heat. Cover with a lid and cook until the vegetables are tender, 10 to 15 minutes. *If using the 50/50 protein option,* stir in the chicken during the last couple of minutes of cooking to allow it to heat through.

4. Remove from the heat, add the lime juice, and season with additional salt or curry paste if necessary.

5. Garnish with fresh herbs and serve with naan or pita, if using. Store leftovers in an airtight container in the fridge for up to 4 days.

KIMCHI FRIED RICE

YIELD: 4 servings

This easy fried rice is packed with gut-friendly foods, like kimchi (spicy fermented cabbage) and refrigerated, day-old rice. Using leftover rice in this recipe serves a dual purpose. It fries better, giving your fried rice a good texture, and it increases the amount of food available to your good gut bacteria!

2 tablespoons low-sodium soy sauce or tamari

2 teaspoons toasted sesame oil or extra-virgin olive oil

1 tablespoon extra-virgin olive oil, divided

2 green onions, thinly sliced, white and green parts divided

2 small cloves garlic, minced

1 cup kimchi, roughly chopped, plus 3 to 4 tablespoons kimchi juice from the jar

2 cups frozen peas and carrots

3 cups day-old cooked brown rice

2 cups frozen riced cauliflower

4 large eggs, lightly beaten

For topping (optional):

Sesame seeds

Roasted seaweed snacks, cut into strips

Gochujang or Sriracha sauce

1. Place the soy sauce and sesame oil in a small bowl and mix well; set aside.

2. Heat 1½ teaspoons of the olive oil in a large skillet over medium heat. Add the white parts of the green onions and the garlic and sauté for 1 minute. Stir in the kimchi and peas and carrots and sauté until warmed through, 2 to 3 minutes.

3. Add the brown rice, riced cauliflower, and soy sauce mixture and cook until warmed through, stirring frequently, 4 to 5 minutes.

4. Meanwhile, heat the remaining 1½ teaspoons of olive oil in a medium skillet over medium heat. Cook the eggs scrambled-style until just set.

5. Fold the eggs into the rice mixture and remove from the heat. Stir in the kimchi juice. Top with the green parts of the green onions and any of the additional toppings, if using. Store leftovers in an airtight container in the fridge for up to 4 days.

GLUTEN-FREE: Use gluten-free tamari/soy sauce.

PLANT-POWERED FACT: Remember resistant starch? (Quick refresher: It escapes digestion—like fiber—and makes its way to the colon where it acts as a prebiotic.) Well, a type of resistant starch forms as rice cools, making cooked-then-cooled rice significantly higher in resistant starch than freshly cooked rice. Even better, reheating leftover cold rice does not lower the resistant starch content.

MEAN GREEN ENCHILADA SKILLET

YIELD: 4 to 6 servings

No filling or rolling for these deconstructed enchiladas served skillet-style and loaded with green veggies. For this pick-your-protein recipe, you have the option of going 50/50 and adding some shredded chicken or going plant-powered with another variety of beans. I highly recommend the Easy Salsa Verde recipe (page 156) a try in this.

---

1 tablespoon extra-virgin olive oil

½ medium red or white onion, chopped

2 cups chopped zucchini (about 1 medium to large)

2 cloves garlic, minced

2 teaspoons chili powder

1 teaspoon ground cumin

5 ounces fresh baby spinach

1½ cups black beans, or 1 (15-ounce) can black beans, drained and rinsed

1 batch Easy Salsa Verde (page 156), or 1 (16-ounce) jar salsa verde

1 cup shredded Monterey Jack cheese, divided

½ cup plain, whole-milk Greek yogurt

½ heaping teaspoon salt

6 (6-inch) corn tortillas, halved then cut into 1-inch-thick strips

1 medium avocado, sliced or cubed, for serving

Fresh cilantro sprigs, for serving (optional)

PICK YOUR PROTEIN:

Plant-Powered: 1½ cups cooked pinto or white beans, or 1 (15-ounce) can pinto or white beans, drained and rinsed

50/50: 1½ cups cooked and shredded chicken (about 8 ounces)

1. Preheat the oven to 450°F.

2. Heat the olive oil in a 12-inch cast-iron or oven-safe skillet over medium heat. Add the onion and zucchini and sauté until softened, about 5 to 7 minutes. Stir in the garlic and spices and sauté until fragrant, about 30 seconds.

3. Add the spinach and cook, stirring often, until all of the spinach has wilted. Remove from the heat and transfer veggies to a large bowl. Do not clean out the skillet.

4. Add the black beans, salsa, half of the cheese, yogurt, salt, and pick-your-protein of choice to the bowl and mix well; season with additional salt to taste. Gently fold in the tortilla strips.

5. Transfer the mixture back to the skillet and sprinkle with the remaining cheese. Place in the oven and bake until the cheese is melted and bubbly, about 7 to 10 minutes.

6. Serve with avocado and cilantro, if using. Store leftovers in an airtight container for up to 4 days.

DAIRY-FREE: Swap unsweetened nondairy yogurt and cheese for the Greek yogurt and Monterey Jack cheese. You can also omit the cheese altogether or top with some of the Plant-Powered Chipotle "Queso" (page 166).

CHIPOTLE PINEAPPLE MUSHROOM TACOS

YIELD: 4 servings

Assorted mushrooms are coated in a sweet and smoky sauce made from pineapple and chipotle peppers and then served taco-style with black bean and pineapple salsa. You can use fresh, frozen, or canned pineapple for this recipe. Fresh tastes best, but as someone who is pineapple-cutting-challenged, I also use the latter two.

2 cups cubed pineapple, divided (see note)

3 tablespoons raw, unfiltered apple cider vinegar

1 to 2 chipotle peppers in adobo sauce

3 cloves garlic, peeled

2 teaspoons chili powder

2 teaspoons smoked or sweet paprika

1 teaspoon dried oregano leaves

½ teaspoon salt

1 tablespoon extra-virgin olive oil

16 ounces assorted mushrooms (such as shiitake, cremini, and/or oyster), sliced

1½ cups cooked black beans, or 1 (15-ounce) can black beans, drained and rinsed

½ small red onion, finely diced

¼ cup chopped fresh cilantro

Juice of 1 lime (about 2 tablespoons)

8 (6-inch) corn or whole-wheat tortillas

1 medium avocado, sliced

1 ounce feta cheese, Cotija, or queso fresco, crumbled (optional)

1. Place 1 cup of the pineapple, vinegar, 1 chipotle pepper, garlic, spices, dried oregano, and salt in a blender or food processor and blend until smooth. Taste and add the other chipotle pepper for a spicier sauce and season with additional salt, if necessary.

2. Heat the olive oil in a large skillet over medium heat. Add the mushrooms and cook until browned, 7 to 10 minutes. Reduce the heat to low, stir in about two-thirds of the sauce, and cook for 5 to 7 minutes to allow the flavors to meld.

3. Meanwhile, make the salsa: Place the remaining 1 cup of pineapple, the black beans, onion, cilantro, and lime juice in a medium bowl and mix well. Season with salt to taste.

4. Warm the tortillas by covering them in a damp paper towel and microwaving on high for 15 to 20 seconds. Divide the mushroom mixture, pineapple and bean salsa, avocado, and cheese among the warmed tortillas and serve with the remaining sauce.

DAIRY-FREE: Swap nondairy Mexican-style shredded cheese or Plant-Powered Chipotle "Queso" (page 166) for the crumbled cheese, or you can omit it altogether.

NOTE

If you use frozen pineapple chunks, thaw and drain them before making the sauce. Alternatively, you can use canned pineapple tidbits or chunks in 100% pineapple juice; drain the pineapple, and reserve the juice for another use.

SPICY ROLL "SUSHI" BOWL

Rolling sushi is truly an art, and one that I haven't quite mastered yet. In the meantime, I enjoy making this deconstructed version that has many of the signature components of sushi, including vinegared rice and seaweed, but requires less artistry to make. The seaweed snacks used here are crispy little sheets of seaweed that are available at most grocery stores, typically in the international section. You can also use a large nori sheet, which is what is used to roll sushi.

1 cup brown rice

2 tablespoons rice vinegar

1 tablespoon honey or pure maple syrup, divided

¼ teaspoon salt

1 tablespoon low-sodium soy sauce or tamari, plus more for serving

3 tablespoons mayonnaise (see note)

2 teaspoons Sriracha sauce, plus more as needed

2 medium carrots, sliced into ribbons or julienned

3 Persian cucumbers, thinly sliced

6 to 8 sheets roasted seaweed snacks, torn or cut into small pieces or strips

1 small avocado, sliced

OPTIONAL ADD-INS: Sesame seeds, microgreens, pickled ginger, sliced radish, shredded red cabbage, and/or diced mango

PICK YOUR PROTEIN:

Plant-Powered: 2 cups frozen, shelled edamame

From the Sea: 2 (5- to 6-ounce) salmon fillets

1. Cook the rice according to the package directions. While the rice cooks, stir together the rice vinegar, half of the honey, and the salt in a small bowl. Once the rice is done, pour the vinegar mixture over the rice while it's still hot and stir until well combined. Set aside.

2. Meanwhile, combine the soy sauce and the remaining honey in a small bowl, then prepare your protein of choice.

If using salmon: Set the oven rack 5 to 6 inches from the top and preheat the broiler to the high setting. Pat the salmon fillets dry and season lightly with salt. Brush the soy sauce mixture on the salmon and let sit at room temperature for 10 minutes. Broil the salmon until lightly charred on top and just cooked through, 6 to 8 minutes, depending on the thickness. Discard the skin and flake the salmon with a fork.

If using edamame: Cook according to the package directions, then toss in the soy sauce mixture.

3. In a small bowl, stir together the mayonnaise and Sriracha. Add additional Sriracha, if desired.

4. Divide the rice among 4 bowls and top with the protein of choice, carrots, cucumber, seaweed snacks, avocado, and any optional add-ins. Drizzle the Sriracha mayo sauce on top and serve with soy sauce. Store leftovers in an airtight container in the fridge for up to 4 days.

NOTE

I prefer avocado or olive oil–based mayos, but you can use any kind, including vegan or reduced-fat. If you're mayo averse, you can omit it and simply drizzle with Sriracha sauce and additional soy sauce, or mix the Sriracha with a little tahini and rice vinegar.

BUILD YOUR OWN PLANT-POWERED NOURISH BOWLS

Nourish bowls, similar to buddha bowls or macro bowls, consist of smaller portions of a variety of nutrient-dense, mostly plant-based foods—typically a leafy green, a whole grain or starchy veggie, a plant protein, and some more veggies (raw and/or cooked)—dressed in healthy fats. Use the formulas in this chart to build your own nourish bowl—you can get a little gourmet and follow the examples to a T or simply throw together whatever components you have in your kitchen. When assembling the bowls, toss everything in haphazardly or artfully arrange the components, layering your grain and leafy greens and sectioning off each topping (so it's Instagram-worthy).

Directions to make 4 bowls of the examples offered on pages 250 and 251.

- **For the base:** For bowls that include a grain, cook 1 cup according to the package directions and season with salt and pepper to taste. Divide among 4 bowls. Add 1 cup of the leafy green listed to each bowl.

- **For the Greek Nourish Bowl:** Divide 1 (15-ounce) can chickpeas (drained and rinsed) among 4 bowls and top each with sliced tomato and cucumber, feta cheese, hummus, olives, mint, and a squeeze of fresh lemon juice.

- **For the Anti-Inflammatory Nourish Bowl:** Preheat the oven to 425°F. Toss 1 (15-ounce) can chickpeas (drained, rinsed, and patted dry), 1 small head cauliflower (chopped into florets), and 3 small beets (peeled and cut into small, ½-inch cubes or wedges) in 1 generous tablespoon extra-virgin olive oil and 1 teaspoon each ground cumin and smoked paprika; season with salt and pepper. Roast on a sheet pan until the veggies are tender and lightly browned, 20 to 25 minutes, tossing halfway through. Divide among 4 bowls and top each with the sauce and hemp hearts. (Note: You also can use precooked beets, in which case, you skip roasting them.)

- **For the Harvest Nourish Bowl:** Preheat the oven to 425°F. Toss 10 to 12 ounces shaved Brussels sprouts in 1½ teaspoons extra-virgin olive oil and toss 1 large sweet potato (cubed) in another 1½ teaspoons oil. Place the sprouts on one half of a sheet pan and the potatoes on the other half; season with salt and pepper. Roast until tender and lightly browned, 20 to 25 minutes, tossing halfway through. Drizzle the sprouts with 1 tablespoon balsamic vinegar and 1 teaspoon honey or maple syrup; toss to coat. Divide the cooked veggies, 1 (15-ounce) can white beans (drained, rinsed, and seasoned with salt and pepper), and 1 apple (chopped) among 4 bowls and top each with pesto and pepitas.

- **For the California Burger Bowl:** For the dressing, combine 2 tablespoons each Dijon mustard, apple cider vinegar, and extra-virgin olive oil, 2 teaspoons honey, and salt to taste. Divide 1 batch of the fries among 4 bowls and top each with a burger, pickled onions, sliced tomato, pickles, avocado, and sauce.

- **For the Gut Glow Nourish Bowl:** Sub miso paste for some or all of the soy sauce in the dressing (optional). Divide 1 batch of the tofu among 4 bowls and top each with shredded carrot, sliced cucumber, kimchi, dressing, and cashews.

- **For the Mango Mojo Nourish Bowl:** Preheat the oven to 425°F. Toss 1 large sweet potato (cut into small cubes), 1 red bell pepper (sliced), and 1 green bell pepper (sliced) in 2 teaspoons of olive oil; season with salt and pepper. Roast on a large sheet pan until veggies are tender and lightly browned, 20 to 25 minutes, tossing halfway. Once done, immediately add 1 (15-ounce) can black beans (drained, rinsed, and seasoned with salt and pepper) to the pan and toss to warm. Add ½ teaspoon ground cumin to the dressing recipe. Divide the cooked veggies, beans, and 1 mango (chopped) among 4 bowls and top each with avocado, minced or sliced jalapeño, dressing, and cilantro.

FORMULA (PER BOWL)	LEAFY GREEN BASE (ABOUT 1 CUP)	SLOW CARB (½ TO 1 CUP COOKED GRAINS OR STARCHY VEGGIES, CHOPPED FRUIT, OR A COMBO)	NONSTARCHY VEGGIES (ABOUT 1 CUP TOTAL)	
			Cooked	Raw
GREEK	Arugula	Quinoa	None	Cherry tomatoes, Cucumber
ANTI-INFLAMMATORY	Kale (massaged, see page 202)	Quinoa	Cauliflower, Golden or regular beets	None
HARVEST	Kale (massaged, see page 202)	Farro, Sweet potato, Apple	Brussels sprouts	None
CALIFORNIA BURGER	Mixed greens	Mixed Root Veggie Fries (page 256)	None	Quick Pickled Onions (page 162), Tomato, Pickles
GUT GLOW	Spinach	Wild rice	None	Carrot, Cucumber, Kimchi
MANGO MOJO	Spinach	Quinoa, Sweet potato, Mango	Bell pepper	Jalapeño

PROTEIN (ABOUT ½ CUP/3 OUNCES PULSES, TOFU, OR TEMPEH)	HEALTHY FATS		FLAVORINGS (SPICES, HERBS, JUICES, ETC.)
	Dressing/Sauce (2 tablespoons home-made or store-bought)	Nuts, seeds, other (about 1 tablespoon, optional)	
Chickpeas Crumbled feta cheese (optional)	Beet & White Bean or Basic Hummus (page 164)	Olives	Chopped fresh mint (optional), Lemon juice
Chickpeas	Golden Tahini Sauce (page 152)	Hemp hearts	Cumin, Smoked paprika
White beans	The Perfect Pesto (page 158)	Pepitas	Balsamic vinegar, Honey or maple syrup
Black Bean Quinoa Burger (page 216)	Dijon mustard, Apple cider vinegar, Olive oil, Honey	Avocado	None
Best Crispy Tofu (page 146)	Orange Ginger Peanut Sauce (page 154)	Chopped cashews	White miso paste (optional)
Black beans	Honey-Lime Dressing (page 200)	Avocado	Cumin, Chopped fresh cilantro

SMALLER FARE

CAULIFLOWER STEAKS WITH ALMOND BUTTER ROMESCO

YIELD: 6 servings

Let's be honest: The only thing these cauliflower "steaks" have in common with real steak is the size and shape (and even that's a stretch). Other than that, this is cauliflower, and steak is steak. But that doesn't mean this dish isn't mouthwateringly delicious in its own way. The easy romesco-style sauce uses almond butter instead of almonds for extra creaminess. You can serve it as a starter, a side, or even a light meal.

2 large heads cauliflower

1 tablespoon extra-virgin olive oil

1 tablespoon fresh lemon juice

½ teaspoon salt

Pinch of black pepper

Chopped fresh parsley, for garnish (optional)

FOR THE ALMOND BUTTER ROMESCO:

2 roasted red bell peppers (see note)

¼ cup sun-dried tomatoes packed in oil, drained

¼ cup unsweetened almond butter

2 tablespoons extra-virgin olive oil

2 cloves garlic, roughly chopped

1 tablespoon sherry vinegar or red wine vinegar

1 teaspoon smoked paprika

½ teaspoon salt

¼ teaspoon crushed red pepper (optional)

1. Remove the leaves from the cauliflower heads and trim the stems, but leave the core intact. Slice three ¾-inch-thick "steaks" from the center of each head. Save the remaining cauliflower pieces for another dish.

2. In a small bowl, whisk together the olive oil and lemon juice. Brush the mixture onto both sides of each cauliflower steak, then season with the salt and pepper.

3. Cook the cauliflower steaks:

To grill: Preheat a grill to medium heat and lightly oil the grill grate. Place the steaks on the grill and cook until lightly charred and tender, 5 to 7 minutes per side.

To roast: Preheat the oven to 425°F. Place the steaks on a sheet pan and roast until golden and tender, 20 to 25 minutes, flipping them halfway through.

4. Meanwhile, make the romesco: Place all of the ingredients in a blender or food processor and blend until smooth.

5. Serve the cauliflower steaks with the romesco and garnish with parsley, if desired. If the sauce is too thick, add warm water 1 tablespoon at a time to thin it.

NOTE

You can either roast your own peppers according to the directions in the Tuscan Red Pepper, Tomato & White Bean Soup recipe on page 208 or use a 16-ounce jar of good-quality roasted red peppers (drained).

MIXED ROOT VEGGIE FRIES

YIELD: 3 to 4 servings

The way to guarantee veggie fries that don't fall limp is a thin coating of starch! Preheating the sheet pan, using parchment paper, and not crowding the oven with more than one pan also helps the fries crisp. In just a few steps, you can turn most of your favorite root vegetables into delicious homemade fries.

1½ pounds root vegetables of choice, such as carrots, parsnips, or sweet potatoes (see note)

2 teaspoons cornstarch, arrowroot starch, or tapioca starch

Heaping ½ teaspoon garlic powder

½ teaspoon paprika

¼ teaspoon black pepper

½ teaspoon salt

1½ tablespoons extra-virgin olive oil or avocado oil

1. Preheat the oven to 425°F. Line a sheet pan with parchment paper and place it in the oven while it preheats.

2. Cut the veggies into ¼- to ⅓-inch-thick and 3-inch-long batons (fry-sized sticks). Try to cut them all to the same thickness so that they cook evenly. Place the cut veggies in a large bowl.

3. In a small bowl, stir together the cornstarch, spices, and salt, then sprinkle over the fries and toss until evenly coated. Pour in the oil, then toss again until evenly coated.

4. Carefully arrange the veggie fries in a single layer on the preheated pan, making sure they don't overlap or touch.

5. Bake for 12 minutes, flip the fries, then bake until browned and crispy, 10 to 15 minutes more. Season with additional salt to taste.

NOTE

It's up to you whether to peel your veggies. I typically peel parsnips and carrots but leave the skin on for potatoes. Be sure to scrub the veggies if you plan to leave the peel on.

PEACH & ARUGULA PESTO SOCCA FLATBREAD

YIELD: 4 to 6 servings

Socca is a simple flatbread (sometimes referred to as a large pancake) made from chickpea flour that's popular in parts of France and in Italy (where it's more commonly referred to as farinata). Topped with pesto, sliced peaches, and a light balsamic glaze, these flatbreads have all the makings of a perfect sweet and savory summer appetizer or light meal.

---

1 cup chickpea/garbanzo bean flour

½ teaspoon salt

1½ tablespoons extra-virgin olive oil, divided

¼ cup thinly sliced red onions

⅓ cup The Perfect Pesto (page 158), made with arugula and hemp hearts

1 large or 2 small ripe peaches, halved, pitted, and thinly sliced

1 to 2 ounces fresh goat cheese, crumbled

Arugula, for serving

FOR THE BALSAMIC GLAZE:

⅓ cup balsamic vinegar

1 tablespoon pure maple syrup or honey

1. Combine the chickpea flour and salt in a medium bowl. Pour in 1 cup of warm water and whisk until the batter is smooth, then whisk in 1 tablespoon of the olive oil. Let sit at room temperature for 15 minutes before preheating the oven.

2. Preheat the oven to 450°F. Place a 10-inch cast-iron or oven-safe skillet in the oven while it preheats.

3. When the oven has come to temperature, carefully remove the skillet from the oven and add the remaining 1½ teaspoons of oil; swirl to coat the bottom of the skillet. Pour the chickpea batter into the skillet and swirl to spread it evenly across the bottom of the skillet. Scatter the onion slices on top.

4. Bake until the socca is set and golden around the edges, 10 to 12 minutes.

5. Spread the pesto on top of the socca and top with the sliced peaches and goat cheese. Return the pan to the oven and bake until the cheese has softened, 5 to 7 minutes.

6. Meanwhile, make the balsamic glaze: Bring the balsamic vinegar and maple syrup to a boil in a small saucepan. Reduce the heat to low and simmer until the sauce coats the back of a spoon, about 5 minutes.

7. Top the socca with some arugula leaves and drizzle with the balsamic glaze before serving.

DAIRY-FREE: Swap nondairy cheese for the goat cheese and nutritional yeast for the Parmesan in The Perfect Pesto.

TAKEOUT TOFU LETTUCE WRAPS

YIELD: 4 servings

These better-than-takeout tofu lettuce wraps can be served as an appetizer or a light meal, or you can easily transform them into a heartier meal by adding some cooked brown rice, quinoa, or soba noodles to the lettuce cups!

1 to 2 heads Little Gem, baby romaine, or butter lettuce, leaves separated

1 batch Best Crispy Tofu (page 146)

2 cups thinly sliced or shredded crunchy veggies, such as bell pepper, carrot, radish, or red cabbage

3 green onions, thinly sliced

½ cup Orange Ginger Peanut Sauce (page 154), for serving

Chopped fresh mint or basil, for serving (optional)

1. Fill the lettuce leaves with the crispy tofu cubes, sliced veggies, and green onions.

2. Top each with peanut sauce and garnish with fresh herbs, if desired.

PEANUT-FREE/NUT-FREE/GLUTEN-FREE: Refer to the Orange Ginger Peanut Sauce recipe for substitutions.

CRUCIFEROUS CRUNCH POWER SALAD

YIELD: 4 to 6 servings

This crunchy, fiber- and phytonutrient-packed salad was inspired by the sweet kale salad kits you can find at many grocery stores that contain a blend of cruciferous veggies (like kale, broccoli, and Brussels sprouts), dried fruit, seeds, and a creamy poppy seed dressing. Serve it cold or warm, as a side or light meal as a complete meal by topping with some extra plant protein (see the tip).

3 cups stemmed and shredded or chopped kale

1 teaspoon extra-virgin olive oil

Salt

2 cups broccoli slaw mix

2 cups shaved, shredded, or very thinly sliced Brussels sprouts

1 medium avocado, diced or sliced

⅓ cup dried berries (such as blueberries, cranberries, or cherries)

¼ cup hemp hearts

¼ cup pepitas or sunflower seeds, toasted

1 batch Poppy Seed Tahini Dressing (page 152)

To serve cold: Place the kale in a large bowl with the olive oil and a pinch of salt. Gently massage the leaves, rubbing them between your fingers until they start to soften, 2 to 3 minutes. Add the broccoli slaw and Brussels sprouts and toss to combine.

To serve warm: Heat the oil in a large skillet over medium heat. Add the kale, broccoli slaw, and Brussels sprouts and sauté until slightly wilted, 3 to 4 minutes.

For both: Drizzle the vegetables with a bit of the dressing and toss. Top with the avocado, dried berries, hemp hearts, and seeds and drizzle with additional dressing.

TIP

Make this salad a meal by adding some extra protein. Keep it simple and easy by topping with 1 (15-ounce) can white beans or chickpeas (drained, rinsed, and seasoned with a pinch of salt and pepper) or get a little gourmet and top with the Chickpea Poppers (page 274) or the Best Crispy Tofu (page 146).

PLANT-POWERED FACT: Like other veggies, cruciferous vegetables are great sources of a variety of vitamins, minerals, and phytonutrients. But one characteristic that sets them apart from the rest is their high content of glucosinolates—inactive phytonutrients that are activated into their potent, disease-fighting forms when they come in contact with enzymes stored separately in these veggies via cutting, chopping, and/or chewing of the veggie. Sulforaphane is one such form that's linked with cardiovascular and brain health benefits and widely studied for its protective role against several forms of cancer.

AUTUMN APPLE FARRO SALAD

YIELD: 4 to 6 servings

Crisp, tangy, and with just the right amount of sweetness, this salad is perfect for serving to friends and family at a holiday gathering (or year-round) or enjoying all to yourself at home. The secret to this flavorful, grain-based salad is cooking the farro in some apple cider (not apple cider vinegar, which you'll add after).

¾ cup farro

1 cup apple cider

1 cup low-sodium vegetable broth

1 bay leaf

Salt

3 cups arugula

1 large Granny Smith or Gala apple, diced or thinly sliced

½ cup chopped pecans or walnuts, toasted

1 to 2 ounces fresh goat cheese, crumbled

FOR THE CIDER VINAIGRETTE:

3 tablespoons extra-virgin olive oil

2 tablespoons minced shallot

2 tablespoons raw, unfiltered apple cider vinegar

1 teaspoon Dijon mustard

Salt and black pepper

1. Place the farro, apple cider, vegetable broth, bay leaf, and ½ teaspoon of salt in a medium saucepan and bring to a boil over high heat. Reduce the heat to low, cover, and let simmer until the farro is tender, 15 to 30 minutes (depending on the farro; check the package directions). Drain any remaining liquid, discard the bay leaf, and let cool.

2. Meanwhile, whisk together the olive oil, shallots, apple cider vinegar, and mustard in a small bowl. Season with salt and pepper to taste.

3. Place the cooked farro, arugula, and apple in a large serving bowl; drizzle with the vinaigrette and toss gently. Top with the pecans and goat cheese before serving.

MOJITO FRUIT SALAD

YIELD: 8 servings

Orange, lime, and mint give this fruit salad a mojito-esque vibe, but this mojito mixture serves another purpose, too. The acidity of the orange and lime juices helps keep the cut fruit fresh a little longer (not that that's much of a concern since this sweet and tangy fruit salad never lasts long).

¼ cup fresh orange juice

Zest and juice of 1 lime

¼ cup fresh mint, chopped

1 small pineapple, cored and cut into chunks

1 pound fresh strawberries, sliced or quartered

2 cups red grapes

4 kiwis, peeled, sliced into half-moons

1. Place the orange juice, lime zest and juice, and mint in a small bowl and mix well.

2. Place the pineapple, strawberries, grapes, and kiwi in a large bowl. Pour the juice mixture over top and mix gently until the fruit is evenly coated.

NOTE

You don't have to peel the kiwis! Sure, the skin is a little fuzzy, but it is edible (and surprisingly pleasant to eat) and packed with nutrients, particularly fiber, folate, and vitamin E. Just be sure to wash them first.

GLOWING GREEN SOUP

YIELD: 4 servings

Everyone needs a nourishing veggie-packed green soup in their recipe repertoire—you know, for when you're feeling a little under the weather or like you just need to reset. This is it, my friend. Made with a variety of green produce, including broccoli (both the florets and the stems) and flavorful fresh herbs, it'll make you feel like you're glowing from the inside out. And when it comes to protein, this green soup delivers when most others fall short. Each bowl provides 12 grams of plant protein, thanks to the cashews, peas, and even the broccoli!

1 cup raw cashews

1 teaspoon salt, divided

1 large head broccoli (about 1 pound)

1 tablespoon extra-virgin olive oil

1 small yellow onion, chopped

1 jalapeño pepper, seeded and chopped

3 cloves garlic, minced

4 cups reduced-sodium vegetable broth

4 cups fresh baby spinach

1 cup frozen green peas

¼ cup packed fresh basil leaves

¼ cup packed fresh mint leaves

¼ cup packed fresh parsley leaves

2 tablespoons fresh lemon juice

NUT-FREE: Serve without the cashew cream (it's still delicious without it) or top with a spoonful of plain Greek yogurt or unsweetened nondairy yogurt.

1. Place the cashews and ⅔ cup of water in a small microwave-safe bowl and microwave on high for 2 minutes. Alternatively, heat the cashews and water in a small saucepan over high heat just until they boil. Pour into a high-powered blender with ¼ teaspoon of the salt; cover and let sit while preparing the soup.

2. Slice the florets from the broccoli head, cutting as close to the base of the florets as you can; set aside. Slice the remaining slender stems and main stalk into thin coins.

3. Heat the olive oil in a large pot over medium heat. Add the onion, jalapeño, and broccoli stems and sauté until softened, about 5 minutes. Stir in the garlic and sauté until fragrant, about 30 seconds.

4. Add the broccoli florets, broth, and the remaining ¾ teaspoon of salt. Bring to a boil, then reduce the heat to medium-low and simmer until the broccoli is tender, about 10 minutes. Add the spinach and peas and cook until the spinach has wilted, stirring frequently, about 1 minute. Remove from the heat.

5. Blend the cashews until completely smooth. Transfer the cashew cream to a small bowl and set aside.

6. To the same blender, add the contents of the pot, fresh herbs, and lemon juice and blend until smooth. (You may have to do this in two batches. Be sure not to cover too tightly to allow the steam to escape.) Season with salt to taste. If the soup is too thick for your liking, add a splash of broth or water to thin it.

7. Serve the soup topped with the cashew cream. (I like to stir some in with my spoon.)

PLANT-POWERED FACT: At the time of my writing this book, chlorophyll supplements are taking social media by storm as the cure-all for a slew of conditions, promising cleared acne, weight loss, "detoxification," and more. If you're unfamiliar with chlorophyll, it's the phytonutrient responsible for the green hue of plants (and algae). Although research on chlorophyll—both in its natural and supplement forms—is lacking and the claims I just mentioned are very much unsubstantiated as of now, it has been shown to possess antioxidant properties and disease-fighting potential, much like other phytonutrients in the rainbow of plant pigments (see page 38). But do yourself a favor: Skip the droppersful of liquid chlorophyll and turn to food instead. Dark leafy greens are the champions of chlorophyll, so it's no surprise that spinach and parsley—main ingredients in this green soup—are two of the foods highest in it. (You'll get some from the other green vegetables and herbs in this soup, too.) Taking a food-first approach means you'll also benefit from the vitamins, minerals, fiber, and other phytonutrients these green foods have to offer.

FULLY LOADED PLANTAIN NACHOS

YIELD: 6 servings

Thinly sliced plantains crisp perfectly in the oven and serve as the base for these loaded nachos. It might seem odd to buy unripe, green produce, but the less ripe the plantains (the greener, the better), the higher the starch content, and the crispier the slices will get. They're topped with "unfried" beans, salsa verde, and your choice of additional protein: go 50/50 or keep it vegetarian. There's even a vegan/dairy-free option, so you can make these nachos to accommodate the dietary needs of anyone and everyone.

---

2 large green plantains, peeled

1 tablespoon avocado oil, extra-virgin olive oil, or melted coconut oil

½ teaspoon salt

1 batch "Unfried" Beans (below)

1 cup Easy Salsa Verde (page 156) or store-bought salsa verde, divided

1 cup shredded Monterey Jack cheese

1 large red bell pepper, chopped

1 medium avocado, halved, divided

⅓ cup Quick Pickled Onions (page 162) or diced red onion

Optional garnishes: fresh cilantro leaves and/or sliced jalapeño pepper

"UNFRIED" BEANS

1 (15-ounce) can pinto beans plus 2 tablespoons liquid from the can, remaining liquid drained and beans rinsed

1 tablespoon extra-virgin olive oil

1 clove garlic, roughly chopped

½ teaspoon ground cumin

½ teaspoon chili powder

¼ teaspoon salt

PICK YOUR PROTEIN:

Plant-Powered: 1 (15-ounce) can black beans, drained and rinsed

50/50: 1½ cups cooked and shredded chicken, or 8 to 10 ounces ground turkey or lean ground beef, browned and crumbled

1. Preheat the oven to 375°F. Line two sheet pans with parchment paper.

2. Use a mandoline or knife to slice the plantains ⅛ inch thick on the diagonal.

3. Place the plantain slices in a large bowl, drizzle with the oil, and toss until well coated. Arrange the slices in a single layer on the prepared sheet pans so that they don't overlap. Sprinkle with the salt.

4. Bake until slightly browned on the edges, 15 to 20 minutes, rotating the pans halfway through. Be sure to monitor them during the last few minutes because they will brown quickly! Remove from the oven and set aside. Increase the oven temperature to 425°F.

5. Meanwhile, make the "unfried" beans: Place all of the ingredients in a food processor and process until roughly pureed.

6. Place your protein of choice and ¼ cup of the salsa in a medium bowl and toss to coat.

7. Arrange all of the plantain chips on one of the lined pans. Distribute the unfried beans, protein of choice, cheese, and bell pepper evenly over the chips. Bake until the cheese is melted and bubbling, 5 to 7 minutes.

8. Meanwhile, pour the remaining ¾ cup of salsa into a blender with half of the avocado and blend until smooth. Dice the other half of the avocado.

9. Dollop the creamy salsa verde over the nachos and top with the diced avocado pickled onions, and, if desired, cilantro and/or jalapeño slices.

DAIRY-FREE/VEGAN: You can use nondairy shredded cheese in place of the Monterey Jack, but my recommendation is to use dollops of Plant-Powered Chipotle "Queso" (page 166).

CHEEZY TAHINI KALE CHIPS

YIELD: 3 to 4 servings

I know kale chips had their moment years ago, but I think it's time they made a comeback, like mom jeans and chunky sneakers. They're light, crispy, nutrient-dense, and can be full of flavor depending on how you season them. This version is sure to turn any kale hater into a kale lover (or at least a kale tolerator). Best enjoyed the day of!

1 large bunch curly kale, washed, stemmed, and dried thoroughly

2 tablespoons tahini

2 tablespoons nutritional yeast, plus more for serving

1 tablespoon extra-virgin olive oil

1 tablespoon fresh lemon juice

½ teaspoon garlic powder

½ teaspoon salt

1. Preheat the oven to 300°F and lightly grease two sheet pans with cooking spray or line them with parchment paper.

2. Tear or chop the kale leaves into 2-inch pieces and place in a large bowl.

3. In a small bowl, mix the remaining ingredients. Pour over the kale leaves and toss. Use your hands to gently massage the tahini mixture into the leaves so that they are evenly coated.

4. Arrange the coated leaves in a single layer on the prepared sheet pans. Bake until crispy, 20 to 25 minutes, rotating the pans halfway through. Let cool for about 5 minutes before enjoying. Sprinkle with additional salt and nutritional yeast, if desired.

CHICKPEA POPPERS

YIELD: 8 servings

These perfectly seasoned crispy roasted chickpeas are so versatile, you can enjoy them on their own as a fiber- and protein-packed snack or as a meal topper—think salads, soups, bowls, and more.

3 cups cooked chickpeas, or 2 (15-ounce) cans chickpeas, drained and rinsed

1½ tablespoons extra-virgin olive oil

1 teaspoon salt

1 tablespoon nutritional yeast

ONE OF THE FOLLOWING SEASONING BLENDS:

Nacho: ½ teaspoon each chili powder, ground cumin, garlic powder, onion powder, and paprika

Garlic Herb: 1 teaspoon salt-free Italian seasoning + 1 teaspoon garlic powder

1. Preheat the oven to 400°F.

2. Place the rinsed chickpeas on a clean, dry kitchen towel or paper towels and rub vigorously to dry them as much as possible, but try not to smush them. You'll remove some of the skins in the process; discard them. It's not necessary to remove all of the skins, but the chickpeas without skins will be slightly crispier.

3. Place the chickpeas on a large sheet pan and roast for 10 minutes. Remove the pan from the oven, add the oil, salt, and seasoning blend of choice, and toss to coat evenly. Return the pan to the oven and continue roasting until golden brown and crispy, 15 to 25 minutes, tossing every 10 minutes.

4. When done, immediately add the nutritional yeast to the hot chickpeas and toss to coat. Let sit for at least 5 minutes before eating.

5. The poppers are best enjoyed the day they're made but can be stored at room temperature in a jar or container with the lid cracked open just slightly for up to 5 days.

TIP

You can season these chickpea poppers with anything and everything. For a super easy ranch version, toss in 2 tablespoons dry ranch seasoning (omit the salt). Or, if you're feeling spicy, toss in 2 tablespoons dry Sriracha seasoning (omit the salt).

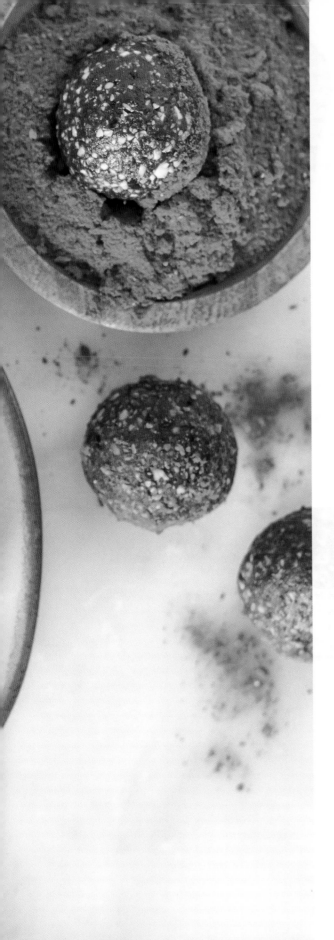

SOMETHING SWEET

BETTER BERRY CRUMBLE BARS

YIELD: 9 servings

Traditional crumbles and crumble bars may be made with fruit, but I wouldn't call them nutritious. So I created my Better Berry Crumble Bars, which are lightly sweetened (mostly from fruit) and pack in around 6 grams of protein and 5 grams of fiber per bar. (Not that you eat dessert with the intention of getting protein and fiber, but it's a nice bonus.)

2 cups rolled/old-fashioned oats, divided

1 cup blanched almond flour

⅓ cup unsweetened applesauce

¼ cup pure maple syrup

¼ cup coconut oil, melted

1 teaspoon pure vanilla extract

½ teaspoon baking powder

⅛ teaspoon salt

1 batch 10-Minute Any Berry Chia Jam (page 160)

1. Preheat the oven to 350°F. Line an 8-inch square baking pan with parchment paper.

2. Process 1 cup of the oats in a food processor or blender until they have a flourlike consistency. Transfer to a large bowl with the remaining 1 cup of oats, almond flour, applesauce, maple syrup, coconut oil, vanilla, baking powder, and salt and mix until well combined and the mixture has a crumbly texture.

3. Set aside a scant cup of the oat mixture, then press the rest into the bottom of the prepared pan. Top with the chia jam and spread into an even layer. Sprinkle the remainder of the oat mixture evenly over the top.

4. Bake until the topping is golden brown, 35 to 40 minutes. Let the bars cool *completely* in the pan before slicing (see note).

5. Store the leftover bars in a covered container in the refrigerator for up to 5 days.

NOTE

I know it's tough to wait to dive into the bars, but allowing them to cool completely in the pan helps them firm up so that they don't fall apart. I recommend putting them in the freezer for about 20 minutes or so once the pan is cool to the touch to speed cooling; then you can cut and eat them more quickly.

DATE CARAMEL CANDIES 2 WAYS

YIELD: 12 turtles or 16 squares

If fruit is "nature's candy," then dates are nature's caramel. Their soft and chewy texture, natural sweetness, and caramel-like flavor make them the perfect substitute for real caramel in these lightened-up yet decadent homemade "candies." Be warned: They are insanely delicious.

DATE CARAMEL BASE:

10 soft pitted Medjool dates

1 tablespoon unsweetened nut or seed butter of choice

½ teaspoon pure vanilla extract

FOR THE TURTLES:

36 raw pecan halves (about ½ cup)

½ cup dark chocolate chips

1 teaspoon coconut oil

Sea salt flakes, for topping

FOR THE PB PRETZEL SQUARES:

½ cup unsweetened peanut butter

1 tablespoon coconut flour

1½ teaspoons pure maple syrup

16 waffle pretzels

⅔ cup dark chocolate chips

1½ teaspoons coconut oil

Sea salt flakes, for topping

Make the caramel base: Place the dates in a small bowl and cover with hot water (about 1 cup, microwaved for 90 seconds); let sit for 10 minutes. Drain the dates well and transfer to a small food processor with the nut or seed butter and vanilla. Process until a thick and sticky "caramel" forms.

For the turtles: Assemble 12 clusters of pecan halves on a parchment-lined cookie sheet or small cutting board. Each cluster will have 3 pecan halves that touch in the middle to form a triangle to make the "legs" of the turtles. Using a spoon and your fingers, dollop the date caramel onto the center of each cluster without completely covering the pecans and press down gently. (You may want to wet your hands to prevent sticking.) Place the chocolate chips and coconut oil in a small microwave-safe bowl and microwave on high in 30-second increments until melted, then spoon over each turtle to cover the caramel. Lightly sprinkle the tops with sea salt flakes. Freeze to harden the chocolate, about 15 minutes.

For the PB pretzel squares: In a small bowl, stir together the peanut butter, coconut flour, and maple syrup. Arrange the pretzels on a parchment-lined cookie sheet or small cutting board and top with about 1½ teaspoons each of the peanut butter mixture followed by the date caramel, pressing down gently. Place in the freezer to firm up, 20 to 30 minutes. Place the chocolate chips and coconut oil in a small microwave-safe bowl and microwave on high in 30-second increments until melted, then use a fork to quickly dip each candy into the chocolate. Lightly sprinkle the tops with sea salt flakes. Freeze to harden the chocolate, about 15 minutes.

The turtles and the PB pretzel squares can be stored in an airtight container in the refrigerator for up to 1 week or in the freezer for up to 1 month. Let sit out for 5 to 10 minutes before consuming the frozen candies.

PLANT-POWERED FACT: Native to Morocco, Medjool dates—known as "the king of fruits"—are just one of over 200 varieties of dates. While Medjool dates are rich in natural sugars, they also rank high in antioxidant polyphenols and provide fiber and a variety of vitamins and minerals—particularly potassium and magnesium.

CHICKPEA HAZELNUT-ELLA

YIELD: 8 servings

This rich chocolate hazelnut hummus-style spread is inspired by THE greatest chocolate hazelnut spread of all time, Nutella. Serve it with sliced fruit, on toast or roasted sweet potato slices (see page 176), or eat it by the spoonful like you would the original (or is that just me?).

1 cup raw hazelnuts

1½ cups cooked chickpeas, or 1 (15-ounce) can chickpeas, drained and rinsed

½ cup canned full-fat or light coconut milk

⅓ cup unsweetened cocoa powder

⅓ cup pure maple syrup

2 teaspoons pure vanilla extract

⅛ teaspoon salt

1. Preheat the oven to 350°F.

2. Arrange the hazelnuts on a bare or parchment-lined sheet pan and roast until lightly toasted and fragrant, 8 to 10 minutes; let cool.

3. Process the toasted hazelnuts in a food processor until you get a consistency similar to that of a nut butter. (Be patient—this will take a couple of minutes!) Add the remaining ingredients and process until smooth and creamy. Stop blending periodically to scrape down the sides of the food processor.

4. Store in an airtight container in the refrigerator for up to 1 week.

OMEGA ENERGY BITES

YIELD: 12 balls (each flavor)

Energy bites are the ultimate make-ahead grab-and-go snack. Made from a base of dates and nuts, these bites will give you an energy boost from the dates' natural sugars along with some fiber and protein. Plus, you'll get a little dose of omega-3s from omega-3-rich seeds, like flax seed and hemp hearts. The Salted Brownie Bites are the omega-3 MVP because they're made with walnuts, which are one of the best plant-based omega-3 sources available. The two flavors provided are just the beginning—once you get bored with them, you can take the base recipe and get creative!

BASE INGREDIENTS:

1 cup raw walnut halves or cashews

3 tablespoons omega-3-rich seeds, such as chia seeds, ground flax seed, or hemp hearts

10 soft pitted Medjool dates

2 tablespoons unsweetened almond butter or other nut butter

1 teaspoon pure vanilla extract

Splash of unsweetened almond milk or water, as needed

FOR THE SALTED BROWNIE BITES:

Use walnut for the nut and ground flax seed for the seed.

3 tablespoons unsweetened cocoa powder

⅛ teaspoon salt

¼ teaspoon pure peppermint extract (optional, for a mint brownie flavor)

FOR THE STRAWBERRY SHORTCAKE BITES:

Use cashews for the nut and hemp hearts for the seed.

1 cup freeze-dried strawberries, plus more for rolling (optional)

1 tablespoon fresh lemon juice

Pinch of salt

1. Place the nuts and seeds in a food processor and process until the nuts are crumbly. Add the dates and process until broken apart. Add the remaining base ingredients as well as the ingredients for the flavor of your choice and continue processing until a thick, slightly sticky "dough" forms. (It might clump into a ball in the food processor and that's OK!) If the dough is too dry, add a splash of almond milk or water.

2. Remove the food processor blade, then scoop out the dough using your hands or a cookie scoop and roll into twelve 1-inch balls.

3. Optional for the Strawberry Shortcake Bites: process some freeze-dried strawberries in a food processor until they have a powderlike consistency. Roll some or all of the bites in the powder.

4. Store in an airtight container in the refrigerator for up to 1 week.

NOTE

When you start to experiment with other flavors of energy bites, you can use any type of raw nut.

CREAMY CHIA PUDDING 2 WAYS

YIELD: 2 to 3 servings

This simple, sweet snack takes on a puddinglike consistency thanks to fiber-rich chia seeds. You can sweeten the pudding entirely with fruit or add a little sweetener.

FOR THE BASE:

½ cup canned light or full-fat coconut milk

½ cup unsweetened nondairy milk

¼ cup chia seeds

1 tablespoon pure maple syrup or honey, or 2 to 3 soft pitted Medjool dates

1 teaspoon pure vanilla extract

Pinch of salt

FOR THE BANANA CREAM PIE VERSION:

2 small ripe bananas, 1 mashed, 1 sliced

½ teaspoon ground cinnamon

¼ cup unsweetened coconut flakes, raw or toasted (optional)

FOR THE CHOCOLATE RASPBERRY VERSION:

2 tablespoons unsweetened cocoa powder

½ cup fresh raspberries

¼ cup chopped walnuts or pecans, raw or toasted (optional)

Combine all of the base ingredients in a medium bowl. *If using dates, put them in a blender along with the milk and blend until completely broken down, then add to the bowl with the remaining ingredients.*

For the Banana Cream Pie version: Add the mashed banana to the bowl with the base ingredients. Sprinkle in the cinnamon and stir to combine.

For the Chocolate Raspberry version: Add the cocoa powder and stir to combine.

For both versions: Cover and let sit in the refrigerator for at least 1 to 2 hours or overnight to thicken. Top with the remaining ingredients for each version before serving.

TIP

Turn the flavor and sweetness of the Banana Cream Pie version up a notch by sautéing the sliced banana à la bananas foster before topping the pudding. When you cook a banana, its sugars start to caramelize, thereby enhancing its natural sweetness. It's easy: Heat 1 teaspoon of coconut oil or butter in a small skillet over medium heat. Add the banana slices and a pinch of cinnamon and sauté until golden, 2 to 3 minutes per side.

LEMON POPPY SEED ZUCCHINI MUFFINS

YIELD: 10 muffins

These gluten-free muffins are full of lemon flavor, lightly sweetened with honey, and perfectly moist—thanks to zucchini and olive oil, which add a healthy dose of phytonutrients and heart-healthy fats. Baking with olive oil might seem strange, but it adds a subtle flavor that helps bring out the taste of the other ingredients.

1 medium zucchini, grated

1 cup blanched almond flour

1 cup oat flour

1 teaspoon baking powder

½ teaspoon baking soda

⅛ teaspoon salt

2 large eggs

¼ cup honey

¼ cup extra-virgin olive oil

Grated zest and juice of 1 large lemon

1 teaspoon pure vanilla extract

1 tablespoon poppy seeds

1. Preheat the oven to 350°F and lightly grease or line 10 wells of a standard-size muffin pan.

2. Place the grated zucchini in a clean, thin dish towel or paper towels and squeeze out as much moisture as possible.

3. In a large bowl, stir together the almond flour, oat flour, baking powder, baking soda, and salt.

4. Add the eggs, honey, olive oil, lemon zest and juice, and vanilla to the bowl and stir until smooth. Stir in the zucchini and poppy seeds.

5. Divide the batter among the prepared wells of the muffin pan filling them about ⅔ full. Bake until a toothpick inserted into the center of a muffin comes out clean, 20 to 25 minutes.

6. Let the muffins cool for 10 to 15 minutes in the pan. Store in an airtight container at room temperature for up to 3 days.

NOTE

Don't have oat flour? Make your own using rolled oats! To make 1 cup oat flour, process about 1¼ cup rolled oats in a blender or food processor until you get a flourlike consistency.

SWEET POTATO TAHINI BROWNIES

YIELD: 12 brownies

Two antioxidant-rich foods unite in these secretly nutritious brownies that come out so decadent and fudgy, you'll forget there's a vegetable in them. Tahini is most often used in savory recipes, but I love the flavor it brings to chocolate-flavored sweets. Just be sure to use a smooth, drippy tahini—like from a new or recently opened jar and not the rock-solid bottom-of-an-old-jar stuff. Don't have/can't find tahini? Just swap it out for your nut butter of choice.

1 packed cup cooked sweet potato flesh (see note)

½ cup tahini

½ cup pure maple syrup

2 tablespoons coconut oil, melted

1 large egg or flax/chia egg (see page 138)

2 teaspoons pure vanilla extract

½ cup oat, white whole-wheat, all-purpose (regular or gluten-free), or spelt flour

⅓ cup unsweetened cocoa powder

1 teaspoon baking powder

¼ teaspoon salt

⅓ cup dark chocolate chips or chunks

1. Preheat the oven to 350°F. Line an 8-inch square baking pan with parchment paper.

2. Place the sweet potato, tahini, maple syrup, coconut oil, egg, and vanilla in a blender or food processor and blend until smooth.

3. In a large bowl, stir together the flour, cocoa powder, baking powder, and salt. Add the sweet potato mixture and stir until smooth. Fold in the chocolate chips.

4. Pour the batter into the prepared baking pan—it'll be thick, so you may need to smooth it out with a rubber spatula.

5. Bake until the edges are visibly baked through and the center is set, 27 to 30 minutes. Let cool completely before slicing and serving.

6. Store leftover brownies in an airtight container in the fridge for up to 5 days.

NOTE

You can make the cooked sweet potato one of two ways. For both methods, first pierce a medium sweet potato several times with a fork. To bake, preheat the oven to 425°F, wrap the sweet potato in foil, place on a sheet pan, and bake until tender, about 40 to 50 minutes. To microwave, place the sweet potato on a microwave-safe plate and microwave on high until tender, 5 to 7 minutes. For both methods, slice the cooked sweet potato down the center and open it to allow it to cool faster. Once mostly cooled, scoop out the flesh and measure 1 cup.

BANANA SPELT CINNAMON ROLLS

YIELD: 2 servings

Ever crave a warm cinnamon roll but don't have the energy or patience to whip up a batch? Well, there's no yeast, no rising, and no oven for these mug cinnamon rolls, so they're ready in 1 minute as opposed to 30. They're made with nutrient-rich spelt flour and banana to take the plant power (and the flavor) up a notch.

1 large ripe banana, divided

1 tablespoon unsweetened nondairy milk, plus more if needed

½ cup spelt flour, plus more for rolling and more for dough if needed

1 teaspoon baking powder

Pinch of salt

2 teaspoons coconut oil, melted

1 tablespoon brown or coconut sugar

½ teaspoon ground cinnamon

1 tablespoon regular or nondairy cream cheese, softened

1 teaspoon pure maple syrup

1. In a small bowl, mash about one-third of the banana until there are no lumps. Thinly slice the other piece of the banana and set aside.

2. Add the milk to the bowl with the banana and stir until smooth. Add the flour, baking powder, and salt and mix until you get a dough. If the dough is too dry and isn't sticking together well, add a splash of milk. If the dough is too wet and is sticking to your hands, add a little more flour.

3. Lightly flour a cutting board and roll out the dough into a rectangle, about ¼ inch thick. Brush the dough with the melted coconut oil and sprinkle with the sugar and cinnamon. Top with the banana slices, trying to keep them in a single layer without overlapping, and then roll the dough. Slice the dough log in half crosswise to make 2 rolls.

4. Transfer each roll to a shallow mug. Microwave both at the same time on high for 1 minute. If they appear wet on top, microwave for an additional 10 to 15 seconds.

5. Meanwhile, combine the cream cheese and maple syrup in a small bowl. Drizzle over the cinnamon rolls before eating.

REFERENCES

Chapter 2

Abumweis, S. S., R. Barake, and P. J. H. Jones, "Plant Sterols/ Stanols as Cholesterol Lowering Agents: A Meta-Analysis of Randomized Controlled Trials," *Food & Nutrition Research* 52 (2008): 1-.3402/fnr.v52i0.1811.

Al-Shaar, L., A. Satija, D. D. Wang, E. B. Rimm, S. A. Smith-Warner, M. J. Stampfer, F. B. Hu, and W. C. Willett, "Red Meat Intake and Risk of Coronary Heart Disease Among US Men: Prospective Cohort Study," *BMJ* 371 (2020): m4141.

American College of Cardiology and American Heart Association Task Force, "ACC/AHA Clinical Practice Guideline: 2019 ACC/AHA Guideline on the Primary Prevention of Cardiovascular Disease," *Circulation* 140 (2019): e596–e646.

Aune, D., D. S. M. Chan, R. Lau, R. Vieira, D. C. Greenwood, E. Kampman, and T. Norat, "Dietary Fibre, Whole Grains, and Risk of Colorectal Cancer: Systematic Review and Dose-Response Meta-Analysis of Prospective Studies," *BMJ* 343 (2011): d6617.

Baer, D. J., W. V. Rumpler, C. W. Miles, and G. C. Fahey, Jr., "Dietary Fiber Decreases the Metabolizable Energy Content and Nutrient Digestibility of Mixed Diets Fed to Humans," *Journal of Nutrition* 127, no. 4 (1997): 579–586.

Bell, E. A., V. H. Catellanos, C. L. Pelkman, M. L. Thorwart, and B. J. Rolls, "Energy Density of Foods Affects Energy Intake in Normal-Weight Women," *American Journal of Clinical Nutrition* 67, no. 3 (1998): 412–420.

Bernard, N. D. S. M. Levin, and Y. Yokoyama, "A Systematic Review and Meta-Analysis of Changes in Body Weight in Clinical Trials of Vegetarian Diets," *Journal of the Academy of Nutrition and Dietetics* 115, no. 6 (2015): 954–969.

Bernstein, A. M., Q. Sun, F. B. Hu, M. J. Stampfer, J. E. Manson, W. C. Willett, "Major Dietary Protein Sources and the Risk of Coronary Heart Disease in Women," *Circulation* 122, no. 9 (2010): 876–883.

Blackburn, G., "Effect of Degree of Weight Loss on Health Benefits," *Obesity* 3, no. S2 (1995): 221s–216s.

Bolte, L. A. et al., "Long-Term Dietary Patterns Are Associated with Pro-Inflammatory and Anti-Inflammatory Features of the Gut Microbiome," *Gut* 70 (2021): 1287–1298.

Bradbury, K. E., N. Murphy, and T. J. Key, "Diet and Colorectal Cancer in UK Biobank: A Prospective Study," *International Journal of Epidemiology* 49, no. 1 (2020): 246–258.

Brassard, D., et al., "Comparison of the Impact of SFAs from Cheese and Butter on Cardiometabolic Risk Factors: A Randomized Controlled Trial," *American Journal of Clinical Nutrition* 105, no. 4 (2017): 800–809.

Brinkworth, G. D., M. Noakes, P. M. Clifton, and A. R. Bird, "Comparative Effects of Very Low-Carbohydrate, High-Fat and High-Carbohydrate, Low-Fat Weight-Loss Diets on Bowel Habit and Faecal Short-Chain Fatty Acids and Bacterial Populations," *British Journal of Nutrition* 101, no. 10 (2009): 1493–1502.

Budhathoki, S., et al., "Association of Animal and Plant Protein Intake with All-Cause and Cause-Specific Mortality in a Japanese Cohort," *JAMA Internal Medicine* 179, no. 11 (2019): 1509–1518.

Buettner, D. and S. Skemp, "Blue Zones: Lessons from the World's Longest Lived," *American Journal of Lifestyle Medicine* 10, no. 5 (2016): 318–321.

Byrne, C. S., E. S. Chambers, D. J. Morrison, and G. Frost, "The Role of Short Chain Fatty Acids in Appetite Regulation and Energy Homeostasis," *International Journal of Obesity* 39, no. 9 (2015): 1331–1338.

Canfora, E. E., J. W. Jocken, and E. E. Blaak, "Short-Chain Fatty Acids in Control of Body Weight and Insulin Sensitivity," *Nature Reviews Endocrinology* 11 (2015): 577–591.

Cani, P. D., M. Osto, L. Geurts, and A. Everard, "Involvement of Gut Microbiota in the Development of Low-Grade Inflammation and Type 2 Diabetes Associated with Obesity," *Gut Microbes* 3, no. 4 (2012): 279–288.

Cena, H. and P. C. Calder, "Defining a Healthy Diet: Evidence for the Role of Contemporary Dietary Patterns in Health and Disease," *Nutrients* 12, no. 2 (2020): 334.

Centers for Disease Control and Prevention, "Heart Disease Facts," last updated September 8, 2020, https://www.cdc.gov/heartdisease/facts.htm.

Chai, B. C., J. R. van der Voort, K. Grofelnik, H. G. Eliasdottir, I. Klöss, and F. J. A. Perez-Cueto, "Which Diet Has the Least Environmental Impact on Our Planet? A Systematic Review of Vegan, Vegetarian and Omnivorous Diets," *Sustainability* 11, no. 15 (2019): 4110.

Chambers, E. S., D. J. Morrison, and G. Frost, "Control of Appetite and Energy Intake by SCFA: What Are the Potential Underlying

Mechanisms?" *Proceedings of the Nutrition Society* 74, no. 3 (2015): 328–336.

Chen, G.-C., D. B. Lv, Z. Pang, and Q.-F. Liu, "Red and Processed Meat Consumption and Risk of Stroke: A Meta-Analysis of Prospective Cohort Studies," *European Journal of Clinical Nutrition* 67 (2013): 91–95.

Cho, C. E., S. Taesuwan, O. V. Malysheva, E. Bender, N. F. Tulchinsky, J. Yan, J. L. Sutter, and M. A. Caudill, "Trimethylamine-N-oxide (TMAO) Response to Animal Source Foods Varies Among Healthy Young Men and Is Influenced by Their Gut Microbiota Composition: A Randomized Controlled Trial," *Molecular Nutrition & Food Research* 61, no. 1 (2017).

Choi, Y., N. Larson, L. M. Steffen, P. J. Schreiner, D. D. Gallaher, D. A. Duprez, J. M. Shikany, J. S. Rana, and D. R. Jacobs, Jr., "Plant-Centered Diet and Risk of Incident Cardiovascular Disease During Young to Middle Adulthood," *Journal of the American Heart Association* 10, no. 16 (2021): e020718.

Clarke, R., C. Frost, R. Collins, P. Appleby, and R. Peto, "Dietary Lipids and Blood Cholesterol: Quantitative Meta-Analysis of Metabolic Ward Studies," *BMJ* 314, no. 7074 (1997): 112–117.

Conceição de Oliveira, M., R. Sichieri, and R. V. Mozzer, "A Low-Energy-Dense Diet Adding Fruit Reduces Weight and Energy Intake in Women," *Appetite* 51, no. 2 (2008): 291–295.

Corrêa-Oliveira, R., J. L. Fachi, A. Vieira, F. T. Sato, and M. A. R. Vinolo, "Regulation of Immune Cell Function by Short-Chain Fatty Acids," *Clinical & Translational Immunology* 5, no. 4 (2016): e73.

Crowe, F. L., P. N. Appleby, R. C. Travis, and T. J. Key, "Risk of Hospitalization or Death from Ischemic Heart Disease Among British Vegetarians and Nonvegetarians: Results from the EPIC-Oxford Cohort Study," *American Journal of Clinical Nutrition* 97, no. 3 (2013): 597–603.

David, L. A., et al., "Diet Rapidly and Reproducibly Alters the Human Gut Microbiome," *Nature* 505 (2014): 449–563.

Davis, J. N., K. E. Alexander, E. E. Ventura, C. M. Toledo-Corral, and M. I. Goran, "Inverse Relation Between Dietary Fiber Intake and Visceral Adiposity in Overweight Latino Youth," *American Journal of Clinical Nutrition* 90, no. 5 (2009): 1160–1166.

Davis, J. N., V. A. Hodges, and M. B. Gillham, "Normal-Weight Adults Consume More Fiber and Fruit Than Their Age- and Height-Matched Overweight/Obese Counterparts," *Journal of the Academy of Nutrition and Dietetics* 106, no. 6 (2006): 833–840.

De Filippis, F., et al., "High-Level Adherence to a Mediterranean Diet Beneficially Impacts the Gut Microbiota and Associated Metabolome," *Gut* 65 (2016): 1812–1821.

de Oliveira Otto, M. C., D. Mazaffarian, D. Kromhout, A. G. Bertoni, C. T. Sibley, D. R. Jacobs, Jr., and J. A. Nettleton, "Dietary Intake of Saturated Fat by Food Source and Incident Cardiovascular Disease: The Multi-Ethnic Study of Atherosclerosis," *American Journal of Clinical Nutrition* 96, no. 2 (2012): 397–404.

Deehan, E. C. and J. Walter, "The Fiber Gap and the Disappearing Gut Microbiome: Implications for Human Nutrition," *Trends in Endocrinology & Metabolism* 27, no. 5 (2016): 239–242.

Dehgen, M., et al., "Association of Dairy Intake with Cardiovascular Disease and Mortality in 21 Countries from Five Continents (PURE): A Prospective Cohort Study," *The Lancet* 392, no. 10161 (2018): 2288–2297.

Den Besten, G., K. van Eunen, A. K. Groen, K. Venema, D.-J. Reijngoud, and B. M. Bakker, "The Role of Short-Chain Fatty Acids in the Interplay Between Diet, Gut Microbiota, and Host Energy Metabolism," *Journal of Lipid Research* 54, no. 9 (2013): 2325–2340.

Desai, M. S., et al., "A Dietary Fiber-Deprived Gut Microbiota Degrades the Colonic Mucus Barrier and Enhances Pathogen Susceptibility," *Cell* 167, no. 6 (2016): 1339–1353.e21.

Du, H., et al., "Dietary Fiber and Subsequent Changes in Body Weight and Waist Circumference in European Men and Women," *American Journal of Clinical Nutrition* 91, no. 2 (2010): 329–336.

Duncan, S. H., A. Belenguer, G. Holtrop, A. M. Johnstone, H. J. Flint, and G. E. Lobley, "Reduced Dietary Intake of Carbohydrates by Obese Subjects Results in Decreased Concentrations of Butyrate and Butyrate-Producing Bacteria in Feces," *Applied and Environmental Microbiology* 73, no. 4 (2007): 1073–1078.

Fung, K. Y. C., L. Cosgrove, T. Lockett, R. Head, and D. L. Topping, "A Review of Potential Mechanisms for the Lowering of Colorectal Oncogenesis by Butyrate," *British Journal of Nutrition* 108, no. 5 (2012): 820–831.

Gardner, C. D., et al., "Effect of Low-Fat vs. Low-Carbohydrate Diet on 12-Month Weight Loss in Overweight Adults and the Association with Genotype Pattern or Insulin Secretion," *JAMA* 319, no. 7 (2018): 667–679.

Glenn, A. J. and K. Lo, "Relationship Between a Plant-Based Dietary Portfolio and Risk of Cardiovascular Disease: Findings from the Women's Health Initiative Prospective Cohort Study," *Journal of the American Heart Association* 10, no. 16 (2021): 21515.

Guasch-Ferré, M., A. Satija, S. A. Blondin, M. Janixzewski, E. Emlen, L. E. O'Connor, W. W. Campbell, F. B. Hu, W. C. Willett, and M. J. Stampfer, "Meta-Analysis of Randomized Controlled Trials of Red Meat Consumption in Comparison with Various Comparison Diets on Cardiovascular Risk Factors," *Circulation* 139 (2019): 1828–1845.

Hall, K. D., et al., "Calorie for Calorie, Dietary Fat Restriction Results in More Body Fat Loss Than Carbohydrate Restriction in People with Obesity," *Cell Metabolism* 22, no. 3 (2015): 427–436.

Hall, K. D., et al., "Effect of a Plant-Based, Low-Fat Diet Versus an Animal-Based, Ketogenic Diet on Ad Libitum Energy Intake," *Nature Medicine* 27 (2021): 344–353.

Hall, K. D., et al., "Energy Expenditure and Body Composition Changes After an Isocaloric Ketogenic Diet in Overweight and

Obese Men," *American Journal of Clinical Nutrition* 104, no. 2 (2016): 324–333.

Harland, J. I. and L. E. Garton, "Whole-Grain Intake as a Marker of Healthy Body Weight and Adiposity," *Public Health Nutrition* 11, no. 6 (2008): 554–563.

Hein, S., A. R. Whyte, E. Wood, A. Rodriguez-Mateos, and C. M. Williams, "Systematic Review of the Effects of Blueberry on Cognitive Performance as We Age," *The Journals of Gerontology* 74, no. 7 (2019): 984–995.

Higgens, J. A., "Whole Grains, Legumes, and the Subsequent Meal Effect: Implications for Blood Glucose Control and the Role of Fermentation," *Journal of Nutrition and Metabolism* (2012): 829238.

Hills, Jr., R. D., B. A. Pontefract, H. R. Mishcon, C. A. Black, S. C. Sutton, and C. R. Theberge, "Gut Microbiome: Profound Implications for Diet and Disease," *Nutrients* 11, no. 7 (2019): 1613.

Howarth, N. C., E. Saltzman, and S. B. Roberts, "Dietary Fiber and Weight Regulation," *Nutrition Reviews* 59, no. 5 (2001): 129–139.

Huang, R.-Y., C.-C. Huang, F. B. Hu, and J. Chavarro, "Vegetarian Diets and Weight Reduction: A Meta-Analysis of Randomized Controlled Trials," *Journal of General Internal Medicine* 31, no. 1 (2016): 109–116.

Ibrügger, S., L. K. Vigsnæs, A. Blennow, D. Škuflić, A. Raben, L. Lauritzen, and M. Kristensen, "Second Meal Effect on Appetite and Fermentation of Wholegrain Rye Foods," *Appetite* 80 (2014), 248–256.

Institute of Medicine, *Dietary Reference Intakes for Energy, Carbohydrate, Fiber, Fat, Fatty Acids, Cholesterol, Protein, and Amino Acids* (Washington, DC: The National Academies Press, 2005).

Kahleova, H., S. Levin, and N. Barnard, "Cardio-Metabolic Benefits of Plant-Based Diets," *Nutrients* 9, no. 8 (2017): 848.

Koeth, R. A., et al., "Intestinal Microbiota Metabolism of L-carnitine, a Nutrient in Red Meat, Promotes Atherosclerosis," *Nature Medicine* 19, no. 5 (2013): 576–585.

Krikorian, R., M. D. Shidler, T. A. Nash, W. Kalt, M. R. Vinqvist-Tymchuk, B. Shukitt-Hale, and J. A. Joseph, "Blueberry Supplementation Improves Memory in Older Adults," *Journal of Agricultural and Food Chemistry* 58, no. 7 (2010): 3996–4000.

Kristensen, M. and M. G. Jensen, "Dietary Fibres in the Regulation of Appetite and Food Intake. Importance of Viscosity," *Appetite* 56, no. 1 (2011): 65–70.

Landfald, B., J. Valeur, A. Berstad, and J. Raa, "Microbial Trimethylamine-N-oxide as a Disease Marker: Something Fishy?" *Microbial Ecology in Health and Disease* 28, no. 1 (2017): 1327309.

Lattimer, J. M. and M. D. Haub, "Effects of Dietary Fiber and Its Components on Metabolic Health," *Nutrients* 2, no. 12 (2010): 1266–1289.

Lau, K., V. Srivatsav, A. Rizwan, A. Nashed, R. Liu, R. Shen, and M. Akhtar, "Bridging the Gap Between Gut Microbial Dysbiosis and Cardiovascular Diseases," *Nutrients* 9, no. 8 (2017): 859.

Li, Y., et al., "Saturated Fats Compared with Unsaturated Fats and Sources of Carbohydrates in Relation to Risk of Coronary Heart Disease: A Prospective Cohort Study," *Journal of the American College of Cardiology* 66, no. 14 (2016): 1538–1548.

Martínez-González, M. A., et al., "A Provegetarian Food Pattern and Reduction in Total Mortality in the Prevención con Dieta Mediterránea (PREDIMED) Study," *American Journal of Clinical Nutrition* 100, no. suppl_1 (2014): 320S–328S.

McCullough, M. L., "Diet Patterns and Mortality: Common Threads and Consistent Results," *Journal of Nutrition* 144, no. 6 (2014): 795–796.

McDonald, D., et al., "American Gut: An Open Platform for Citizen Science Microbiome Research," *mSystems* 3, no. 3 (2018): e0031–18.

Morowitz, M. J., E. Carlisle, and J. C. Alverdy, "Contributions of Intestinal Bacteria to Nutrition and Metabolism in the Critically Ill," *Surgical Clinics of North America* 91, no. 4 (2011): 771–785.

Morris, M. C., C. C. Tangney, Y. Wang, F. M. Sacks, D. A. Bennett, and N. T. Aggarwal, "MIND Diet Associated with Reduced Incidence of Alzheimer's Disease," *Alzheimer's & Dementia Journal* 11, no. 9 (2015): 1007–1014.

Morris, M. C., C. C. Tangney, Y. Wang, F. M. Sacks, D. A. Bennett, and N. T. Aggarwal, "MIND Diet Slows Cognitive Decline with Aging," *Alzheimer's & Dementia Journal* 11, no. 9 (2015): 1015–1022.

Morris, M. C., Y. Wang, L. L. Barnes, D. A. Bennett, B. Dawson-Hughes, and S. L. Booth, "Nutrients and Bioactives in Green Leafy Vegetables and Cognitive Decline," *Neurology* 90, no. 3 (2018): e214–e222.

Morrison, D. and T. Preston, "Formation of Short Chain Fatty Acids by the Gut Microbiota and Their Impact on Human Metabolism," *Gut Microbes* 7, no. 3 (2016): 189–200.

Neelakantan, N., J. Y. H. Seah, and R. M. van Dam, "The Effect of Coconut Oil Consumption on Cardiovascular Risk Factors," *Circulation* 141, no. 10 (2020): 803–814.

Nestel, P. J., A. Chronopulos, and M. Cehun, "Dairy Fat in Cheese Raises LDL Cholesterol Less Than That in Butter in Mildly Hypercholesterolaemic Subjects," *European Journal of Clinical Nutrition* 59 (2005): 1059–1063.

Newby, P. K., K. L. Tucker, and A. Wolk, "Risk of Overweight and Obesity Among Semivegetarian, Lactovegetarian, and Vegan Women," *American Journal of Clinical Nutrition* 81, no. 6 (2005): 1267–1274.

O'Keefe, S. J. D., "Fat, Fiber and Cancer Risk in African Americans and Rural Africans," *Nature Communications* 6 (2015): 6342.

Orlich, M. J., P. N. Singh, J. Sabaté, K. Jaceldo-Siegl, J. Fan, S. Knutsen, W. L. Beeson, and G. E. Fraser, "Vegetarian Dietary Patterns and Mortality in Adventist Health Study 2," *JAMA Internal Medicine* 173, no. 13 (2013): 1230–1238.

Ou, J., F. Carbornero, E. G. Zoetendal, J. P. DeLany, M. Wang, K. Newton, H. R. Gaskins, and S. J. D. O'Keefe, "Diet, Microbiota, and Microbial Metabolites in Colon Cancer Risk in Rural Africans and African Americans," *American Journal of Clinical Nutrition* 98, no. 1 (2013): 111–120.

Pan, A., Q. Sun, A. M. Bernstein, M. B. Schulze, J. E. Manson, M. J. Stampfer, W. C. Willett, and F. B. Hu, "Red Meat Consumption and Mortality: Results from Two Prospective Cohort Studies," *JAMA Internal Medicine* 173, no. 7 (2012): 555–563.

Pan, A., Q. Sun, A. M. Bernstein, M. B. Schulze, J. E. Manson, W. C. Willett, and F. B. Hu, "Red Meat Consumption and Risk of Type 2 Diabetes: 3 Cohorts of US Adults and an Updated Meta-Analysis," *American Journal of Clinical Nutrition* 94, no. 4 (2011): 1088–1096.

Papanikolaou, Y. and F. L. Fulgoni III, "Bean Consumption Is Associated with Greater Nutrient Intake, Reduced Systolic Blood Pressure, Lower Body Weight, and a Smaller Waist Circumference in Adults: Results from the National Health and Nutrition Examination Survey 1999–2002," *Journal of the American College of Nutrition* 27, no. 5 (2008): 569–576.

Pérez-Escamilla, R., J. E. Obbagy, J. M. Altman, Y. P. Wong, J. M. Spahn, and C. L. Williams, "Dietary Energy Density and Body Weight in Adults and Children: A Systematic Review," *Journal of the Academy of Nutrition and Dietetics* 112, no. 5 (2012): 671–684.

Pimentel, D. and M. Pimentel, "Sustainability of Meat-Based and Plant-Based Diets and the Environment," *American Journal of Clinical Nutrition* 78, no. 3 (2003): 660S–663S.

Quagliani, D. and P. Felt-Gunderson, "Closing America's Fiber Intake Gap," *American Journal of Lifestyle Medicine* 11, no. 1 (2017): 80–85.

Rock, C. L., et al., "American Cancer Society Guideline for Diet and Physical Activity for Cancer Prevention," *CA: A Cancer Journal for Clinicians* 70, no. 4 (2020).

Rolls, B. J., "The Relationship Between Dietary Energy Density and Energy Intake," *Physiology & Behavior* 97, no. 5 (2009): 609–615.

Rolls, B. J., L. S. Roe, and J. S Meengs, "Reductions in Portion Size and Energy Density of Foods Are Additive and Lead to Sustained Decreases in Energy Intake," *American Journal of Clinical Nutrition* 83, no. 1 (2006): 11–17.

Rosell, M., P. Appleby, E. Spencer, and T. Key, "Weight Gain over 5 Years in 21,966 Meat-Eating, Fish-Eating, Vegetarian, and Vegan Men and Women in EPIC-Oxford," *International Journal of Obesity* 30 (2006): 1389–1396.

Russell, W. R., et al., "High-Protein, Reduced-Carbohydrate Weight-Loss Diets Promote Metabolite Profiles Likely to Be Detrimental to Colonic Health," *American Journal of Clinical Nutrition* 93, no. 5 (2011): 1062–1072.

Satija, A., S. N. Bhupathiraju, E. B. Rimm, D. Spiegelman, S. E. Chiuve, L. Borgi, W. C. Willett, J. E. Manson, Q. Sun, and F. B. Hu, "Plant-Based Dietary Patterns and Incidence of Type 2 Diabetes in US Men and Women: Results from Three Prospective Cohort Studies," *PLoS Medicine* 13, no. 6 (2016): e1002039.

Satija, A., S. N. Bhupathiraju, D. Spiegelman, S. E. Chiuve, J. E. Manson, W. C. Willett, K. M. Rexrode, E. B. Rimm, and F. B. Hu, "Healthful and Unhealthful Plant-Based Diets and the Risk of Coronary Heart Disease in US Adults," *Journal of the American College of Cardiology* 70, no. 4 (2017): 411–422.

Satija, A. and F. B. Hu, "Plant-Based Diets and Cardiovascular Health," *Trends in Cardiovascular Medicine* 28, no. 7 (2018): 437–441.

Schulze, M. B., M. Schulz, C. Heidemann, A. Schienkiewitz, K. Hoffmann, and H. Boeing, "Fiber and Magnesium Intake and Incidence of Type 2 Diabetes," *JAMA Internal Medicine* 167, no. 9 (2007): 956–965.

Sedlak, T. W., et al., "Sulforaphane Augments Glutathione and Influences Brain Metabolites in Human Subjects: A Clinical Pilot Study," *Molecular Neuropsychiatry* 3, no. 4 (2018): 214–222.

Sender, R., S. Fuchs, and R. Milo, "Revised Estimates for the Number of Human and Bacteria Cells in the Body," *PLoS Biology* 14, no. 8 (2016): e1002533.

Silva, Y. P., A. Bernardi, and R. L. Frozza, "The Role of Short-Chain Fatty Acids from Gut Microbiota in Gut-Brain Communication," *Frontiers in Endocrinology* 11 (2020): 25.

Song, M., T. T. Fung, F. B. Hu, W. C. Willett, V. Longo, A. T. Chan, and E. L. Giovannucci, "Animal and Plant Protein Intake and All-Cause and Cause-Specific Mortality: Results from Two Prospective US Cohort Studies," *JAMA Internal Medicine* 176, no. 10 (2016): 1453–1463.

Sonnenburg, E. D. and J. L. Sonnenburg, "Starving Our Microbial Self: The Deleterious Consequences of a Diet Deficient in Microbiota-Accessible Carbohydrates," *Cell Metabolism* 20, no. 5 (2014): 779–786.

Sonnenburg, J. L. and F. Bäckhed, "Diet-Microbiota Interactions and Moderators of Human Metabolism," *Nature* 535, no. 7610 (2016): 56–64.

Springmann, M., et al., "Options for Keeping the Food System Within Environmental Limits," *Nature* 562 (2018): 519–525.

Streppel, M. T., L. R. Arends, P. van't Veer, D. E. Grobbee, and J. M. Geleijnse, "Dietary Fiber and Blood Pressure: A Meta-Analysis of Randomized Placebo-Controlled Trials," *JAMA Internal Medicine* 165, no. 2 (2005): 150–156.

Tang, W. H. W., Z. Wang, B. S. Levison, R. A. Koeth, E. B. Britt, X. Fu, Y. Wu, and S. L. Hazen, "Intestinal Microbial Metabolism of Phosphatidylcholine and Cardiovascular Risk," *New England Journal of Medicine* 368 (2013): 1575–1584.

Threapleton, D. E., D. C. Greenwood, C. E. L. Evans, C. L. Cleghorn, C. Nykjaer, C. Woodhead, J. E. Cade, C. P. Gale, and V. J. Burley, "Dietary Fibre Intake and Risk of Cardiovascular Disease: Systematic Review and Meta-Analysis," *BMJ* 347 (2013): f6879.

Tomova, A., I. Bukovsky, E. Rembert, W. Yonas, J. Alwarith, N. D. Barnard, and H. Kahleova, "The Effects of Vegetarian and Vegan Diets on Gut Microbiota," *Frontiers in Nutrition* 6 (2019): 47.

Tonstad, S., T. Butler, R. Yan, and G. E. Fraser, "Type of Vegetarian Diet, Body Weight, and Prevalence of Type 2 Diabetes," *Diabetes Care* 32, no. 5 (2009): 791–796.

Tonstad, S., K. Stewart, K. Oda, M. Batech, R. P. Herring, and G. E. Fraser, "Vegetarian Diets and Incidence of Diabetes in the Adventist Health Study-2," *Nutrition, Metabolism & Cardiovascular Diseases* 23, no. 4 (2013): 292–299.

US Environmental Protection Agency, "Greenhouse Gas Emissions: Overview of Greenhouse Gases," accessed June 2, 2021, https://www.epa.gov/ghgemissions/overview-greenhouse-gases.

Valdes, A. M., J. Walter, E. Segal, and T. D. Spector, "Role of the Gut Microbiota in Nutrition and Health," *BMJ* 361 (2018), k2179.

Venegas, D. P., J. K. De la Fuente, G. Landskron, M. J. González, R. Quera, G. Dijkstra, H. J. M. Harmsen, K. N. Faber, and M. A. Hermoso, "Short Chain Fatty Acids (SCFAs)-Mediated Gut Epithelial and Immune Regulation and Its Relevance for Inflammatory Bowel Diseases," *Frontiers in Immunology* 10 (2019): 277.

Vighi, G., F. Marcucci, L. Sensi, G. Di Cara, and F. Frati, "Allergy and the Gastrointestinal System," *Clinical & Experimental Immunology* 154, no. Suppl 1 (2008): 3–6.

Wang, B., M. Yao, L. Lv, Z. Ling, and L. Li, "The Human Microbiota in Health and Disease," *Engineering* 3, no. 1 (2017): 71–82.

Wang, D. D., Y. Li, S. E. Chiuve, M. J. Stampfer, J. E. Manson, E. B. Rimm, W. C. Willett, and F. B. Hu, "Specific Dietary Fats in Relation to Total and Cause-Specific Mortality," *JAMA Internal Medicine* 176, no. 8 (2016): 1134–1145.

Wang, F., J. Zheng, B. Yang, J. Jiang, Y. Fu, and D. Li, "Effects of Vegetarian Diets on Blood Lipids: A Systematic Review and Meta-Analysis of Randomized Controlled Trials," *Journal of the American Heart Association* 4, no. 10 (2015): e002408.

Wang, X., X. Lin, Y. Y. Ouyang, J. Liu, G. Zhao, A. Pan, and F. B. Hu, "Red and Processed Meat Consumption and Mortality: Dose-Response Meta-Analysis of Prospective Cohort Studies," *Public Health Nutrition* 19, no. 5 (2016): 893–905.

World Cancer Research Fund/American Institute for Cancer Research, *Diet, Nutrition, Physical Activity and Cancer: A Global Perspective. Continuous Update Project Expert Report 2018.* https://www.wcrf.org/wp-content/uploads/2021/02/Summary-of-Third-Expert-Report-2018.pdf.

World Health Organization, "Cardiovascular Diseases Data and Statistics," accessed June 2, 2021, https://www.euro.who.int/en/health-topics/noncommunicable-diseases/cardiovascular-diseases/data-and-statistics.

J. Ranganathan, D. Vennard, R. Waite, P. Dumas, B. Lipinski, and T. Searchinger, "Shifting Diets for a Sustainable Food Future," Working Paper, Installment 11 of *Creating a Sustainable Food Future.* Washington, DC: World Resources Institute. Accessible at http://www.worldresourcesreport.org.

Yeoh, Y. K., et al., "Gut Microbiota Composition Reflects Disease Severity and Dysfunctional Immune Responses in Patients with COVID-19," *Gut* 70 (2021): 698–706.

Yokoyama, Y., K. Nishimura, N. D. Barnard, M. Takegami, M. Watanabe, A. Sekikawa, T. Okamura, and Y. Miyamoto, "Vegetarian Diets and Blood Pressure: A Meta-Analysis," *JAMA Internal Medicine* 174, no. 4 (2014): 577–587.

Zheng, D., T. Liwinski, and E. Elinav, "Interaction Between Microbiota and Immunity in Health and Disease," *Cell Research* 30 (2020): 492–506.

Zhong, V. W., L. Van Horn, P. Greenland, M. R. Carnethon, H. Ning, J. T. Wilkings, D. M. Lloyd-Jones, and N. B. Allen, "Associations of Processed Meat, Unpressed Red Meat, Poultry, or Fish Intake with Incident Cardiovascular Disease and All-Cause Mortality," *JAMA Internal Medicine* 180, no. 4 (2020): 503–512.

Zong, G., Y. Li, L. Sampson, L. W. Dougherty, W. C. Willett, A. J. Wanders, M. Alssema, P. L. Zock, F. B. Hu, and Q. Sun, "Monounsaturated Fats from Plant and Animal Sources in Relation to Risk of Coronary Heart Disease Among US Men and Women," *American Journal of Clinical Nutrition* 107, no. 3 (2018): 445–453.

Chapter 3

Bhatt, D. L., et al., "Cardiovascular Risk Reduction with Icosapent Ethyl for Hypertriglyceridemia," *New England Journal of Medicine* 380 (2019): 11–22.

Bouzari, A., D. Holstege, and D. M. Barrett, "Vitamin Retention in Eight Fruits and Vegetables: A Comparison of Refrigerated and Frozen Storage," *Journal of Agricultural and Food Chemistry* 63, no. 3 (2015): 957–962.

Bradbury, J., "Docosahexaenoic Acid (DHA): An Ancient Nutrient for the Modern Human Brain," *Nutrients* 3, no. 5 (2011): 529–554.

Davis, B. C. and P. M. Kris-Etherton, "Achieving Optimal Essential Fatty Acid Status in Vegetarians: Current Knowledge and Practical Implications," *American Journal of Clinical Nutrition* 78, no. 3 (2003): 640S–646S.

De Palma, G., I. Nadal, M. C. Collado, and Y. Sanz, "Effects of a Gluten-Free Diet on Gut Microbiota and Immune Function in Healthy Adult Humans," *Gut Microbes* 1, no. 3 (2010): 135–137.

Dewanto, V., X. Wu, K. K. Adom, and R. H. Liu, "Thermal Processing Enhances the Nutritional Value of Tomatoes by Increasing Total Antioxidant Activity," *Journal of Agricultural and Food Chemistry* 50, no. 10 (2002): 3010–3014.

Elango, R., M. A. Humayun, R. O. Ball, and P. B. Pencharz, "Evidence That Protein Requirements Have Been Significantly Underestimated," *Current Opinion in Clinical Nutrition and Metabolic Care* 13, no. 1 (2010): 52–57.

Etamadi, A., R. Sinha, M. H. Ward, B. I. Graubard, M. Inoue-Choi, S. M. Dawsey, and C. C. Abnet, "Mortality from Different Causes Associated with Meat, Heme Iron, Nitrates, and Nitrites in the NIH-AARP Diet and Health Study: Population Based Cohort Study," *BMJ* 357 (2017): j1957.

Jenkins, D. J. A., S. B. Mejia, L. Chiavaroli, E. Viguiliouk, S. S. Li, C. W. C. Kendall, V. Vuksan, and J. L. Sievenpiper, "Cumulative Meta-Analysis of the Soy Effect over Time," *Journal of the American Heart Association* 8, no. 13 (2019): e012458.

Kris-Etherton, P. M., W. S. Harris, and L. J. Appel, "Omega-3 Fatty Acids and Cardiovascular Disease," *Arteriosclerosis, Thrombosis, and Vascular Biology* 23 (2003): 151–152.

Lebwohl, B., et al., "Long Term Gluten Consumption in Adults Without Celiac Disease and Risk of Coronary Heart Disease: Prospective Cohort Study," *BMJ* 357 (2017): j1892.

Li, L., R. B. Pegg, R. R. Eitenmiller, J.-Y. Chun, and A. L. Kerrihard, "Selected Nutrient Analyses of Fresh, Fresh-Stored, and Frozen Fruits and Vegetables," *Journal of Food Composition and Analysis* 59 (2017): 8–17.

Lorenzson, V. and W. A. Olsen, "In Vivo Responses of Rat Intestinal Epithelium to Intraluminal Dietary Lectins," *Gastroenterology* 82, no. 5 Pt. 1 (1982): 838–848.

Mariotti, F. and C. D. Gardner, "Dietary Protein and Amino Acids in Vegetarian Diets—A Review," *Nutrients* 11, no. 11 (2019): 2661.

Mayo, B., L. Vázquez, and A. B. Flórez, "Equol: A Bacterial Metabolite from the Daidzein Isoflavone and Its Presumed Beneficial Health Effects," *Nutrients* 11, no. 9 (2019): 2231.

Meija, S. B., et al., "A Meta-Analysis of 46 Studies Identified by the FDA Demonstrates That Soy Protein Decreases Circulating LDL and Total Cholesterol Concentrations in Adults," *Journal of Nutrition* 149, no. 6 (2019): 968–981.

Miller, S. R. and W. A. Knudson, "Nutrition and Cost Comparisons of Select Canned, Frozen, and Fresh Fruits and Vegetables," *American Journal of Lifestyle Medicine* 8, no. 6 (2014): 430–437.

The National Academies of Sciences, Engineering, and Medicine, *Genetically Engineered Crops: Experiences and Prospects* (Washington, DC: National Academies Press, 2016).

Rickman, J. C., D. M. Barrett, and C. M. Bruhn, "Nutritional Comparison of Fresh, Frozen and Canned Fruits and Vegetables. Part 1. Vitamins C and B and Phenolic Compounds," *Journal of the Science of Food and Agriculture* 82, no. 6 (2007): 930–944.

Saunders, A. V., W. J. Craig, and S. K. Baines, "Zinc and Vegetarian Diets," *Medical Journal of Australia* 199, no. 4 (2013): S17–S21.

Shi, L., S. D. Arntfield, and M. Nickerson, "Changes in Levels of Phytic Acid, Lectins and Oxalates During Soaking and Cooking of Canadian Pulses," *Food Research International* 107 (2018): 660–668.

Shwarma, S. P., H. J. Chung, H. J. Kim, and S. T. Hong, "Paradoxical Effects of Fruit on Obesity," *Nutrients* 8, no. 10 (2016): 633.

Simon, S., "Soy and Cancer Risk: Our Expert's Advice," American Cancer Society website, April 29, 2019, https://www.cancer.org/latest-news/soy-and-cancer-risk-our-experts-advice.html/.

United States Department of Agriculture, *Pesticide Data Program, Annual Summary, Calendar Year 2019,* Agricultural Marketing Service, October 2020, https://www.ams.usda.gov/sites/default/files/media/2019PDPAnnualSummary.pdf.

Vasconcelos, I. M. and J. T. A. Oliveira, "Antinutritional Properties of Plant Lectins," *Toxicon* 44, no. 4 (2004): 385–403.

Winter, C. K. and J. M. Katz, "Dietary Exposure to Pesticide Residues from Commodities Alleged to Contain the Highest Contamination Levels," *Journal of Toxicology* 2011 (2011): 589674.

World Health Organization, "Antibiotic Resistance," World Health Organization website, July 31, 2020, https://www.who.int/news-room/fact-sheets/detail/antibiotic-resistance.

World Health Organization, "Food, Genetically Modified," World Health Organization website, accessed June 3, 2021, https://www.who.int/health-topics/food-genetically-modified#tab=tab_1.

Yau, T., X. Dan, C. C. W. Ng, and T. B. Ng, "Lectins with Potential for Anti-Cancer Therapy," *Molecules* 20, no. 3 (2015): 3791–3810.

Chapter 4

Asnicar, F., et al., "Microbiome Connections with Host Metabolism and Habitual Diet from 1,098 Deeply Phenotyped Individuals," *Nature Medicine* 27, no. 2 (2021): 321–322.

Aune, D., D. S. M. Chan, R. Lau, R. Vieira, D. C. Greenwood, E. Kampman, and T. Norat, "Dietary Fibre, Whole Grains, and Risk of Colorectal Cancer: Systematic Review and Dose-Response Meta-Analysis of Prospective Studies," *BMJ* 353 (2011): d6617.

Aune, D., N. Keum, E. Giovannucci, L. T. Fadnes, P. Boffetta, D. C. Greenwood, S. Tonstad, L. J. Vatten, E. Riboli, and T. Norat, "Nut Consumption and Risk of Cardiovascular Disease, Total Cancer, All-Cause and Cause-Specific Mortality: A Systematic Review and Dose-Response Meta-Analysis of Prospective Studies," *BMC Medicine* 14, no. 1 (2016): 207.

Aune, D., N. Keum, E. Giovannucci, L. T. Fadnes, P. Boffetta, D. C. Greenwood, S. Tonstad, L. J. Vatten, E. Riboli, and T. Norat, "Whole Grain Consumption and Risk of Cardiovascular Disease, Cancer, and All Cause and Cause Specific Mortality: Systematic Review and Dose-Response Meta-Analysis of Prospective Studies," *BMJ* Jun 14 (2016): 353.

Aune, D., T. Norat, P. Romundstad, and L. J. Vatten, "Whole Grain and Refined Grain Consumption and the Risk of Type 2 Diabetes: A Systematic Review and Dose-Response Meta-Analysis of Cohort Studies," *European Journal of Epidemiology* 28, no. 11 (2013): 845–858.

Bäckhed, F., C. M. Fraser, Y. Ringel, M. E. Sanders, R. B. Sartor, P. M. Sherman, J. Versalovic, V. Young, and B. B. Finlay, "Defining a Healthy Human Gut Microbiome: Current Concepts, Future Directions, and Clinical Applications," *Cell Host & Microbe* 12, no. 5 (2012): 611–622.

Baer, D. J., S. K. Gebauer, and J. A. Novotny, "Walnuts Consumed by Healthy Adults Provide Less Available Energy Than Predicted by the Atwater Factors," *Journal of Nutrition* 146, no. 1 (2016): 9–13.

Bamberger, C., A. Rossmeier, K. Lechner, L. Wu, E. Waldmann, S. Fischer, R. G. Stark, J. Altenhofer, K. Henze, and K. G. Parhofer, "A Walnut-Enriched Diet Affects Gut Microbiome in Healthy Caucasian Subjects: A Randomized, Controlled Trial," *Nutrients* 10, no. 2 (2018): 244.

Bao, Y., J. Han, F. B. Hu, E. L. Giovannucci, M. J. Stampfer, W. C. Willett, and C. S. Fuchs, "Association of Nut Consumption with Total and Cause-Specific Mortality," *New England Journal of Medicine* 369 (2013): 2001–2011.

Bazzano, L. A., A. M. Thompson, M. T. Tees, C. H. Nguyen, and D. M. Winham, "Non-Soy Legume Consumption Lowers Cholesterol Levels: A Meta-Analysis of Randomized Controlled Trials," *Nutrition, Metabolism & Cardiovascular Diseases* 21, no. 2 (2011): 94–103.

Carlson, J. L., J. M. Erickson, B. B. Lloyd, and J. L. Slavin, "Health Effects and Sources of Prebiotic Dietary Fiber," *Current Developments in Nutrition* 2, no. 3 (2018): nzy005.

Chun, O. K., N. Smith, A. Sakagawa, and C. Y. Lee, "Antioxidant Properties of Raw and Processed Cabbages," *International Journal of Food Sciences and Nutrition* 55, no. 3 (2004): 191–199.

Clifford, M. N., "Diet-Derived Phenols in Plasma and Tissues and Their Implications for Health," *Planta Medica* 70, no. 12 (2004): 1103–1114.

Derrien, M. and J. E. T. van Hylckama Vlieg, "Fate, Activity, and Impact of Ingested Bacteria Within the Human Gut Microbiota," *Trends in Microbiology* 23, no. 6 (2015): 354–366.

Dovani-Davari, D., M. Negahdaripour, I. Karimzadeh, M. Seifan, M. Mohkam, S. J. Masoumi, A. Berenjian, and Y. Ghasemi, "Prebiotics: Definition, Types, Sources, Mechanisms, and Clinical Applications," *Foods* 8, no. 3 (2019): 92.

Fantino, M., C. Bichard, F. Mistretta, and F. Bellisle. "Daily Consumption of Pistachios over 12 Weeks Improves Dietary Profile Without Increasing Body Weight in Healthy Women: A Randomized Controlled Intervention," *Appetite* 144 (2020): 104483.

Gausch-Ferré, M., X. Liu, V. S. Malik, Q. Sun, W. C. Willett, J. E. Manson, K. M. Rexrode, Y. Li, F. B. Hu, and S. N. Bhupathiraju, "Nut Consumption and Risk of Cardiovascular Disease," *Journal of the American College of Cardiology* 70, no. 20 (2017): 2519–2532.

Gibson, G. R., et al., "Expert Consensus Document: The International Scientific Association for Probiotics and Prebiotics (ISAPP) Consensus Statement on the Definition and Scope of Prebiotics," *Nature Reviews Gastroenterology & Hepatology* 14 (2017): 491–502.

Guarneiri, L. L., C. M. Paton, and J. A. Cooper, "Pecan-Enriched Diets Alter Cholesterol Profiles and Triglycerides in Adults at Risk for Cardiovascular Disease in a Randomized, Controlled Trial," *The Journal of Nutrition* Aug 12 (2021): nxab248.

Harland, J. I. and L. E. Garton, "Whole-Grain Intake as a Marker of Healthy Body Weight and Adiposity," *Public Health Nutrition* 11, no. 6 (2008): 554–563.

Hermsdorff, H. H. M., M. A. Zulet, I. Abete, and J. A. Martínez, "A Legume-Based Hypocaloric Diet Reduces Proinflammatory Status and Improves Metabolic Features in Overweight/Obese Subjects," *European Journal of Nutrition* 50 (2011): 61–69.

Holscher, H. D., H. M. Guetterman, K. S. Swanson, R. An, N. R. Matthan, A. H. Lichetenstein, J. A. Novotny, and D. J. Baer, "Walnut Consumption Alters the Gastrointestinal Microbiota, Microbially Derived Secondary Bile Acids, and Health Markers in Healthy Adults: A Randomized Controlled Trial," *Journal of Nutrition* 148, no. 6 (2018): 861–867.

Huang, J., L. M. Liao, S. J. Weinstein, R. Sinha, B. I. Graubard, and D. Albanes, "Association Between Plant and Animal Protein Intake and Overall and Cause-Specific Mortality," *JAMA Internal Medicine* 180, no. 9 (2020): 1–12.

Iraporda, C., A. Errea, D. E. Romanin, D. Cayet, E. Pereyra, O. Pignataro, J. C. Sirard, G. L. Garrote, A. G. Abraham, and M. Rumbo, "Lactate and Short Chain Fatty Acids Produced by Microbial Fermentation Downregulate Proinflammatory Responses in Intestinal Epithelial Cells and Myeloid Cells," *Immunobiology* 220, no. 10 (2015): 1161–1169.

Jayalath, V. H., et al., "Effect of Dietary Pulses on Blood Pressure: A Systematic Review and Meta-Analysis of Controlled Feeding Trials," *American Journal of Hypertension* 27, no. 1 (2014): 56–64.

Jenkins, D. J. A., et al., "Effect of Legumes as Part of a Low Glycemic Index Diet on Glycemic Control and Cardiovascular Risk Factors in Type 2 Diabetes Mellitus: A Randomized Controlled Trial," *JAMA Internal Medicine* 172, no. 21 (2012): 1653–1660.

Kim, S. J., et al., "Effects of Dietary Pulse Consumption on Body Weight: A Systematic Review and Meta-Analysis of Randomized Controlled Trials," *American Journal of Clinical Nutrition* 103, no. 5 (2016): 1213–1223.

Kristensen, M. D., N. T. Bendsen, S. M. Christiansen, A. Astrup, and A. Raben, "Meals Based on Vegetable Protein Sources (Beans and Peas) Are More Satiating Than Meals Based on Animal Protein Sources (Veal and Pork)–A Randomized Cross-Over Meal Test Study," *Food & Nutrition Research* 60 (2016): 10.3402/fnr.v60.32634.

La Fata, G., P. Weber, and M. H. Mohajeri, "Probiotics and the Gut Immune System: Indirect Regulation," *Probiotics and Antimicrobial Proteins* 10, no. 1 (2018): 11–21.

Liu, X., Y. Li, W. C. Willett, J.-P. Drouin-Chartier, S. N. Bhupathiraju, and D. K. Tobias, "Changes in Nut Consumption Influence Long-Term Weight Changes in US Men and Women," *BMJ Nutrition, Prevention & Health* 2, no. 2 (2019): bmjsph-2019-000034.

Luu, H. N., et al., "Prospective Evaluation of the Association of Nut/Peanut Consumption with Total and Cause-Specific Mortality," *JAMA Internal Medicine* 175, no. 5 (2015): 755–766.

Marco, M. L., et al., "Health Benefits of Fermented Foods: Microbiota and Beyond," *Current Opinion in Biotechnology* 44 (2017): 94–102.

Martínez, I., et al., "Gut Microbiome Composition Is Linked to Whole Grain–Induced Immunological Improvements," *ISME Journal* 7, no. 2 (2013): 269–280.

Melini, F., V. Melini, F. Luziatelli, A. G. Ficca, and M. Ruzzi, "Health-Promoting Components in Fermented Foods: An Up-to-Date Systematic Review," *Nutrients* 11, no. 5 (2019): 1189.

Mellen, P. B., T. F. Walsh, and D. M. Herrington, "Whole Grain Intake and Cardiovascular Disease: A Meta-Analysis," *Nutrition, Metabolism & Cardiovascular Diseases* 18, no. 4 (2008): 283–290.

Mollard, R. C., B. L. Luhovyy, S. Panahi, M. Nunez, and G. H. Anderson, "Regular Consumption of Pulses for 8 Weeks Reduces Metabolic Syndrome Risk Factors in Overweight and Obese Adults," *British Journal of Nutrition* 108, no. S1 (2012): S111–S122.

Naghshi, S., O. Sadeghi, W. C. Willett, and A. Esmaillzadeh, "Dietary Intake of Total, Animal, and Plant Proteins and Risk of All Cause, Cardiovascular, and Cancer Mortality: Systematic Review and Dose-Response Meta-Analysis of Prospective Cohort Studies," *BMJ* 320 (2020): m2412.

Oghbaei, M. and J. Prakash, "Effect of Primary Processing of Cereals and Legumes on Its Nutritional Quality: A Comprehensive Review," *Cogent Food & Agriculture* 2, no. 1 (2016): 1–29.

Pan, A., D. Yu, W. Demark-Wahnefried, O. H. Fanco, and X. Lin, "Meta-Analysis of the Effects of Flaxseed Interventions on Blood Lipids," *American Journal of Clinical Nutrition* 90, no. 2 (2009): 288–297.

Queipo-Ortuño, M., M. Boto-Ordóñez, M. Murri, J. M. Gomez-Zumaquero, M. Clemente-Postigo, R. Estruch, F. C. Diaz, C. Andrés-Lacueva, and F. J. Tinahones, "Influence of Red Wine Polyphenols and Ethanol on the Gut Microbiota Ecology and Biochemical Biomarkers," *American Journal of Clinical Nutrition* 95, no. 6 (2012): 1323–1334.

Rezac, S., C. R. Kok, M. Heermann, and R. Hutkins, "Fermented Foods as a Dietary Source of Live Organisms," *Frontiers in Microbiology* 9 (2018): 1785.

Sabaté, J., "Nut Consumption and Body Weight," *American Journal of Clinical Nutrition* 78, no. 3 (2003): 647S–650S.

Tan, S. Y. and R. D. Mattes. "Appetitive, Dietary and Health Effects of Almonds Consumed with Meals or as Snacks: A Randomized, Controlled Trial," *European Journal of Clinical Nutrition* 67, no. 11 (2013): 1205–1214.

Tighe, P., G. Duthie, N. Vaughan, J. Brittenden, W. G. Simpson, S. Duthie, W. Mutch, K. Wahle, G. Horgan, and F. Thies, "Effect of Increased Consumption of Whole-Grain Foods on Blood Pressure and Other Cardiovascular Risk Markers in Healthy Middle-Aged Persons: A Randomized Controlled Trial," *American Journal of Clinical Nutrition* 92, no. 4 (2010): 733–740.

Tzounis, X., A. Rodriguez-Mateos, J. Vulevic, G. R. Gibson, C. Kwik-Uribe, and J. P. E. Spencer, "Prebiotic Evaluation of Cocoa-Derived Flavanols in Healthy Humans by Using a Randomized, Controlled, Double-Blind, Crossover Intervention Study," *American Journal of Clinical Nutrition* 93, no. 1 (2011): 62–72.

Vendrame, S., S. Guglielmetti, P. Riso, S. Arioli, D. Klimis-Zacas, and M. Porrini, "Six-Week Consumption of a Wild Blueberry Powder Drink Increases Bifidobacteria in the Human Gut," *Journal of Agricultural and Food Chemistry* 59 (2011): 24.

Wastyk, H. C., et al., "Gut-Microbiota-Targeted Diets Modulate Human Immune Status," *Cell* 184, no. 16 (2021): 4137–4153.

Winham, D. M. and A. M. Hutchins, "Perceptions of Flatulence from Bean Consumption Among Adults in 3 Feeding Studies," *Nutrition Journal* 20 (2011): 128.

Ye, E. Q., S. A. Chacko, E. L. Chou, M. Kugizaki, and S. Liu, "Greater Whole-Grain Intake Is Associated with Lower Risk of Type 2 Diabetes, Cardiovascular Disease, and Weight Gain," *Journal of Nutrition* 142, no. 7 (2012): 1304–1313.

RECIPE INDEX

BASICS

Best Crispy Tofu

Cooking Beans 101

Tahini Sauce/
Dressing 5 Ways

Orange Ginger
Peanut Sauce

Easy Salsa Verde

The Perfect Pesto

10-Minute
Any Berry Chia Jam

Quick Pickled
Onions

Beet & White Bean
Hummus

Plant-Powered
Chipotle "Queso"

BREAKFASTS

Berry Bliss Smoothie

Caramel Apple Smoothie

Chocolate Cherry Smoothie

Happy Belly Smoothie

Tahini Date Shake

The Green Machine Smoothie

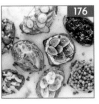
Not Your Basic Breakfast Toast

Creamy Cauli-Powered Steel-Cut Oatmeal

Superseed Overnight Oats

Make-Ahead Breakfast Burritos

Peaches & Cream Quinoa Porridge

Banana Buckwheat Blender Pancakes

Eggplant Shakshuka

Make Your Own Muesli

MAINS

196 Strawberry & Feta Quinoa Salad

198 Spring Niçoise Salad

200 10-Minute Lentil-Walnut Taco Salad

202 Less Kale Caesar

204 Spiced Green Tahini Salad

206 Rainbow Soba Salad

208 Tuscan Red Pepper, Tomato & White Bean Soup

210 Lemony Greek-Style Soup

212 Miso Mushroom & Barley Stew

214 Smoky Butternut Squash Three-Bean Chili

216 Black Bean Quinoa Burgers

218 Hummus Power Sandwich

220 Portobello Pitas

222 Smashed Bean Sammies or Wraps

224 Farmers' Market Quiche

226 Sheet Pan Pesto Gnocchi, Sausage & Veggies

228 "Meaty" Bolognese

230 Creamy Caulifredo

232 Lasagna Roll-Ups with Plant Ricotta

234 Zoodles & Noodles Primavera

236 Roasted Ratatouille Rigatoni

238 One-Pot Chickpea & Cauliflower Curry

240 Kimchi Fried Rice

242 Mean Green Enchilada Skillet

244 Chipotle Pineapple Mushroom Tacos

246

Spicy Roll "Sushi" Bowl

248

Build Your Own Plant-Powered Nourish Bowls

SMALLER FARE

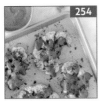

254

Cauliflower Steaks with Almond Butter Romesco

256

Mixed Root Veggie Fries

258

Peach & Arugula Pesto Socca Flatbread

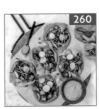

260

Takeout Tofu Lettuce Wraps

262

Cruciferous Crunch Power Salad

264

Autumn Apple Farro Salad

266

Mojito Fruit Salad

268

Glowing Green Soup

270

Fully Loaded Plantain Nachos

272

Cheezy Tahini Kale Chips

274

Chickpea Poppers

SOMETHING SWEET

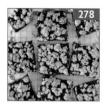

Better Berry
Crumble Bars

Date Caramel
Candies 2 Ways

Chickpea
Hazelnut-ella

Omega Energy Bites

Creamy Chia
Pudding 2 Ways

Lemon Poppy Seed
Zucchini Muffins

Sweet Potato Tahini
Brownies

Banana Spelt
Cinnamon Rolls

GENERAL INDEX